*Identity and
Interpersonal Competence*

I had learnt from experience that many false opinions may be exchanged for true ones, without in the least altering the habits of mind of which false opinions are the result. The English public, for example, are quite as raw and undiscerning on subjects of political economy since the nation has been converted to free-trade, as they were before; and are still further from having acquired better habits of thought or feeling, or being in any way better fortified against error, on subjects of a more elevated character. For, though they have thrown off certain errors, the general discipline of their minds, intellectually and morally, is not altered. I am now convinced, that no great improvements in the lot of mankind are possible, until a great change takes place in the fundamental constitution of their modes of thought.

JOHN STUART MILL, *Autobiography*

Identity and Interpersonal Competence

A New Direction in Family Research

Nelson N. Foote
and
Leonard S. Cottrell, Jr.

THE UNIVERSITY OF CHICAGO PRESS
CHICAGO & LONDON

Library of Congress Catalog Card Number: 55-11957

THE UNIVERSITY OF CHICAGO PRESS, CHICAGO & LONDON
The University of Toronto Press, Toronto 5, Canada

Foreword

This volume offers, as indicated by its subtitle, a new direction in family research. It took imagination, originality, and courage for its authors to essay a breakthrough on a new frontier of research. They chose the difficult and daring course. It would have been much easier to follow the traditional path and project current trends in family research. In proposing a new direction, the authors are challenging research workers to close two large gaps in our procedures. Many of us are unaware or only dimly conscious of their existence. One of these has been the lack of a clearly defined theoretical focus for research on the family. The other is the enormous gap which lies between our research and its utilization by family-serving agencies and organizations.

In closing the gap of the lack of a central conception of the nature of the family, the authors make use of emerging insights from social psychology and social psychiatry. They find as essential and central for research an understanding of marriage and the family in terms of interpersonal relations. It is in interpersonal relations that man achieves the highest development of his humanity and gains the greatest satisfaction and happiness. It is also in interpersonal relations that men and women may be most thwarted and dehumanized and rendered most miserable. Thus competence in interpersonal relations is a means by which members of the family are able to interact effectively in achieving their common ends and their individual self-expression and development.

Second, the authors show how the new direction in family research utilizes recent perceptions of the relation of social science research to social action.

In modern physics, chemistry, and biology the findings of theoretical studies are immediately put to work in research of value for human welfare. It is paradoxical that social science research, by contrast, should so often be kept remote from practical application and use. The authors point out how this gap can be closed. They indicate how research can be reoriented to

v

be of effective assistance to family-serving agencies. These organizations arose historically and developed to meet family breakdowns. Accordingly, their techniques have been remedial and therapeutic. Recently they have become more and more interested in prevention. But current findings of family research seem of little or no help in achieving this new orientation.

The new direction in family research takes account of this receptive attitude and stresses planning, prevention, and evaluation. It recognizes that health and economic security are basic to human welfare. In these aspects of family living, great gains have been made through social planning and programs of prevention. Accordingly, family-serving agencies are now free to give almost undivided attention to the problem of the underdeveloped potentialities of human beings. The development of competence in interpersonal relations becomes the great preventive of personal disorganization and of unsolved family conflicts leading to family disruption. The essential service to be offered to the family and its members by schools, churches, and family-life education agencies is assistance in the development of interpersonal competence.

While this volume has been in preparation, the Family Study Center of the University of Chicago has been developing research with this new orientation. It has sponsored studies of three components of competence in interpersonal relations—autonomy, empathy, and creativity—by the method of participant experimentation. It has offered workshops in the summers of 1954 and 1955 giving practical demonstrations of these new techniques. These have been attended by college and high-school teachers of courses on marriage and the family, social workers, ministers, family-life education workers, and others.

This book will attract a wide audience. It will excite discussion. It will stimulate research. Its final test will be its success in providing a new focus of family research and in bringing together for fruitful co-operation the social scientist and the prospective consumers of research, namely, the professional workers in agencies, organizations, and institutions that are serving families.

ERNEST W. BURGESS

Acknowledgments

THE INITIAL impetus for this work came in 1948, when the Grant Foundation indicated to the Social Science Research Council its interest in the preparation of "a comprehensive research planning report, taking account of the need for research findings which can be applied by agencies serving the family, and of new knowledge and techniques which should contribute to the advance of research on problems in marriage and family relations."

With funds supplied by the foundation, the Social Science Research Council, through its Committee on Family Research, sponsored a preliminary survey of recent developments in research and practical programs designed to serve the family in American society. Members of the committee were: Ernest W. Burgess, *chairman*, Leonard S. Cottrell, Jr., Stanley P. Davies, A. Irving Hallowell, Emily H. Mudd, and Robert R. Sears.

While the working papers produced in this survey did not eventuate in a conventional research planning report, they did serve to stimulate the present authors to go further in their study of recent trends in both research and family agency programs and to attempt a formulation of what appeared to them to be some desirable new directions for research and application in this area.

We gratefully acknowledge our indebtedness to those who have given so generously of support, encouragement, technical assistance, and criticism. While only the authors can be held to account for the deficiencies of the work, it is certainly correct to say that whatever of merit it contains is due in very substantial part to the contributions of many people.

Not only did the Grant Foundation provide the necessary funds in support of the enterprise, but the patient understanding, encouragement, and bold and imaginative advice of its executive director, Perrin C. Galpin, were indispensable in the completion of this assignment.

Mention has already been made of the initiative and early developmental functions provided by the Social Science Research Council's Committee on Family Research. It would be difficult to overestimate the worth of its counsel and guidance, as well as the intensive and often vehement criticisms provided by individual members who read earlier drafts of the manuscript.

The preparation of working memoranda by Ernest W. Burgess, Helen Canon, Harold E. Jones, Carson McGuire, Emily H. Mudd, Lois B. Murphy, Vincent Nowlis, Max Rheinstein, Lemo D. Rockwood, Robert R. Sears, and Guy E. Swanson provided a rich and stimulating set of background materials upon which to base our own efforts.

At several stages in our survey of the literature and preparation of bibliographies, we had the able assistance of a number of people, notably Albert J. Reiss, Guy E. Swanson, and Edith W. Williams.

Various staff members of the Family Study Center at the University of Chicago have contributed both directly and indirectly to certain aspects of this report. In particular, meticulous bibliographic and stenographic assistance was provided by Winifred Locke and earlier by Noreen K. Haygood.

Geraldine R. Foote not only assisted with bibliography, proofreading, and indexing but gave invaluable help through her constant encouragement and illuminating criticism of various sections of the manuscript.

NELSON N. FOOTE
LEONARD S. COTTRELL, JR.

Table of Contents

ix

I Introduction: Social Science as Systematic Self-scrutiny

A GUESSING GAME of more than playful significance can be played among persons who have spent a few days sociably together, as in a series of parties or at a resort: one person attempts to describe the kinds of families from which the group members came, with no prior knowledge of their personal histories. The game is most successfully played when the group includes mainly young adults but also some older and younger people. Still more clues can be secured if the attitudes of the group members toward waiters or clerks can be observed. Hits or misses are determined by checking guesses against the facts, and score is kept by noting the correct guesses and comparing them with the record of other guessers, or with the results that might be obtained by chance alone.

A practiced observer of normal sensitivity and adult experience can usually make a surprisingly large number of correct guesses. The kind of questions to which he can most frequently give accurate answers are these:

1. Did the person have any brothers or sisters?
2. Were these brothers or sisters older or younger?
3. How much was he loved by his mother? Father? (Another adult?) With which did he tend to identify more?
4. Was his family close and demonstrative, or cold and distant?
5. Were his parents young or old when he was born?
6. Was his mother or his father dominant, or were they equal in authority?
7. Was either parent repeatedly cruel or arbitrary in disciplining him?
8. Which parent was more influential in the person's career choices?

9. Were his parents, or his brother and sisters, approving or critical of his achievements?
10. Which parent was the more intellectual? Action-oriented? Sociable?

Sometimes, though less frequently, even such characteristics as the presence and importance of grandparents, adoptive status, father's occupation, mother's education, the family's social status, and some quite idiosyncratic circumstances can be guessed. As the guesser goes from the common relations of authority and affection among parents and children into these more peculiar features of another person's upbringing, his chances of being right go down; his chances of being right by luck alone, however, decrease still faster. Yet the validity of some of his faintest premonitions can be quite astounding to his audience.

Indeed, the more accurate in detail the guesser becomes, the more likely it is that the game will encounter two specific hazards. The person whose family origins are so closely described may suspect and charge that he has been previously investigated and resent the implied invasion of his privacy, or he may be embarrassed by the disclosure of such intimate and perhaps ungratifying facts to the remainder of the group. Yet, if this game is played correctly, the guesser has depended for clues entirely upon what each particular subject has already disclosed about himself through the characteristic patterns of his interaction with others. Whether consciously or not, each person tells his history publicly in his behavior, and could only conceal it by withdrawing from society, an act that in itself is diagnostic and occasionally observed.

There is nothing mysterious or occult about the inferences employed. They are all derived from the theorem that one reproduces one's earlier family relations in one's interpersonal relations beyond the family. Father-figures, mother-figures, brother-figures, sister-figures, rivals, servants, authorities, as first experienced in the family, furnish the prototypes for apprehending and responding to all later intimates. Especially in the rapid development of intimate association with strangers, the prototypical family constellation is most recognizably reproduced, and the characteristic actions which it guides form the "person" that becomes known to others. When a person is most spontaneously free, these same expressive acts are usually subjectively taken by him to be his natural self. A person's identity in such a group is thus—or can be—simultaneously his self as privately conceived. Yet even his reactions to constraints upon his self-expression tell something of the figures he fears; in this sense, all his acts are representative. And it is precisely upon the evidence of many small but representative encounters witnessed between each subject of this game and the others that successful guesses and generalizations can be made. In later discussion, the basis for errors through insufficient evidence or mistaken inference may be brought out, but no evidence used is found invalid. (Such checking back is useful for improving the skill of the guesser.)

To be sure, no single episode leads directly back to a specific family pattern. Rather, by recurrence of similar episodes in orderly relationship to episodes of other kinds, the generic constellation is pieced together. As more information is added, the more the pattern hangs together and even indicates missing evidence to be sought for by reviewing a wider range of incidents. For instance, a girl bumps a boy and blushes; he speaks to her cordially and thereafter her eyes follow him about the room; a younger boy tries to gain her attention, but is ignored; she appears respectful toward a male teacher and defends him against gibes by other girls; after a downpour, she organizes the drying-out of clothes by the other girls; her female teacher speaks equivocally of her as independent. Is it possible that her father was a widower, and let her play the role of a "little mother" to her small sister—which she did out of a desire to please him, whom she admires? Even with these many observed details, much of the complex is missing from which a successful guess might be made; but at least the principle employed is evident. If it is remembered that boys who have dated her found her somewhat repressed and inclined toward intellectual conversation, further confirmation may be added, but also complications may emerge which reduce the plausibility of the previous guess.

From experience in playing this game, several limitations become evident. The older the person—the further he has left his parental family behind, in time or in any other sense—the less does his present behavior tell about his past. And if his succeeding experience has been markedly heterogeneous, with strong emotional attachments intervening between his original family and his present circle of intimates, the less does the present constellation tell about the original. If the person's cultural or subcultural background is markedly foreign to the guesser's, of course the latter has more difficulty in interpreting the biographical significance of behavior. Patterns of sociability among teen-agers still living at home, by contrast, almost transparently reveal the structure of their families.

Although there is thus no mystery as to why successful guessing is not really guessing or intuition, but complex inference from objective evidence, explanation of the procedure does not diminish the uncanny feeling of some of the subjects that they are being laid bare. Even when the bits of evidence are painstakingly pointed out and are admitted to be public knowledge, the sense of exposure may persist and give rise to mild dismay on the part of beholders as well. What might develop if the procedure were explored systematically and no longer used mainly as a game is a matter for speculation. But questions are raised by the demonstration of the underlying theorem which are far more important than the mild shock of the shyer players.

If postdiction is this easy, why is prediction so hard? And if prediction from previous to future behavior is hard, does not this fact qualify the deterministic assumption which underlies and characterizes much research and writing in social science? And finally, what might this game of revelation disclose about the role of the social scientist and his ultimate audience?

KNOWLEDGE FOR WHOM?

The subject matter of social science is the behavior of human beings. When people are the subjects of any particular study, their permission if not their active co-operation is indispensable. Whether people will permit themselves to be observed, whether they will answer questions truthfully or at all, whether they will carry out experimental tasks, whether indeed they will give of their means to maintain the professional investigator, are all field problems which have to be solved before any new knowledge of their behavior can be gained. After their infancy, it is only in their public behavior that human beings remain indifferent or unaware of observers. One alternative is for the observer to secretly intrude on people's privacy.

To be admitted with their consent as an observer to their private behavior requires the establishment of trust in the investigator and eventually of some kind of reciprocity, some *quid pro quo*. The significance of these commonplaces of social research may be overlooked or unrecognized when social research is thought to be too closely analogous to natural science.

It would be unrealistic to insist that social science cannot be conducted as if it were natural science. Much or most of what goes on under this name follows the model of natural science. Its phenomena—its subject matter and subjects—are assumed to be passive objects, indifferently receptive to contemplation or manipulation, and findings of a sort do accrue. Moreover, the goodwill of persons used in this way seems almost inexhaustible, with a manageable modicum of recalcitrant exceptions. But meanwhile the potentialities of the alternative assumption remain relatively unexplored.

Social science is the only branch of science which needs the co-operation of its subjects and where the results are of interest to the subjects. This is acknowledged every time the subjects of a survey are promised a later look at the findings. To recognize the subjects' stake in the social sciences does not infringe the principles of scientific methods; it only demands an acceptance of empirical fact. Yet acceptance of such a pregnant axiom fundamentally affects everything that the social scientist does. The potentialities to be derived from this axiom are so extensive as to raise the question of why they have attracted so little attention up till now. The predominant prestige of the contemplative-manipulative model of natural science may be the reason, or perhaps the blame lies in the social scientist's failure to appraise his professional role. Due to its origins, social science has been pursued mainly as an avocation or as a derivative branch of liberal education; only recently has social research become a full-time paid occupation.

In defining his profession, the social scientist may conceive

himself as serving several employers or audiences. He may conceive himself as applying his techniques to predicting or manipulating the behavior of one group on behalf of another, such as
buyers and sellers, voters and office-seekers, workers and managers. Or he may evaluate his distinctive product as not being
of immediate practical value and himself as patronized by affluent
minorities or the public at large, in the manner of the artist and
his patron. Or he may conceive of himself as carrying on an
activity of highest relevance and worth for the subjects of his
research. In any case, since he no longer is the amateur supporting his inquiries out of his own earnings as a teacher or writer,
he must justify his salary and compete for it with the other
claims on his sponsors. At present, to judge from relative salaries,
his worth as evaluated by manipulators, by patrons, and by
subjects, appears to descend in just that order. Yet in terms of
appreciation by his audience, the value of his findings and of
his services may, at least potentially, mount in the opposite
direction.

There is a fourth audience for research, an influential and
close one to the social scientist. While the esteem of one's colleagues is professionally important it should be evident that
since all researchers are equally dependent upon outside sponsorship, they can only in a short run sponsor each other, by
drawing upon their net collective assets; beyond the short run,
they must find the support of a public. To guarantee one's standing among one's fellow-professionals, it is frequently sufficient
to display mere virtuosity, but this cannot for long satisfy the
sponsor, for he demands some product in return.

The product of social science which is of most value to its
sponsor is a generalization relevant to the conduct of his life,
whether simply as a person or in the discharge of his profession,
whatever that may be. The special function of family research
is to produce generalizations ultimately useful in family living,
or useful to agencies concerned with family living. Yet precisely
as such research moves closer to full relevance, a significant
paradox or ambivalence in the reception of its findings becomes
conspicuous. This ambivalence arises from the desire for privacy
which is more intensely felt by the subjects of family research

than in any other branch of social science, except perhaps in criminology. And even in criminal behavior, the interests in finding out and not being found out are not united in the same persons. In family research they are, so that here the need for confronting and clarifying this ambivalence becomes vital.

A man's home is his castle, says the ancient principle of family law. By what right can the investigator intervene to gather his data: only by leave of the subject himself, limited by the abuse his patience will tolerate. By what reward or promise can his consent be obtained, by what reciprocity? Some researchers pay their subjects, then wonder about the validity of what they buy. Some utilize friends, who are bound by other obligations, but this raises the sampling problem. Some exploit students, and others, employees. Fair results are probably obtained by mildly exploiting the goodwill of the average man, who will offer much without reward, given a minimum bit of trust. But the fullest and most valid results appear to come when the subject's own interest in the accuracy and scope of the results is mobilized. And this is so when the results are most relevant to his current concerns, and least imposed by a foreign spy. To be sure, as interviewers know, a person may more freely speak to a stranger than to a relative or friend, but this again is because such a disclosure is cathartic for him; the interviewer, for that moment, is the uncritical listener he needs, to whom he will not have to account later. In spite of these qualifications, the proposition can be bluntly put: The kind of research that will best reward the subject is about those questions where the answers mean as much to him as to his investigator.

The "him" can be extended to cover groups as well. The older notion of applied research is one in which the practitioner in an agency takes down and reads the journals which record previous research. If lucky, he finds an instance or two of a study cognate with his own experience and situation. By comparison with what has been found by others he may form a better impression of how he and his agency are doing. But increasingly, it has become apparent that the most relevant research of all will usually be some new research, done directly upon the persons or agencies seeking to know more about their own operation. In this sense, applied research is any client-oriented inquiry from a psychoanalysis to an agency evaluation; it is not a mere matter of injecting textbook principles into the vocabulary of the clients. It is systematic self-scrutiny in which the researcher plays the role of reflector, rememberer, thorough examiner, and in a very limited sense, objective judge of conduct. Research so conceived adds dimensions and devices for self-regulation to the persons and groups which before they did not possess, or experienced only through flashes of genius. In this sense social science represents the democratization of critical insight about behavior; it is both the product and means of generalized access to social knowledge and self-control.

The problem of trust implied in a nonmanipulative social science runs both ways; but there are some who will cry that only the few can be trusted with realistic knowledge about themselves. Going back to our opening game, it is a regular occurrence to hear it described by the professionally anxious as intensely traumatic, a menace and hazard that ought to be prohibited. Instead of a game, it is put on a par with the "slam book" of the public high schools, that dire expedient by which the adolescent seeks to learn what his best friends, parents, and teachers will not tell him. Despite the efforts to stamp it out, the slam book seems to survive, wherever the mystery of self is most intensely shared. In the officer candidate school, it used to have official sanction, as the "buddy sheet" of fame and scorn.

Now wherein lies the avid curiosity and the avid opposition toward these and other schemes by which adult and adolescent try to establish with greater firmness what others think of them? Why the great conflict over showing to subjects the results of psychological tests? Certainly harm can be done, and the greater the significance of the information, the greater the harm. The question of harm is a function of timing and audience: when and by whom and before whom is the vital information to be disclosed? But just as certainly, it is vital information, and not too much thought seems required to conclude that it is exactly the type of valued finding mentioned above. The kind of generalization of greatest moment to researcher and subject alike is the kind that enables the latter to define himself and thereby govern his conduct. The social science which best repays its cost and justifies the researcher in the division of labor is that which reveals people to themselves objectively and authoritatively, but also appropriately in terms of timing and development. If realism cannot be stomached, then social science must make way for the return of hypocrisy and superstition, as well it might, since social scientists themselves are so little prepared to exploit and develop their major strength—the interest of their subjects in the findings of research. Indeed some retreat from justifying their profession, as if it were crime or an illicit assertion of values to stand for realism and the open publication of results in the study of social behavior.

Let us take into account just what it might mean, within the limits of family research, as conducted by professionals, to assume that the subjects of the research are also to be its consumers? One can be as precise and impersonal in answering this question as the etiquette of scientific writing normally demands. In the Appendix to this volume is listed every contribution to the formal literature of American family research for the past ten years. By convention, the titles are supposed to describe the content, and if they do not, it is probably because the content also deviates from straight description, analysis, or explanation. By definition, however, despite such marginal cases, every item included deserves the title of research. They record observations of specified subjects; they refer to the family as the principal unit considered, as against the individual or other institutions; they approach the family through many disciplines, but only those guided by the methods of scientific investigation. In our earlier considerations of this array of writings, it was supposed that systematic criteria could be applied for evaluating all these products of the postwar decade from the standpoint of design and technical standards of the research craft. This may yet become feasible, through another project, but the over-all reason why it was abandoned in this study was the recognition that professional standards are not enough. The compelling measure of the worth of any item, from which technical standards must finally be derived, is the bearing it has upon the life of the subjects it describes—its reflexivity quotient. This is not the place to take the reader through that list, though he may wish to do so himself, keeping this question in mind: How many titles bear upon his behavior as a family member and product in any imaginable way whatsoever? The summary judgment of several of those who have scanned not merely the titles but the articles and books themselves, is that very few have any such bearing at all. Family research has generally not been directed squarely to the questions raised by taking its subjects into account; it is plainly possible to raise a new series of questions by doing this.

These are harsh words and a severe challenge to the family researchers of the next decade, but only if the assumption is retained, that the relevance of research to its subjects is the concern of the scientists. If this is assumed to be of no concern, then what follows will seem of small account.

The strongest defense of family research can be made on the same grounds as the harshest criticism. Compared with most other fields of social research, the family field is distinguished by the extent and degree of its relevance to the life problems of its subjects: marital selection and success, personality development, continuity and stability amid social change. There is much family research of only academic interest, but the ratio of this to research of functional significance to family members is relatively lower than for studies like those on communities or individual attitudes, which appear in the same journals.

Moreover, during the past ten years, there has been a mounting demand for knowledge about the problems of family living especially among young adults. On many university campuses, often in the face of resistance by academic departments of social science who are averse to having their stock of generalizations tested by practical application, course after course, in preparation for marriage and parenthood, has been installed because of petitions by students. Enrollment in such courses has mounted faster than the supply of persons equipped and willing to teach them. If the great state universities are representative of the general college population, then the young people's groups in churches may also be taken as representative of at least the more organized non-college segment in each community, since churches enroll more members than any other institution outside of schools. In such groups, the postwar demand for the knowledge or training for successful adult family roles has grown to an unprecedented extent. The impulse may be vague, ill-defined, and ill-served; but it is real, insistent, and valid.

Its validity, to be sure, continues to be debated by the academic and scientific fraternity. These phrases from a leading family researcher on so-called functional textbooks designed for use in such courses are fairly representative: "Advice-giving . . . hortatory . . . lack of objectivity, scientific proof for statements . . . simple writing . . . does not recognize complexities . . . goes by what is commercially o.k. . . . we don't know enough to do this sort of job . . . divinely authoritative . . . a fraud." Those who retort to this start with the needs of young people, the lack of an authoritative tradition to guide them, and young people's ability to select critically from the alternative hypotheses to which they are exposed by wider knowledge of family patterns and outcomes. In view of the extent of recent demand for enlightenment about the problems of family living, to reserve scientific knowledge for the professional few is to turn the many over to quacks. No doubt what is in print to date, either as research or as functional textbook, falls far short of what it attempts, but this is a different question from whether the demand is valid and reasonable. If the demand for knowledge that is useful in governing behavior is not valid, then the demand of family researchers for support of their work must likewise seem unjustified to the public. But if the demand for usable knowledge is valid, then the research that is done must be judged by its success in achieving such relevance.

It is quite true that there are writers, including some of evident sincerity, who try to employ research to lend authority to their own a priori views on proper behavior. And some opponents of research correspondingly fear that research will weaken acceptance of the customary patterns they uphold. Neither of these groups of writers is interested in research as self-examination of behavior; both, however, are more conscious of the potentialities of research for changing behavior than those exponents of its neutrality who insist that the best research is the least relevant to action, and is merely a kind of recreation for the researcher.

One cannot know in advance where the systematic scrutiny of one's own or a group's behavior will lead; to engage in such research is an adventure of uncertain outcome, yet one in which each change of direction, or decision to persist, will depend upon the weight of evidence. Because human beings live in time and make history, because they do not simply repeat old patterns but continually develop, research applied to self-examination will more frequently suggest alterations of behavior than confirm old patterns. It may thus seem as risky to apply the criterion of relevance in selecting research problems for the next decade as it seems harsh to apply it retrospectively to the work of the past decade. Yet not to ask, how much difference do the findings of a study make to the persons studied, is to seem indifferent to the state and status in which the social scientist will be kept.

THE FULCRUM OF INTERVENTION

Whoever you are, your successive families have had a larger share in constituting your identity as a person than any other institution of society.

You are scarcely responsible for the characteristics with which you have been endowed by your parents, but you steadily acquire self-conscious responsibility for the use you make of these endowments. As you move beyond the influence of your parents, you tend to rely upon your most intimate peers for confirming you in the further identities you formulate; you rely especially upon that member of the other sex and another family whom you marry. And ultimately, the conditions you establish for the development of your children are more likely to be taken by yourself as the gauge of your self-realization than any public report of your career.

Your occupation—if you are an adult—may seem more determinative of who and what you are than any activities outside your work. Yet your family of orientation—which you did not choose—almost certainly cast a decisive weight in your choice of vocation. And your family of procreation furnishes major

criteria for continuing or changing your job, residence, or avocations.

It is easy to grant the dependence of the newborn infant upon
a family or family-substitute; but when adult independence is so
vastly cherished and striven for, it is hard to concede that the
isolated individual is a myth—an ideal, which no one seriously
entertains for long. To reject this extreme, however, is not to
embrace the other.

That the family joins self to society is trite, yet the very ease
with which the connection can be taken for granted may also
inhibit its scientific exploration. The realization of interdependence clutches attention forcibly on occasions of grief. Only by
ties of affection and identification does the person psychologically transcend the isolation of his brief existence, and when these
ties sever, he confronts independence with pain and misgiving.
To penetrate deep into family dynamics when that is appropriate may equally stir the foundations of personal being. The
study of the family may avoid this risk, but only by missing its
mark.

Seen from the inside by the actor, the study of the family
produces knowledge about the matrix of his identity and thereby his progressive development as a person. Seen by the outside
observer, trends in research upon the family as an institution—
for example, even questions of family size—appear to converge
upon the same developmental approach. Personality remains always to some degree undefined, inchoate, potential, whereas the
family seems visible, structured, and relatively accessible for
observation of its forms and experimentation with its functions.

When in the past men have theorized about how to bring
the course of events closer to their desires, they have often got
caught on one or the other of two extreme poles—the entire
community or the separate individual. Yet, one can deal directly neither with a wholly isolated individual nor with the community at large—each is at best a useful abstraction. The potent
entities—the organs and groupings among which the work and
loyalties of community members are distributed—are the specific
institutions. Among these the family is elemental. The effects
of virtually all other institutions upon persons are mediated

through families. Whether one's interest, therefore, is in influencing single persons or whole societies, the point of greatest leverage for intervention is the family.

For example, revolutionary movements have characteristically discerned that greater changes occur between than within generations, and they have thus sought to capture and organize the loyalty of youth. Those who have wished to stabilize traditional practices have likewise tried to get permanent commitments in adolescence. The major outlines of adult identity tend to become established during this period when the person is moving from his parental to his marital family. In no other such brief period are decisions made of greater import for the next generation. Whether the person who commences a new family cycle will re-create a link in the chain of transmission identical with his parents' depends upon how well prepared he is to do better or worse or the same.

As the intersection of specialized points of view, the family itself is resistant to definition. Is kinship biological or legal? Is intimate co-operation in a common household the distinguishing characteristic? What ontological reality can be imputed to the interlocking network of significant others which is termed the family constellation? Can such an institution be validly conceived in the manner of the flyer who scans the houses in a town and thereby estimates the number of families? Or is the family rather an abstract form, represented ideally in game or sacrament, but poorly approached in real life? What is the family, as such, or is nothing known "as such"?

However elusive to segmented science, to a person, his family is normally central and whole. If the investigator wants to grasp it as a unit, therefore, and not simply as reflexes—or rules or roles or rites—then it behooves him to take the view of the acting member, the one for whom and to whom the family exists unsegmented and complete. That is the premise on which we begin.

TYPES OF GENERALIZATION

If science is our guide, and the object of science is valid generalization, then what kind of generalization can be deduced from looking at the family from the standpoint of the individual?

For it has become a truism among students of the family that every person sees his family in a different perspective.[1] A family could thus be described as the nexus of separate but intercontingent careers; or, psychologically, as the constellation of significant others (whether or not legally and biologically related) upon whom one most depends for developing and affirming one's identity. Conversely, a person's career might almost be described as the history of his efforts to realize the potentialities and transcend the limitations imposed by his family. Stating it either way seems to emphasize the unique instead of the regular, but this may be due to the dearth of developmental concepts.

A science may be possible which classifies the forms taken by families at particular moments, analogous to the work of those who photograph snowflakes before they melt. But from the standpoint of the actor in the family, it is less important to assemble extensive taxonomies of the ephemeral forms of interaction than to connect one event with another in the sequence of time. It is common in social science to speak as often of antecedents and consequents as of independent and dependent variables. Whichever terminology is used, the type of generalization most useful to the actor is that which relates his family experiences to his development as a person, and states those institutional or institutionalizable conditions which lead to various outcomes. That family research ought to be oriented to producing this type of generalization is the second premise of this report.

The developmental generalization does not, like news, deal with the particular and the unique. News deals with events apart from causes; this is its virtue as well as shortcoming. It cannot guide action save as the significance of events is generalized: Y follows X, and may again. The journalist and scientist are poles apart in their approach to events, at least at the outset of their inquiry. The journalist gathers additional facts from the context of the event in order to distinguish them further as peculiarly news; the aspect he favors in his report is the esoteric. The scientist, however, wants to put events in a class, and locate the

1. Alfred Adler, "The Family Constellation," *Understanding Human Nature* (Cleveland: The World Publishing Company, 1941), chap. viii, pp. 149–57.

conditions under which they recur. His goal is to reduce strangeness to familiarity, understanding, and regular expectation.

The development of identity in a person or a group, is established by the pattern of recurrence of related events. The paradox of personality is that it changes; identity is the thread which unites episode to episode, as much as they are united, but it is a wandering thread, and often not one thread but several. Moreover, there are many transitions and turning points, and each is a dramatic event, which may be appraised as news or as development—as either a subtle or discordant variation on a previous theme.

Thus, a description of a person may simply depict an event where he was present, as for example in the statement: He came, he listened, he left. Similarly, a description of a group may be as follows: They met in the Grand Hotel from four to seven, and then they dispersed. But if any further attempt is made, not to add details of the newsy sort, but to order what happened in terms of antecedents and consequents, then the episodes are generalized along lines of persistent pattern, of identity and development. And without stopping for evaluation, in the sense of approval or disapproval, this description gains significance for the subjects precisely as it estimates closely emerging trends. The event is not news to them; they know it already, though it may be news to others. It is the meaning of that event, in terms of the past and the future, of realization or frustration of intent, that makes the generalizing account of relevance to each subject.

It is not mere fact-finding to describe a person. No one thinks another can tell the whole truth about himself, and no one can tell it about another, though some may vainly try and disregard the protests. Yet alone and unaided, the person knows little about himself. It is not that the self is wholly composed of appraisals by others; that is as fallacious as the opposite view, that the self is a set of existent traits, as objective and describable as two eyes and two ears. The truth lies in between, but it is ever a partial truth, an obsolescing definition, and a problem for intermittent review and renewal.

Let us mention another game. In any small group of more-or-less intimates, on a round-robin basis, ask each to write on a card five adjectives that best describe each of the others. Write the names of the person described and of his describer on the card; collect the cards, and sort them out, so that for each person the characterizations number one less than the total in the group. Now first read off the lists of traits attributed to any member of the group, omitting his name and letting it be guessed. With rare exceptions, he is readily identified. But do not confirm the guesses until the round has been made, lest identity be guessed through the process of elimination. Or, make all players write down their guesses without consulting each other. Then sort the cards again, this time by describer instead of described. Take only one card from each of these piles, choosing it at random. Read first the name of describee, and then the five adjectives by which some player has judged him best described. Then ask who judged him thus. Assuming the group is not too big nor strange, the guesses will be as good this time as the time before. One carries this only as far as the fun permits, and that may not be very far. For the disquieting fact is that the describer discloses not only his notion of what the other is like, but in the eyes of others, discloses himself in his choice of terms. For each adjective reveals a relationship between one person and another, and not simply and clearly the traits of the other person.

For a further excursion in self-revelation, the game may be played with an extra card for each player, on which he records his own five best self-describing terms. Comparison of these with versions of himself by others is often a jar, but it can be as pleasing as hurting, though there is seldom unanimity in the descriptions. A second playing has another advantage. Opinions change as a result of disclosures, and further adjectives come to mind, which reveal new slants about the person described, and this is especially so when the previous series is excluded from reuse. When the reciprocity involved is recognized, it affects further attributions. For the reciprocity includes not only the relational origin of the traits attributed but also the mutual willingness to state one's views of others as if they were factual truth. Self-awareness that one is thereby simultaneously identifying one's self leads to reflection on how one wishes to be represented. The game may thus arouse some anxiety, unless it is handled with care and mutual trust, as for example in a large family at its best. But given such trust and curiosity, the speed and intensity of the effect of such mutual attribution are greater than that achieved in family life.

When people help each other in self-examination they greatly alter their notions about themselves. Self-examination alters relations within the group, confirms some tendencies, and discourages others. In a group of affectionate friends, the adjectives used are as potent to cultivate growth as the views of the hostile to curb it. A person flourishes in one group, fails in another, and remains unchanged in a third because no appraisal has been given, it being either repressed or ignored. The secret of self-examination and the secret of families, friends, and foes is that only those can hurt or help us whose view—whether hostile, helpful, or a mixture of both—is close enough to us to be known and respected.

From the static view of personality, nothing could result from such a game. According to this there is only one truth, which does not change, and it is only enlarged by additional knowledge. But the developmental view recognizes the reflexive effect of another person's evaluation. Each description is all the more constitutive as its speaker supposes it fact, and acts accordingly toward the person he so described. If all behavior were determined by the ascriptions of others, then the self would be left with no room for movement, or for self-determination; when consensus prevails there is no choice. But there are always discrepancies in the estimations of others. Even the smallest child soon learns to distinguish between his father's and mother's differing evaluation of his behavior. And given the chance, one gravitates toward that audience which helps one develop one's self. At least this hypothesis of the thematic selection from the stream of events appears the only one which can offer the person potential control over the course of his own development and prevent the diffusion of his identity in episodic flux.

Some ascriptions by others are taken as true, some not, and some are problematic and are either rejected or assimilated. Some we wish were true, some not, and there are some perplexing maybe's. A common example of ascription is the recommendation of a potential employee, which as a rule is withheld from the person considered, but if known by the employee, of grave importance in his self-definition. Another example is in the decision-making before marriage, when one tests one's own notions of what the other is like by asking advisers for their opinion. One fashions an image of one's self and of significant others from multiple ascriptions, and exhibits, confirms, and reiterates them in one's behavior. ·If responsible professionals want to influence a person, they must begin with his family—with the circle of others that is of greatest account for everyone. The family, though it may not do its job, remains outside of the counseling clinic, the other most sheltered spot for self-examination with the aid of others. And even the counseling clinic is rarely as effective as the family in its influence on the outcome of a case.

Just as there are numerous academic disciplines which bear upon family behavior from one theoretical aspect or another, so there is a wide range of public and private agencies which attack one kind of practical family problem or another—medical, economic, protective, psychological, educational, or recreational. And just as the disciplines tend to segment the family, so do the professions. For example, a strong case has recently been made that family welfare agencies, in the interest of efficiency and effectiveness, ought to co-ordinate their efforts in order to deal with problem families rather than with family problems.[2] The ultimate measure of the effectiveness of any such agency is taken to be the observable change it produces in the behavior of its clients. But the multiple conditions affecting behavior are so interconnected within the family that efforts which deal only with one aspect of a person, and that disregard this network have only partial results. Family research, therefore, is here confined to generalizations at the level of the family unit. When reduced analytically to the constituent aspects and processes, it is with the idea of reconstituting them as a more direct means of realizing the family's functions in personal growth.

The very phrase "family research" raises many problems about what to include or exclude. Fortunately the issue of reductionism

---

2. Bradley Buell and Associates, *Community Planning for Human Services* (New York: Columbia University Press, 1952).

has been threshed out so fully that it may suffice simply to state that a study of the family on its own level is intended. Investigations of sexual physiology, attitude formation, or budget ratios are the type of related studies which are excluded from the definition of family research used here. Family research is not regarded as more basic than other studies; one level of abstraction is scientifically as valid as another.

A more familiar but less resolved question of which problems are basic is whether hypotheses set up for testing in actual practice are necessarily more limited in scope and value than generalizations not applied nor applicable in practice. The premise adopted here holds that the type of generalization most worthy of pursuit is neither basic nor applied; it is both. The wider the universe to which it applies, the more basic in the sense of general. Given the decision to remain at one level of analysis, such as family processes, and not to reduce the problem to another level, and given also the aim of generalizing as far as possible, it is only a play upon words to put hypotheses in basic or applied terminology. One can say either, "under these conditions, the following will happen" or "create these conditions and what you desire will happen." As a generalization of antecedents and consequents, both mean the same. The choice of relevant problems in family research comes down to stating what changes in dependent variables are those desired. These cannot be selected according to a priori principles or mere extrapolation of previous trends; intelligent choice depends on a right reading of what is wanted in concrete situations.

THE EMERGENCE OF RESEARCH PROBLEMS

For better or for worse, scientific research on family behavior in the United States during the past generation has been primarily stimulated by, and directed to, crises. Three periods of crisis can be construed, corresponding roughly with the three decades since World War I.

The overthrow of small-town supremacy in moral standards during the twenties detached large numbers from the control and support of traditional sexual morality. The intellectual ferment which ensued was reflected scientifically in three representative monographs: Katherine B. Davis, *Factors in the Sex Life of Twenty-two Hundred Women* (1929), G. V. Hamilton, *A Research in Marriage* (1929), and Robert L. Dickinson and Lura Beam, *A Thousand Marriages* (1931). During the thirties, family research was predominantly concerned with the success and failure of families as units and of individuals as marriage partners. Three monographs best exhibited the former emphasis, *The Family Encounters the Depression*, by Robert C. Angell (1936), *The Family and the Depression*, by Ruth S. Cavan and Katherine Ranck (1938), and *The Unemployed Man and His Family*, by Mirra Komarovsky (1940); two others inaugurated the latter, *Psychological Factors in Marital Happiness*, by Lewis M. Terman (1938), and *Predicting Success or Failure in Marriage*, by Ernest W. Burgess and Leonard S. Cottrell, Jr. (1939). The coming of World War II forced popular and scientific attention upon the crises caused by the separation of children from parents, and husbands from wives. The two short books by Anna Freud and Dorothy T. Burlingham, *War and Children* (1943) and *Infants without Families* (1944), though written in England, have had much influence in arousing American interest in the effects of identification and separation upon child development, as has *Maternal Care and Mental Health*, by John Bowlby (1952), a summary of previous studies. *Men under Stress*, by Roy R. Grinker and John P. Spiegel (1945), traced many soldier neuroses to family background, while Reuben Hill's *Families under Stress* (1950) drew attention to the burdens placed upon marriage ties by the uncertainties of soldier return.

Despite the heuristic value of the sequence described, the succeeding crises which have engaged the students of American families are not to be divided neatly into separate eras of problems. Too many exceptions and omissions can be found. The dilemmas of morality and sex adjustment, of family loyalty and personal success, of national emergency and private careers, are far from decisively resolved. Nonetheless, since the influence of the altered situation of the fifties will anyhow manifest itself in the choice of research problems, it seems the part of wisdom to attempt self-consciously to assess the direction in which it is likely to press investigators.

It is much less plausible to define the present state of affairs as a crisis than either the depression or the war, yet the impression is widespread that some kind of crisis continues—an unremitting state of impending threat or tension, which some have ironically termed "the permanent emergency." So far no major study has attempted comprehensively to assess the consequences for families of this vague and generalized uneasiness, though certain insightful commentators have endeavored to grasp its main outlines.[3] The important monographs in family research, as examination of their dates of publication shows, have tended to appear in the wake of the problematic state of social affairs which evoked them. Successor monographs, to be practically relevant, must anticipate the effects of the social trends distinctive of the nineteen-fifties. Ten salient trends can be sketched:

1. *The persistent tension of the global political situation* is reflected in various forms of doubt, fear, and suspicion. The most tangible consequence of the cold war is the peace-time draft with its fluctuating quotas. The threat of military service interferes with young men confidently launching vocational and educational careers, and indirectly complicates the expectations of their potential wives. It would be a tenuous argument to attribute divorce or mental disease rates to the international impasse, but it seems plausible that there may be a connection between it and the rise in juvenile delinquency. The dramatization of violence currently pervades social life in activities ranging from children's play and the comics to the best-seller list.

2. *The rapidity of industrial development*, though generally desired, forces continual readjustment upon virtually all segments of society, though some are affected more often and intensely than others. As employment in the "middle-class" tertiary industries gains at the expense of arduous manual labor in primary and secondary industries, occupational mobility becomes a common experience. While the network of relationships based on occupation is thus reorganized, consumption patterns likewise shift

3. David Riesman *et al.*, *The Lonely Crowd: A Study of the Changing American Character* (New Haven: Yale University Press, 1950). Also, Harold Taylor, "Growing Up in a Cold War," an address given by the president of Sarah Lawrence College before the Annual Conference of the Play Schools Association, April 14, 1951; obtainable mimeographed from Play Schools Association.

qualitatively and substantially with inflation and general rise in real family incomes. Even where most gratifying, these gains often have unsettling effects in the development of persons and families. Mass distribution methods and industrial research confront consumers with a frequently bewildering array of incentives to buy. At the same time, amidst general prosperity, the massive fluctuations in particular segments of the national economy are especially disruptive to certain disadvantaged populations—unemployed workers in heavy manufacturing, farmers, aged people on small fixed incomes, the lowest-salaried, the dependent. Moreover, the strenuous pace of competition for advancement puts severe strains on even the most successful.

3. *Large-scale types of organization—both public and private* —create a widespread belief that security and success are functions of the ability to control, influence, or gratify others. Most persons encounter substantial deviations from ostensible rules and standards of employment; *ad hoc* modifications of practice emerge constantly even in bureaucratic organizations. Efforts in industry to diffuse power and widen participation in the decision-making of corporations have only very partially resolved the perpetual question of government in all joint enterprises. The issue seems less pressing among the traditionally self-employed, but their proportion is constantly diminishing and their independence is continually being vitiated by larger bodies. The feeling of individual powerlessness and apathy, prophesied by sociologists like Durkheim, seems to describe the state of mind of considerable numbers, and may help to account for the prevalence of psychological and social isolation. On the other hand, the problems posed by large organizations also help to account for the immense amounts of discussion, experimentation, and efforts to stimulate and organize more direct participation, which are to be found in every community. Small-group movements among the alcoholic, the obese, new mothers, and parents of mental defectives are less related to large organizations, but illustrate efforts toward group self-control in urban life.

Under this caption of large-scale organization should perhaps be included the mounting problems of urban congestion, which the trend to the suburbs does not diminish and in some respects aggravates. City life has never been pre-eminently congenial to family life, and possibly it is becoming less so.

4. *The rate of movement of Americans from place to place,* in both work and play, exaggerated during the war but con-tinued since, has tended to dissolve fixed communities, extended family structures and fabrics of mutual friendship. Migration brings about innumerable circumstances for which conventions are no guide. Physical distance between generations helps to widen the distance between them in belief and practice. Social mobility further widens these separations, which are only slight-ly counteracted by common exposure to the mass media. Cosmo-politan choice of mates—heterogamy and intermarriage—is spurred by this restless moving about (yet heterogamy now seems less likely than was formerly thought to interfere with marital harmony).[4]

For those who can assimilate diversity of experience at the rate at which they are exposed to it there is much to be said for it in terms of the enrichment of personal competence which it brings. For example, divorce is lowest among the most migratory income and education levels—those in professional occupations. Still, the specialists in child development are increasingly alert to the fact that changes of residence are the possible beginning of a child's progressive alienation from his peers. Likewise, the psychologists recognize that spatial mobility occasionally aggravates isolating processes among adults. Migration might thus be termed strong medicine, good for those who can take it and bad for those who cannot.

5. *The wide-scale and rapid growth of leisure*—through shortened working hours, vacations, lengthened schooling, and retirement—has created vast new wants which American culture as yet does not fully satisfy. The aspiration for leisure is often associated with lack of involvement in work, but lack of involve-ment extends widely into leisure pursuits as well, leading to shal-low and restless pursuit of a good time. Recreation has been little studied by social scientists, but the few who have studied it rec-ognize the various effects of the different uses of leisure upon

4. Anselm Strauss, "Strain and Harmony in American-Japanese War-Bride Marriages," *Marriage and Family Living,* XVI, No. 2 (May, 1954), 99–106.

personality development. Strong avocational interests lead to effects generally desired, whereas inability to become deeply involved in either work or play leads at best to boredom and often to quite undesired outcomes. Thus, to some observers, the plenitude of leisure portends a crisis, unless in play people can find an approved and effective avenue of self-development.

6. *The relations of freedom and equality between the sexes* have more nearly approached a single standard than ever before. World War II greatly extended economic, social, and educational opportunities to women. Even the recent peak of divorces, which has been declining only slowly, may in part be favorably interpreted as an expression of women's greater freedom to pick, and choose: unhappy marriages are less likely to endure simply because the wife has no alternative; and marriages which are to endure must rely more than previously upon fulfilling the fundamental requirements of identification and mutual obligation. Admission of women to military service symbolized the end of major official resistance, though peripheral areas of discrimination against the employment and education of women remain.

The effects of the profound transformation by which women leave the home and cease to be segregated from men at work and play are seen in countless ways. A positive index is the easy camaraderie among the younger generation. The "sociologically ideal" courtship in which the parties each have a wide range of choice and come thoroughly to know each other through varied experiences together has become generally feasible.

On the negative side, particularly among the more educated and leisured women, the feelings of futility, boredom, and self-doubt seem prevalent. Their occurrence is widespread but hard to assess more precisely. Though frequently described as a problem of conflicting roles, as between family and career, such an explanation appears somewhat too simple, if not out of date, to judge from the recent spate of books by some highly insightful and informed social and psychological analysts who are themselves women.[5] The problem seems to be more that of formulat-

5. Simone de Beauvoir, *The Second Sex* (New York: Alfred A. Knopf, Inc., 1953). Though written in France, this book has been widely read in the United States and is the most profound of this wave.

ing a satisfactory new identity as a woman, which will be confirmed by experience and the approval of others, than of making a choice between definite existing alternatives. Not only is the current discontent and restlessness over the reformulation of women's roles—in marriage and out—manifest in popular discussion and literature, but official bodies—both public and private—seem to be seriously concerned with it. The range of formal response runs from the United Nations Commission on the Status of Women through the U.S. Women's Bureau and the Commission on the Education of Women of the American Council on Education down to speakers before the local AAUW's (American Association of University Women) and PTA's (Parent-Teacher Association). The ultimate outcome of this intellectual ferment is bound to affect profoundly the character of marriage and family living in the United States.

7. *To have or not to have children* has become more fully a matter of judgment and planning, with the consequence of marked fluctuations in fertility among those classes which exercise superior foresight and exert most influence on the other segments of the community. Among rural families and the more traditional urban groups, where children's labor contributes to family income, children have been wanted in the past as additional hands. However, among the increasing other groups, where each child as an uncompensated cost tends to be evaluated against alternative expenditures of money and effort, a sufficient motive must be found in other terms than economic worth for the child not to be accidental and unwanted. Thus results not only the smallness of contemporary families but the heightened self-consciousness with which couples approach parenthood, instead of taking it for granted. When the population is graded according to income and education, it is found that the major contributors to the continuing baby boom of the early 1950's have been the same white-collar groups among whom family limitation was most pronounced in the 1930's. It is among these that early marriage has gained most rapidly since.[6] These families,

6. John Hajnal, "Differential Changes in Marriage Patterns," *American Sociological Review*, XIX, No. 2 (April, 1954), 148–54; Hajnal, "Analysis of Changes in the Marriage Pattern by Economic Groups," *American Sociological Review*, XIX, No. 3 (June, 1954), 295–302.

through the mass media and the public schools, furnish the model for other families, and the deliberateness of their approach to parenthood has become a pervasive cultural influence.

It could be argued that population dynamics—almost by definition—should not be taken as a conditioning factor external to families. On the other hand, from the standpoint of any given family, it is obvious that the example of family size set by others, the general atmosphere of optimistic or pessimistic expectation, and such tangibles as the availability of large houses and uncrowded schools are rather influential conditions. Families are more likely to feel they must adapt to them, than that they can appreciably modify them. To relate family size positively to family income is coming to be both a cultural and statistical pattern among the prototype strata.

8. *Personality has become an object of popular concern*, as much as the soul was formerly. The belief in fostering the optimal development of children, in psychosocial respects as well as physically and mentally, is propagated through countless media and organizations, among which the parent-teacher associations are pre-eminent and characteristic of the American scene. Due to the desire for scientific sanction for the practices adopted, it is not too early to speak of the professionalization of parenthood, or at least of motherhood. Except for those who remain thoroughly confident of traditional recipes for child-rearing, many parents exhibit some uncertainty and even anxiety over the satisfactory performance of their own roles and their children's development. This effortfulness may therefore somewhat limit the joy and ease with which they conduct their family living. Popular concern with mental health and hygiene, which are professionally recognized as primarily the responsibility of the home, adds a special edge to the concern of certain families. Stray psychiatric thought lends a faintly ominous tinge to some of the literature intended for normal parents of normal children, and may thereby accentuate—among those who expose themselves to it—the hazards as against the satisfactions of family life. It is possible that in retrospect this decade will be seen as transitional to one in which professional emphasis will be upon the joys of competent performance as parents, rather than upon the difficulties

and threats of failure. It is unlikely, however, that a later decade will witness any decline of parental self-awareness, as long as better knowledge and recommended practice continue to be evolved.

9. *Scientific research as a major industry in which increasing resources are being invested is spurring the growth of social science.* Despite the panicky reactions of a few to the rate of transition caused by the application of science and technology, the weight of opinion continues to support science as the proper mode of approach to knowledge and control of the future. Research resources, both human and material, continually increase, guaranteeing that the spiral of change will accelerate. Not "getting back to solid ground," therefore, but finding means to keep afloat in an increasingly fluid situation, is the only response which can provide a realistic sense of security. In turning from more static concepts to the dynamic notion of enhancing social skills for handling unpredicted circumstances, social science is helping to prepare later generations for the continuous transformation of living conditions which natural science brings about.

10. *The social sciences appear to be embarking upon a broadly experimental phase with strong emphasis upon application of results to real-life situations and policy decisions.* Research into economic development, cultural change, race relations, industrial relations, administrative functioning, agency evaluation, mental health, military problems, and public opinion are among the more recent examples of the large-scale application of social science. After a brief period of descriptive study, there seems now to be a rapid increase in all fields toward experimental studies. Paradoxically, this experimental phase in applied research seems to lead to renewed attention to fundamental theoretical and methodological questions, as is illustrated by the new developments of decision theory in statistics. And as this happens, those fields of study where emphasis on application has previously been slight begin to feel the effects of this approach. The study of the family has been one of the fields in which the distance between the pure researchers and the practitioners interested in application has been great, and where experimental study has been almost nil.

While this experimental trend in the social sciences is the precipitating condition for formulating recommendations for future family research, it is not to be taken as any more relevant in selecting and formulating the research problems of highest priority than the other nine factors. Other observers of the general social scene in America may very well list ten somewhat different most important factors to be taken into account in assessing the present situation. It is hoped, however, that the ten set forth will include most of those which would be named by others. To summarize, the ten points are: (1) Persistent tension of the world political situation, (2) Rapidity of industrial development, (3) Growth of large-scale types of organization, (4) Restless movement of Americans from place to place, (5) Wide-scale and rapid growth of leisure, (6) Relations of freedom and equality between the sexes, (7) Deliberateness of decisions to have children, (8) Personality as an object of popular concern, (9) Growth of scientific research as a major industry, (10) Rise of experimentation in social science. If these are indeed the general social conditions of widest import for American families, their re-examination is probably more meaningful than to repeat the hackneyed observation that every individual and his family are immersed in change.

What conclusion is to be drawn as to the appropriate directions for future research may not be self-evident. Nonetheless after much reflection about the significance of these trends, we feel confident that the task of future family research must be to generalize the conditions under which the person becomes competent to handle the dynamic world he confronts. To be sure, all the social sciences are enlisted in helping to make that world more manageable, but the special duty of family studies is to focus upon the intimate processes by which a person is constituted through interaction with those upon whom his identity most depends.

RELIANCE ON REASON

Comments and conclusions about marriage and the family no doubt could be traced back to the first time Mrs. Neanderthal leaned out of her cave to gossip with a neighbor. If we assume, however, that a method of forming reliable generalizations was first applied to the study of the family in the last century, then it may be proper to trace scientific family research to LePlay's first family budgets in France in 1855. But for the sake of limiting the discussion, it is preferable to go no further back than the period of the depression, when the social sciences first came into their own in the United States.

Scientific research on the family in the United States, before President Hoover appointed his famous Commission on Recent Social Trends, was the scanty and sporadic activity of scattered individuals. Few universities in 1930 possessed departments of sociology, and, except for civics, almost no high schools offered courses in social studies, and home economics meant household management. The reports of Hoover's commission and other careful findings laid the basis for the first great programs of social security. As neatly put by Willard Waller, the tradition of rugged individualism had rested upon the workings of a system of rugged familism, bolstered by rural neighborliness. And now that events showed that the system was no longer working, a different system for guaranteeing the economic and protective functions of the family institution had to be devised.

It was early in the thirties that Professor Ogburn set forth his theory of the changing functions of the family, which has since become a standard orientation of family studies. He pointed out[1] how the family institution of the colonial period performed not only economic and protective functions for its members, but also religious, recreational, and educational tasks, nearly all of which were later split off and assigned to such specialized institutions in the community as factories, hospitals, government agencies, churches, theaters, schools, and mass communication media. This has left the family with mainly such primary functions as child-rearing, companionship, and the regulation of sexual conduct. Having united his account of the changes in the form and material conditions of the family with this concise analysis of the trends in its various functions, Ogburn's analysis, though often elaborated, has not been surpassed as an organizing schema. It is

7. William F. Ogburn, *Recent Social Trends in the United States* (New York: McGraw-Hill Book Co., 1933), esp. chap. xiji, "The Family and Its Functions." Also "The Changing Family," *Publications of the American Sociological Society*, XXIII (1929), 124–33.

one of the opening ideas in what is perhaps the most notable analytic treatment of the family institution since then—Alva Myrdal's *Nation and Family*, published in this country on the eve of World War II.

Americans were just getting away from the "fire-fighting" of economic emergencies, and gathering resources for setting positive and constructive goals for family welfare, in the manner foreshadowed by Mrs. Myrdal's prophetic book about Sweden, when World War II plunged them into a new series of emergencies. The not fully completed Social Security Building in Washington was taken over by war production bodies, and all over the country, action agencies dealing with the problems of families were catapulted into new directions of endeavor. Relief offices became employment bureaus. Teachers who had been supervising school lunch programs—where surplus food was given to malnourished children—had to take over day nurseries so that mothers could work in factories.

The depression is estimated by most observers to have had a centripetal net effect upon families. The literature, scientific and popular, on marriage and the family during the thirties, stressed more the treatment of economic strains than it did the disintegration of emotional bonds. But the war, while relieving the economic strain, increased the stresses on emotional solidarity, and the emphasis in research and discussion reversed accordingly.

With the end of the war, observers of the family might have quite naturally expected to return to the situation which had been left behind in 1940. Yet the trends cited, that have become visible since the war, prove how unlike any previous decade the present has become.

If forthcoming family research is to have a practical bearing upon American families, it will be less by offering to shore up the traditional functions of the family institution than by declaring its dedication to those ends for which the institution will remain primarily instrumental. In functional terms these might be called affectional needs, but the objectives postulated by this study do not have the permanent and universal character that is imputed to needs; they are rather emergent values distinctive of the present. In America of the fifties, family research will thrive best as a guide in planning the development of competence in interpersonal relations.

A planning orientation, unlike a functionalist orientation, pushes the question of values into the foreground. An analysis of the malfunctioning of an inherited stock of institutions or practices may be carried on along functionalist lines without seeming to implicate the investigator or the values which motivate him; the investigator is taken to be external to the system; the values are taken as given. But if research is supposed to contribute to the guidance of responsible policy-makers—to be relevant to the progressive revision of ends and the reconstruction of means—then the position of the researcher must be conscientiously stated and his value-commitments exposed to public inspection. In this respect, the work of Mrs. Myrdal serves as a model.[8] Fortunately, in the field of family research, the workers have rarely been loath to reveal their value-positions; if anything, perhaps they have been too willing to do so.

If the orientation we here adopt contains anything novel in the way of premises, it is in uniting the concept of personality with the concept of planning, or, more exactly, of democratic personality with democratic planning. No doubt every social system of the past may have planned for its own perpetuation by indoctrinating the young with its traditional norms. But while our perspective emerges rather logically out of the ethos of individualism as challenged by contemporary conditions, it is probably new to some—to judge from popular discussions of parental discipline—to visualize the deliberate, widespread development of personalities equipped by experience and skill for the discovery and realization of a variety of ends, and not merely stamped out for obedience to fixed commandments.

The concept of planning no doubt differs as much from the earlier interpretations of the values of individualism as the Ogburn-Burgess picture of the contemporary urban family differs from the self-sufficient colonial family. Yet the concept of democratic planning is as authentic an expression of an evolving

8. Alva Myrdal, *Nation and Family: The Swedish Experiment in Democratic Family and Population Policy* (London: Kegan Paul, French, Trubner and Co., 1945), esp. chap. vii, "Goals for a Population Policy," pp. 100–112.

American ethos as is the small, companionate "unity of interacting personalities" with its apartment, car, and television set. The keynote of any democratic conception of planning is sounded by the term "participation." The potentialities of each individual will be developed most fully as he joins with others in creating those social conditions which are optimal for the development of the potentialities of all. This is simply a more dynamic formulation of the principle of respect for the individual, which is usually held to be the central value of American society.

OBJECTIVES OF THIS REPORT

However long it may have been implicit in his own thinking and in that of others, the concept of competence in interpersonal relations was first explicitly stated by Dr. Harry Stack Sullivan in 1947;[9] though since then, attention to "mastery" and "coping behavior" has become current among neo-Freudians. As yet, no clear conceptual definition of such competence has been formulated in these or other circles; so that definition of the term is one of the first tasks of any program of research into the conditions of its development. It is also necessary to distinguish competence from other criteria or objectives of family functioning, such as adjustment or emotional maturity, that is, to make it plain to what it does not refer, and why. Like these other comprehensive notions, the concept of interpersonal competence needs to be broken down into its various components, if it is to be grasped in detail and utilized with precision in research. The next chapter will therefore be devoted both to definition and analysis.

Contemporary emphasis in social research upon the measurement of criterion variables could be indefinitely detaining. Operational definition of the components of interpersonal competence, however, is a large order of research by itself, which cannot be encompassed in this volume. Our major objective is to set forth a series of reproducible conditions, variation of which in certain interrelated ways is thought to facilitate or retard the development of interpersonal competence. To evaluate the influ-

9. Harry Stack Sullivan, "Tensions Interpersonal and International: A Psychiatrist's View," *Tensions That Cause Wars*, ed. by Hadley Cantril (Urbana: The University of Illinois Press, 1950), pp. 79–138.

ence of the conditions specified, measures of outcome are indispensable and yet only instrumental; their elaboration is not taken to be the end of family research. Thus the target of this volume appears in the third chapter, where specific antecedent-consequent hypotheses are proposed for investigation. Some of these were adapted from previous literature, and some were derived from theoretical speculation and discussion between the authors. A much larger number was briefly considered and either rejected as too improbable to be worth testing, or as too impractical, in the sense of not being reproducible by families or family agencies, even on an experimental basis. Thus, the ones listed are selected hypotheses. Part of the sociological and psychological theory from which the hypotheses were derived is sketched in passing, but as a rule the source is either assumed to be self-evident to the theoretically oriented reader or it is briefly cited. This economy of space may be justified by the authors' having written elsewhere on the interactional and developmental approaches in social psychology.[10]

Having confined the hypotheses to those which are deemed reproducible by families or family agencies, the next chapter then scans the various types of family agencies now available, how ready they are to apply and test in action the hypotheses most relevant to their own programs. Inevitably the sketch of each type of agency will be found deficient by those in that specialty. However, the principal object of chapter iv is not to present a comprehensive survey which takes account of all deviations and exceptions to the general trends postulated. Rather, it is to furnish at least a crude gauge by which any agency can estimate where it stands in terms of readiness to experiment along the lines proposed. In addition, this bird's-eye summary of the current state of program planning among family agencies may help to introduce outsiders—especially academic researchers in the separate family-related disciplines—to the broad scope of interdisciplinary-interprofessional collaboration for family wel-

10. Leonard S. Cottrell, Jr., "The Analysis of Situational Fields in Social Psychology," *American Sociological Review*, VII, No. 3 (June, 1942), 370–82.
Nelson N. Foote, "Identification as the Basis for a Theory of Motivation," *American Sociological Review*, XVI, No. 1 (February, 1951), 14–21.

fare. Perhaps the reader will tolerate some injustice to the trees if the forest seems fairly sketched.

When any organization self-consciously sets up program objectives and adopts a matter-of-fact professional attitude toward the means applied it is forced to look at the various stages in the planning process. An attempt is made to generalize this planning process, which again may not exactly match the experience of any particular agency while yet roughly applying to all. As a general model of foresightful action and the progressive revision of values and concepts through systematic scrutiny of experience, this analytical scheme also has some relevance for those families who aspire to prudence in governing their own careers.

Finally, the two general lines of thought about family research and agency planning are brought together in chapter vi in the methodological concept of participant experimentation. Some unwelcome aspects of planning such as the dependence on professionals and the experimentation with families are avoided by the suggested procedure for the establishment of autonomous quasi-families. These intimate groups of limited duration can supply some of the deficiencies of actual families in a way which enhances the competence of their members rather than usurping their functions.

The Appendix, which presents all family research published in the United States between 1945 and 1954, affords a means for the reader to judge for himself how this program extends or diverges from trends discernible from that decade to this. In particular, the family researcher in choosing his problems for today can relate his context to the work of his colleagues and perhaps come forth with a more apt thesis.

II *Interpersonal Competence*

COMPETENCE IS A SYNONYM for ability. It means a satisfactory degree of ability for performing certain implied kinds of tasks. Each of the abilities described below as components of interpersonal competence is found to some degree in any normal person, regardless of his previous experience. Nevertheless, as with virtually all human abilities by practice and purposeful training wide differences result. In this sense, interpersonal competence although based upon inherited potentialities, and directly contributing to self-conceptions, may be compared to acquired skills. To conceive of interpersonal relations as governed by relative degrees of skill in controlling the outcome of episodes of interaction is to diverge greatly from some other explanations of characteristic differences in behavior.

SOME POSSIBLE MISUNDERSTANDINGS

The term "social skills" is now quite widely used. It might seem more advantageous and less awkward to employ it, rather than "interpersonal competence." Unfortunately, however, it has already accumulated a number of connotations which hinder its conveying what is intended here. Thus social skill often indicates correct etiquette or polish. At other times it means success in achieving popularity through display of coveted virtues.

Social skill is also used instead of a word such as rhetoric. In some of the numberless books on self-help and human relations readers are initiated into the various tricks and routines for persuading others—into the sort of skills that are necessary for salesmanship and supervision. While selling and supervision are legitimate activities, and success in these no doubt makes some use of interpersonal competence, skill in influencing others would be a very limited and limiting objective to impose upon family life.

Countless educational media—though ostensibly not commercially or manipulatively minded—likewise profess to furnish training for leadership, which is described in the language of social skill. Again, however, their emphasis tends to be on institutional ends, to the relative neglect of self-realization in day-to-day family living. But it is fairly often observed that a person can function quite successfully in his job or committee post, though his behavior as a husband or father is unsatisfactory to all concerned. Conversely, even the development of extraordinary competence in interpersonal relations—though it may help—cannot guarantee success in business or politics.

Despite these warnings against confusing interpersonal competence with the social skills of success literature, a word can be said in defense of the impulse which moves writers and readers of self-help books on human relations. Immense numbers of our fellow-citizens feel inept in their interpersonal relations; they sense narrow limits to their ability to influence or even to conciliate others. Their belief that something can be done about their ineptitude is hopeful and constructive. Were they to adopt the pessimistic alternative, and construe their fate as recalcitrant to all thought or effort, the result would undoubtedly be grave for them and the community at large.

Certainly no professional person in the field of family relations can lightly condemn the millions who read the endless stream of books, pamphlets, and columns upon marital and child-rearing problems. Yet this too is a kind of self-help literature. The mounting demand for functional courses in marriage and parenthood may be interpreted in part as a response to the fact that knowledge and skill in these matters can no longer be simply absorbed through watching one's parents. The motives which inspire this demand are not merely intended to repair a deficit. More often the reader is confident that better practices are to be found than tradition affords; or he explicitly declares that he wants to do a better job than his parents did. In nearly all such expressions the assumption is evident that differing outcomes depend upon relative degrees of competence.

Among experienced educators in the family field, there is general agreement that mere rules and prescriptions cannot give this eager audience the competence they desire. Applied inappropriately, the most intelligent advice can have untoward results. What the advice-seeking public requires in addition is the resource to utilize general knowledge effectively in varied circumstances. Moreover, as such adaptability of response develops, the craving for categorical rules frequently, as in other fields of learning, abates; the second baby is less likely to be raised from the book. To be sure, the need for straight information on technical matters cannot be gainsaid. But specifically with regard to the intimate interpersonal episodes of family life, general information and abstract principles are of minor effect in enhancing competence; demonstration and practice are superior means of changing behavior.

The possible sources of confusion about the meaning of competence are less troublesome than a moral issue which the term may evoke. In his earliest book, Sullivan spoke forthrightly of the achievement of power in interpersonal relations.[1] Negative reactions to the connotations of the word "power" appear to have convinced him that more was to be gained by dropping than by keeping it. Yet perhaps a later generation of readers can suspend judgment long enough to consider afresh the ambiguity of attitudes toward power in society, at least at the level of the family. This might enable us to dispose of any lingering notion that interpersonal competence implies the mechanical manipulation of others.

The philosopher Bertrand Russell in his book *Power: A New Social Analysis* defines power simply as the ability to produce intended effects, a definition which might also stand for competence. The resistance sometimes engendered by referring to power in interpersonal relations can be traced back to a fear of one person controlling another. Implied in this fear is the assumption that the dominated person will be exploited or forced to serve ends of which he disapproves. Where dominator and dominated are assumed to seek the same goals, the question of domination is less often raised.

1. Harry Stack Sullivan, *Conceptions of Modern Psychiatry* (Washington: The William Alanson White Psychiatric Foundation, 1947), pp. 6–11. From lectures given in 1940.

The democratic values of freedom and equality imply plurality of values and presume that the values of some shall not be imposed upon others. In government, protection against domination by the stronger is approached through distributing power as widely as possible, and by various checks and balances for maintaining this distribution. It is logically absurd to speak of eliminating power; the threat of domination is countered by equalizing power. Some self-styled realists claim that power is never restrained except by equal and opposite power, and that to expect any self-restraint by the powerful is to think wishfully. Yet, if some self-restraint by fathers and husbands, as well as majorities vis-à-vis minorities, could not be counted upon, the powers of the weaker parties could never develop sufficiently to match the strength of their potential oppressors. Thus, even if power is taken to be the relative strength to dominate or resist, there is every reason to learn how to control the conditions of its growth.

As the pragmatist philosophers have pointed out, power (in Russell's sense) is the means of access to all other values. Power may be employed to realize favored or opposed values, to suppress or to foster the development of other persons. The mere fact of possessing power is not evil per se. There is no way of increasing power which guarantees against its misuse, and one cannot realize good ends if one is powerless.

So construed, the pursuit of power in interpersonal relations is ethically neutral. In proposing the enhancement of interpersonal competence we are not advocating any one set of institutional values as against any other.

The analogy to free public education is fairly exact. Unless citizens are equipped with the knowledge and the skill with which to communicate and judge public policy they cannot participate equally in governing the commonwealth. The purpose of free (and compulsory) public education has always been to make all citizens competent to exercise their voice in making public decisions. In a country where only a small class is literate, self-government is hardly feasible, and so the lifting of educational levels generally has become a democratic value. In this same sense, the diffusion of interpersonal competence is a democratic value. It can be employed for good or evil, yet from the stand-point of any one person, it is good to have more of it. As an anti-democrat, a person would at least want it for himself, but as a democrat, he would logically want to see everyone at least as competent as himself. As a program, therefore, the development of interpersonal competence could well be regarded as a proper extension of the value of free public education.

The neutral or general value of interpersonal competence, considered as a prerequisite for the achievement of any other values of personality and family life, appeals to neo-Freudians as well as to pragmatists. Alfred Adler was perhaps the earliest to stress the incessant effort by the person from infancy onward to gain control of his world. And Adler also saw from the out-set that the "power-seeker"—the neurotic individual who delib-erately maneuvers to dominate others—is a person who, having been unsuccessful in winning their favorable response by nor-mal means, strives to construct a situation in which he can extort involuntary deference.[2] Erich Fromm says the same of self-love and selfishness. Karen Horney, though denying the derivation of her thoughts from Adler, repeats almost the identical theme throughout her several works. Erik Erikson postulates the quest for mastery as a virtually universal motive. Yet none of these thinkers could be accused of advocating the domination or manipulation of others, not even of children by parents. All are advocates of some variant of self-realization. And all recognize the dependence of optimal development along self-chosen lines upon one's social relations with others.

At the level of common sense observation, people are seen to differ markedly in their aptitude or ineptitude for dealing satis-factorily with others. At the level of theoretical speculation, in-terpersonal competence as a general phenomenon appears to be based on what certain existentialist philosophers call transcend-ence.[3] This term summarizes the uniquely human processes of

2. Alfred Adler, "The Family Constellation," *Understanding Human Nature* (Cleveland: The World Publishing Company, 1941).

3. Ortega y Gasset, "The Self and the Other," *Partisan Review*, XIX, No. 4 (July–August, 1952). Simone de Beauvoir, *The Second Sex* (New York: Al-fred A. Knopf, Inc., 1953). Robert Ulich, *The Human Career: A Philosophy of Self-transcendence* (New York: Harper and Brothers, 1955).

suspended action, memory, revery, foresight, reflection, and imagination, by means of which a person from birth onward escapes progressively from the control of his immediately given environment and begins to control it. It is by this freedom from the irresistible instincts and external stimuli, which chain the responses of lower animals, that the human being is enabled to modify his surroundings, to plan and create, to have a history and a future. His detachment from the present situation provides both the opportunity and the necessity for him to declare his own identity and values as an adult.

This capacity for transcending the immediately given and thus affecting and reconstructing it invites several levels of explanation, ranging from neurology to prehistory. The explanation most relevant here is the one based on man's ability to use symbols. Symbolization affords representation at will of that which is not present, and recombination of its elements—whether in language, dreams, art, or play. It is more than possible that inquiries into the abstract realms of symbolic processes will produce findings more potent in the development of interpersonal competence than the more proximate behavioral hypotheses ventured in the next chapter. It takes wings of greater breadth than the authors' however to fly in such thin air. We applaud those who will make the attempt while sticking closer to earth ourselves.

Instead of attempting, therefore, to further elaborate a general concept of the origins of interpersonal competence, our main strategy of definition will be analytical, to name its parts, as manifested in observable behavior. These we take to be: (1) health, (2) intelligence, (3) empathy, (4) autonomy, (5) judgment, and (6) creativity. The final number and order of these components, as well as the names assigned to them, are the result of reflection, as well as extensive reference to previous literature and current discussion. Nonetheless they arose initially in quite different form through intensive pondering of what qualities distinguish inept from competent performance in interpersonal relations.

It may seem somewhat inconsistent to take pains to distinguish interpersonal competence from social skills and to insist upon the unfamiliar phrase, while on the other hand assigning to the components of competence terms which have acquired competing meanings and interpretations in previous research. It is advantageous, however, to utilize terms with established significance, and to draw upon the treasuries of previous research, even if both are somewhat wide of the target erected; in this case, these advantages outweigh those of neologism. Given that the general notion of interpersonal competence sets the framework for defining each of its components, it is hoped that each component will be interpreted as an acquired ability for effective interaction, rather than in some other context. To illustrate, creativity may refer elsewhere to artistic talent or scientific genius, but here it is confined to resourcefulness in devising new and effective responses to problematic interpersonal situations. Each component will be separately and more fully defined below, but each is conceived as a component of total competence. In any performance all six aspects of competence are manifested simultaneously, though one may be more obviously put to test than another. And the degree to which each can be cultivated independently remains an empirical question.

The abilities designated are possessed by individual family members in varying degrees, however much they may derive from common family experience or affect family structure and functioning. Nor is this the only reason for speaking of interpersonal rather than family competence. By including all intimate relationships such as fiancé, chum, or sibling long absent, futile controversy over who is a family member is avoided. Since our dependent variable is personality development, every significant other in the family constellation must be taken into account; and, as will be seen in a later chapter, the concept of quasi-families arises both to explain certain suggestive developments in urban sociability and to suggest self-conscious experimentation with identity-forming small groups.

SOME PRIOR FORMULATIONS

A number of theorists have endeavored broadly to classify the relationships among people according to the motives these relationships are said to express. Many years ago, for example, Albion W. Small designated the six basic interests which he believed to generate all human associations:[4] health, wealth, sociability, knowledge, beauty, rightness. Among the many schemes for classifying motives which have been proposed, this early list is of special interest because, as has been called to our attention by Mr. Howard Stanton, Small's list is nearly cognate with the elements of interpersonal competence. Why such resemblances should occur is itself an inviting topic for speculation.

An intriguing coincidence of the same order was also discovered in the 1952 Annual Report of the Superintendent of Schools of New York City, which lists "what we want for our children" as: (1) adequate knowledges and skills, (2) good social character for living in a democracy, (3) good health, (4) sound thinking, (5) creative expression and appreciations, (6) adjustment of the world of work. And Miss Ethel Kawin, Director of the Parent Education Project at the University of Chicago, in a progress report dated March 31, 1954, presented what an advisory panel of qualified scholars had approved as "the major essential characteristics of mature, responsible citizens," and what such citizens require for "competent participation of the individual in a democratic social system": (1) feelings of security and adequacy, (2) understanding of self and others, (3) democratic values and goals, (4) problem-solving attitudes and techniques, (5) self-discipline, responsibility, and freedom, (6) constructive attitudes toward change.

Beyond the obvious differences and similarities of these lists and the elements of competence, two less visible assumptions involved deserve emphasis: that their authors aspired to completeness in the range of species under the genus imputed, and that the motives of persons and the goals of institutions do, can, or ought to congrue.

Some other writers, more therapeutically and less educationally oriented, have attempted to define analytically the characteristics of mental health. At the 1953 National Conference on Social Work, for example, Dr. Marie Jahoda grappled with this quite metaphorical concept before an interdisciplinary sympo-

---

4. Albion W. Small, *General Sociology* (Chicago: The University of Chicago Press, 1905).

sium on the family.[5] She first criticized previous conceptions which confused psychological health with (1) the absence of disease, (2) statistical normality, (3) psychological well-being (happiness), or (4) successful survival. These criteria were inappropriate, she asserted, because they neglected the social matrix of human behavior:

> It follows that we must not conceive of psychological health as the final state in which the individual finds himself, for this state is dependent upon external events over which he has no control. Rather we should think of it as a style of behavior or a behavior tendency which would add to his happiness, satisfaction, and so on, if things in the external world were all right. Psychological health, then, manifests itself in behavior that has a promise of success under favorable conditions.

Although Dr. Jahoda only adumbrated two tentative examples of the positive criteria she recommends, she did set another basic question for family research: What are the psychologically relevant attributes of an environment which permit the manifestation of psychologically healthy behavior? This research task differs markedly from the etiology of mental disease.

Dr. Albert Dorfman, a pediatrician at the University of Chicago, in a 1952 seminar at the Family Study Center, pointed out that any systematic effort to define normality in child development must include, even for small children, not only physical well-being, but such aspects of their behavior as effectiveness, originality, adaptability, trust, and confidence in self. He sought the assistance of social scientists in constructing precise measures of these variables, so that their development might be more readily traced.

5. Marie Jahoda, "The Meaning of Psychological Health," *Social Casework*, XXXIV, No. 8 (October, 1953), 349–54.
The entire symposium, reported in this same issue, is of especial interest as a notable step toward redefinition of the aims of the caseworker. A highly contemporary statement of aims by one authority was: "to help clients with their struggles to master difficult life situations." When this is linked with the classical vocabulary of Mary E. Richmond, one of the founders of social work, who held that the special field of the caseworker is "the development of personality through the conscious and comprehensive adjustment of social relationships," it appears that the earliest and latest periods of social work may be more like each other in this respect than the middle period was to either. Perusal of Miss Richmond's *What Is Social Casework?* (New York: Russell Sage Foundation, 1922), especially chapter v, fortifies this impression.

In his major work to date,[6] Erik H. Erikson promulgates a scheme of eight stages in personality development from infancy to maturity. This scheme is far more profound than the many which simply cut up the process of development into chronological intervals. Erikson entitles each of his stages according to the favorable or unfavorable personality characteristics in which they result. These emerge from successful or unsuccessful negotiation of the problems peculiar to each stage: (1) trust versus basic mistrust, (2) autonomy versus shame and doubt, (3) initiative versus guilt, (4) industry versus inferiority, (5) identity versus role diffusion, (6) intimacy versus isolation, (7) generativity versus stagnation, (8) ego integrity versus despair. Without committing themselves completely to Erikson's apparatus of stages, the editors of the fact-finding report of the Mid-century White House Conference on Children and Youth adapted the favored products for designating the attributes of healthy personality. The cultivation of these products is set forth as an implied objective for the various social institutions making up the community: (1) the sense of trust, (2) the sense of autonomy, (3) the sense of initiative, (4) the sense of duty and accomplishment, (5) the sense of identity, (6) the sense of intimacy, (7) the parental sense, (8) the sense of integrity.[7] That the concept of interpersonal competence converges with certain other trends of current thought is thus as evident as that it diverges from certain lines of conceptualization.

WHAT COMPETENCE IS NOT

Not all researchers agree that it is desirable to set up as their major dependent variable some central measure of family functioning. Among those who do think so, a considerable variety of variables is favored. Some appear to refer to attributes of the family as a kind of reified entity, as for example, solidarity. But upon examination it usually turns out that such a measure is applied to the behavior of individuals defined as family members,

6. Erik H. Erikson, *Childhood and Society* (New York: W. W. Norton and Co., 1950).

7. *Personality in the Making: The Fact-Finding Report of the Mid-century White House Conference on Children and Youth*, eds. Helen L. Witmer and Ruth Kotinsky (New York: Harper and Brothers, 1952).

and then their scores are more or less arbitrarily combined as a family score. Other measures explicitly refer to individual behavior, but in ways that relate it to the behavior of others in familial or other interpersonal relations. The most widely employed measures of this type are happiness, adjustment, and emotional maturity. To approach family behavior in terms of interpersonal competence is a fairly substantial reorientation from these more established ways of interpreting family interaction.

To speak of competent personalities is not to refer to ingrained virtues or fixed traits. What is generally meant by a personality trait is not some constantly evident attribute like blue eyes, but a standardized response to standardized situations. Nevertheless it is usually described adjectivally as if it were a constant, the presence of which transcends or pervades the actor's behavior in all situations. Actually, this is what competence does, and in that limited sense competence answers the notion of a trait better than what are usually called traits, e.g., authoritarianism.

The trait concept, as commonly formulated in psychological literature, is inadequate as a theory of behavior; to attempt directly to inculcate some desired trait is therefore frequently unworkable in practice, and indoctrination is improper as an end. Any notion of molding personalities to fit preconceived standards is likely to construe human beings as things or objects, passively subject to manipulation by superior authorities who stand upon some detached pedestal. Behavior, however, is dynamic, episodic, situationally specific.

Traits, as descriptive categories for distinguishing recurrent aspects of behavior, are applied by some people to other people, and imply a relationship between observer and observed; it is thus that in social life they serve to regularize expectations, though they can do so only roughly and incompletely, for the contingencies are too variable. Reciprocal attributions and imputations are subject to unceasing diversification and disagreement. They are stable bases for reliable prediction only to the extent that the representative situations which evoke them are stabilized through implicit commitments of all the parties involved. Every person repeatedly steps beyond the range of standard expectation in the course of his development; in a dynamic social world novel situations are pandemic. Outside those situations in which conventional responses are appropriate, trait psychology is as ineffectual in guiding the observer or experimenter as rigid iteration of previous responses would be frustrating to an actor.

There is something to be said for the trait notion from the standpoint of an actor's effort to create a harmonious style of life, but this conception—of a more or less self-conscious pattern of decisions—is quite removed from what is normally meant by traits; style of life is a holistic notion, employing themes to relate items or events.

One of the more plausible versions of trait psychology as applied to the study of the family is its incorporation in the idea of compatibility. In its most common form, as applied to marital selection, the traits of one partner are seen as ideally fitting those of another, analogous to the way in which a key fits a lock. In this interpretation the relationship between two people is put either in terms of similarity or complementarity, and it is explained as the predictable product of matching or mismatching of attributes. This is the simplest and most static view which could be taken; actually theories based upon this original notion are woven principally of qualifications and auxiliary hypotheses intended to account for the numerous negative cases. How, for example, do ostensibly compatible people become incompatible, and vice versa? And how do incompatible people marry to begin with?

Contradictions particularly multiply when the matching notion is applied to children and parents. The latter have presumably instilled their own traits into their offspring, yet incompatibilities arise. The emphasis on matching is sometimes carried to extreme lengths in adoption cases, though this has no warrant from research. To suppose that happy marriage and successful parenthood depend upon felicitous concurrence of compatible traits, and that wise selection can avert the hazards of family life, is neither a logical nor an empirical conclusion. Most of the important questions lie in areas that this approach cannot reach, or where it cannot be experimentally tested.

Out of the reaction against the atomistic and static approach of trait psychology, there has arisen a more holistic and dynamic concept—adjustment. This became, and for the present still remains, predominant in both research and practice. There are many measures of adjustment, differing so widely that proponents of each can no doubt with some validity deny the applicability of any general criticism of this concept. Nonetheless the various usages of adjustment can probably for present purposes be sufficiently distinguished from competence by pointing out certain of their most common meanings.

One usage has the "contented cow" overtones of adjustment terminology; the implication is that human beings react only to disturbances which upset their putative equilibrium, and that the objective of all action is the restoration of tensionless rest. Another usage which has come in for increasing attack is the one that implies reliance upon others to provide instigations to action. If each lets himself be directed by others, critics ask, who guides the whole, and, for that matter, who is responsible for each? The so-called environment to which the individual is assumed to be adjusting is mainly a social environment; are the good adjusters to subordinate themselves to the poor adjusters? A third implication which is being currently challenged is the notion of immediate happiness and security as ultimate values, and the rejection of trial, sacrifice, and risk as evils. One of the most recent standard textbooks on the family defines maladjustment as consisting of conflict, frustration, disapproval, and deprivation; by this view Romeo and Juliet were totally maladjusted.

Logically, the concept gets into insuperable difficulties as soon as its users commence to speak of good adjustment and poor adjustment; all pretense of its being a value-neutral term vanishes at this point. The critics allege that adjustment as either an imputed or recommended end masks a conservative ethic; and this cannot be removed without abandoning the use of the term as a means of differentiating desired from undesired states of affairs, or else plainly adopting a value position other than defense of some given status quo.

The practical motive for research on adjustment seems to be the attainment of a state of affairs having a specific behavioral and emotional content deemed "good." But one man's happiness is another man's gloom. We reject such a formulation because (*a*) while we no doubt share the middle-class norms which are idealized, they too often imply a sort of subcultural ethnocentrism that neither can nor should be forced upon other segments of society, (*b*) it treats conflict as evil in itself, and conceives it unrealistically as unnatural and expungeable, and (*c*) by setting up a stable state of affairs as the end of action by family agencies, it dooms such action to inevitable futility, while closing the door to the exploration and the discovery of new experience and forms in family life. Joint involvement in constructive activity is much more than absence of disagreement.

Quite apart from the intricate and unresolved methodological problem of getting operational definitions and objective measures of adjustment and maladjustment, the basic concept seems to have passed the peak of its popularity a decade or so ago. Research devoted to determining the conditions of adjustment in families evokes less and less interest, while critics multiply. The historian of ideas may eventually associate it with the period of the depression, while the notion of traits may perhaps be associated with a still earlier period in which a man's character was alleged to be his fate, a fate predestined because impervious to change.

Thus interpersonal competence is neither a trait nor a state. Competence denotes capabilities to meet and deal with a changing world, to formulate ends and implement them. The incessant problem of equipping human beings to handle their affairs and to progress toward the discovery of new values and new means is not solved by authoritarian indoctrination of static attributes and beliefs. To rely upon such methods would not only be surbversive of the most fundamental of American democratic values but would ultimately result in failure of the system which sought to maintain itself by these means.

On the other hand, there are no grounds for assuming that human nature will "unfold" into competent personalities if merely given freedom. Somewhere between these extremes lies a conception of personalities not inflexibly bound to and molded by the past, nor by utopian absolutists eager to sacrifice the present generation, but capable of utilizing past experience and future aspirations in an effective organization of present effort; not dependent upon direction from without but capable of integrating their goals with those of others and collaborating in their realization; in short, able to cope with their world whether the formulas devised by predecessors fit or not.

The developmental approach, while considerably more suitable than concepts of compatibility and adjustment for evaluating family functioning, is still somewhat encrusted with earlier associations. The notion of maturity, for example, is a rather ambiguous term, which deserves scrutiny. In the normal physical development of a child from infancy to adulthood, the final stage of growth is usually called maturity. When applied to the development of the child's personality, however, the idea of maturity frequently becomes a misleading organic analogy. And when a phrase like "emotional maturity" begins to be used as an epithet by which some adults pronounce moral judgments upon others, its utility has almost vanished.

From the standpoint of interpersonal behavior, personality development is a continuous process. Not only must there be intermittent adaptation to those conditions beyond the control of the person, but a person must constantly set himself a fringe of new objectives. This is especially so in a dynamic society, for it is only thus that a person can resist the welter of conflicting influences which play upon him daily, and organize a more or less unified scheme of autonomous action.

The confusion of age norms with stages of growth is one of the more harassing connotations of the maturity concept because of its incomplete emergence from biology and child psychology. This confusion is especially acute in the more rivalrous subcultures of the American community, where children's progress relative to other children is watched with a jealous eye by their parents. An adequate concept of personality development recognizes the full potential range of qualitative differentiation; it requires the measurement of development of a child or an adult against his previous self or his authentic peers, rather than against extraneous competitive norms. To impose competitive norms in a punitive manner is often discouraging or destructive for development, though intended to be motivating.

As central concepts in family research, adjustment has not superseded compatibility, nor has maturity outdated adjustment, in any neat and clear-cut manner; at most there has been a series of successive emphases. This is particularly true in connection with the concept of adaptability, which was first used effectively in family research by Robert C. Angell in the early 1930's, yet has recently been more fully elaborated by Burgess and Wallin,[8] as particularly appropriate to companionate family relationships. Despite its early use, adaptability appears to be a concept which is transitional from adjustment to competence as a way of looking at family behavior. As used by Burgess and Wallin, it partakes also of a realistic developmental approach: persons do not automatically, if their development is unimpeded, become adapted to a wide range of situations; rather, they acquire adaptability through formulating diverse ways of coping with problematic situations, and if conditions do not permit this kind of learning, they may acquire instead quite maladaptive modes of performance.

There are other terms current in the research literature which might be compared and contrasted with the idea of competence, but we prefer to leave their further consideration to another place or to other writers, while we return now to the further exploration of the elements which compose our central variable.

THE COMPONENTS OF COMPETENCE

Each of the component aspects of competence in interpersonal relations can be considerably elaborated and investigated. The decision as to how far to go in any particular instance depends on the particular project in mind and the amount of resources available. Here it is deemed suitable only to outline roughly a recognizable conceptual definition of each component, and not to attempt operational definition or the construction of any measures. We can then go on to consider some hypotheses about

8. Robert C. Angell, *The Family Encounters the Depression* (New York: Charles Scribner's Sons, 1936); Ernest W. Burgess and Paul Wallin, *Engagement and Marriage* (Chicago: J. B. Lippincott and Co., 1953), chaps. xviii and xix.

the purposeful development of each of the six components of competence.

1. *Health.*—In this component we include much more than mere absence of disease. Rather it signifies the progressive maximization—within organic limits—of the ability of the organism to exercise all of its physiological functions, and to achieve its maximum of sensory acuity, strength, energy, co-ordination, dexterity, endurance, recuperative power, and immunity. A popular synonym is "good physical condition." In some medical research circles, there is, in this positive sense, considerable discussion of the better operational criteria of health to take the place of such crude indices as, for example, gain in weight among children. Research in psychiatry and psychosomatic medicine has been finding not only that sexual competence and fertility depend on psychosocial development, but also physical health in general.[9] But the relationship runs in both directions.

Without good health, interpersonal episodes often diverge in outcome from wanted ends. Fatigue is a common example of this. While it can be and often is a symptom of complications in living, with certain other people it may also originate new difficulties. The overworked mother will lose her patience unless her reserve of energy, her ruggedness of physique, can carry her through the critical periods. The ailing person of either sex may find his dependence is not only a burden to others but means that he cannot complete the tasks that he formerly could. Endurance of strain makes physical demands, but the capacity to bear strain is not a constant; it can be cultivated in advance of its use. A striking example is the frequent recovery from despair and breakdown of interpersonal relations through vacation and rest, hygiene and recreation. On the positive, nontherapeutic side —in terms of optimal development—a benevolent spiral seems to extend from radiant health to a cheerful mien, from a cheerful mien to a friendly response, and back again to competence. The physiological substrates of interpersonal acts have been little

9. Henry B. Richardson, *Patients Have Families* (New York: The Commonwealth Fund, 1948). Also, Metropolitan Life Insurance Company, *Statistical Bulletin*, XXXVI (New York: Metropolitan Life Insurance Company, 1955), published monthly. Innes H. Pearse, M.D., and Lucy H. Crocker, *The Peckham Experiment* (New Haven: Yale University Press, 1945).

studied within each social context; the body-mind dualism lingers on in the choice of research problems; by treating health as an element of competence, fresh possibilities arise, for the physiologist as well as the social psychologist.

Efficient criteria of health which are appropriate to the various developmental periods are needed, and so are economical devices for measuring these criteria. Also needed are hypotheses where the health component is regarded as a consequent as well as an antecedent, and finally there should be programs to test these hypotheses. Such hypotheses can of course range over the entire social, biological, and physical environment. For purposes of this report we limit our definition of the field to the relation of families or quasi-families to the development and maintenance of this component of competence.

2. *Intelligence.*—Since this component has been studied continuously and widely for over two generations, it would be presumptuous to elaborate upon it here. Scope of perception of relationships among events; the capacity to abstract and symbolize experience, to manipulate the symbols into meaningful generalizations, and to be articulate in communication; skill in mobilizing the resources of environment and experience in the services of a variety of goals; these are the kinds of capacities included in this category. It is significant that the construction of measures of intelligence is as controversial as ever, and that in any particular research project, the appropriateness and validity of the measure adopted is always a question of judgment.

The research implications of this component are toward appraisals of the findings of past research within the competence frame of reference and the design of research to fill the gaps in relevant knowledge. Of special interest will be the study of the interrelations of this component with the others we list.

In the planning-action context, the most promising line will be the appraisal of the effectiveness of present programs in creating the relevant antecedent conditions for maximizing the intelligence component, and the design of new sets of conditions which will strengthen or replace those currently operative. The conception of intelligence as a variable subject to planned development is exemplified in certain previous research studies[10] and a number of ambitious experimental programs of action, e.g., the X. G. project of the New York City public schools.

Health and intelligence have been far less often assumed to be variables subject to change through experimental programs than the remaining components of competence, yet they are no less psychosocial in their development. Research and action in respect to the following four components of competence may be less hampered by the weight of previous assumptions.

3. *Empathy.*—People appear to differ in their ability correctly to interpret the attitudes and intentions of others, in the accuracy with which they can perceive situations from others' standpoint, and thus anticipate and predict their behavior. This type of social sensitivity rests on what we call the empathic responses.[11] Empathic responses are basic to "taking the role of the other" and hence to social interaction and the communicative processes upon which rests social integration. They are central in the development of the social self and the capacity for self-conscious behavior. No human association, and least of all democratic society, is possible without the processes indicated by this term. For this reason we must include empathic capacity as one of the essential components of interpersonal competence. The sign of its absence is misunderstanding; to measure its presence in the positive sense is a task now being attempted by a few investigators.

The kind of interaction experienced in the family as well as in other groups appears to depend heavily upon the degree to which empathic capacity develops, but experimental research on fluctuations in this element of competence has hardly begun. This lack in research is paralleled by a lack of explicit programs in action agencies aimed at the development of this type of skill. Yet it is so fundamental to social life of every kind that some

10. Harold M. Skeels, Ruth Updegraff, Beth L. Wellman, and Harold M. Williams, "A Study of Environmental Stimulation: An Orphanage Preschool Project," *University of Iowa Studies in Child Welfare,* Vol. XV, No. 4, New Series, No. 363, December 1, 1938 (Iowa City: University of Iowa, 1938).

11. For a fuller treatment, see: Leonard S. Cottrell, Jr., and Rosalind F. Dymond, "The Empathic Processes," *Psychiatry,* XII, No. 4 (November, 1949), 355–59.

social psychologists have come close to defining their field as the study of empathy.

4. *Autonomy.*—In the conception of the competent personality which we are defining in terms of its components, one essential element is perhaps best denoted by the word "autonomy," though the ordinary usage of the term does not include all the significance we shall assign to it here. Our present referents, expressed as aspects, are: the clarity of the individual's conception of self (identity); the extent to which he maintains a stable set of internal standards by which he acts; the degree to which he is self-directed and self-controlled in his actions; his confidence in and reliance upon himself; the degree of self-respect he maintains; and the capacity for recognizing real threats to self and of mobilizing realistic defenses when so threatened. That is, autonomy is taken to be genuine self-government, construed as an ability, not a state of affairs. A narrower definition, close to operational, is ease in giving and receiving evaluations of self and others.

Commencing with Piaget in the 1920's, the number of writers who have attempted to deal with autonomy has been growing steadily, but the process of making clearer what is meant by this term (or its near-equivalents like ego-strength and integrity) has as yet produced no satisfactory agreement upon its referents. Some writers treat it as a trait, some as a value, some as a set of rules for behavior, and some as a highly subjective, desired state of affairs.[12] We believe that progress in definition and measurement of this obviously very important though subtle complex will come most rapidly if definition is sought in terms of an acquired ability for handling those kinds of problematic interpersonal situations where self-esteem is threatened or challenged.

12. Andras Angyal, *Foundations for a Science of Personality* (New York: The Commonwealth Fund, 1941). Erik H. Erikson, *Childhood and Society* (New York: W. W. Norton and Co., 1950). Joanna Field (pseud.), *A Life of One's Own* (Harmondsworth, Penguin Books, 1952). Erich Fromm, *Man for Himself: An Inquiry into the Psychology of Ethics* (New York: Rinehart, 1947). Robert Lindner, *Prescription for Rebellion* (New York: Rinehart, 1952). Rollo May, *Man's Search for Himself* (New York: W. W. Norton and Co., 1953). Henry A. Murray *et al.*, *Explorations in Personality* (Cambridge: Harvard University Press, 1938). Jean Piaget, *The Moral Judgment of the Child* (Glencoe: The Free Press, 1948). David Riesman, *The Lonely Crowd* (New Haven: Yale University Press, 1950).

5. *Judgment.*—While critical judgment has long been understood to be acquired slowly with experience, more or less according to age, its operational definition and measurement is still a difficult task. Certain of the educational psychologists have perhaps gone furthest in differentiating this ability from intelligence, and in analyzing the conditions by which an educational or other agency may cultivate judgment among its pupils.[13]

Judgment refers here to the ability which develops slowly in human beings to estimate and evaluate the meaning and consequences to one's self of alternative lines of conduct. It means the ability to adjudicate among values, or to make correct decisions; the index of lack of judgment (bad judgment) is mistakes, but these are the products of an antecedent process, in which skill is the important variable. Obviously neither small children nor incapacitated adults can make sound decisions in the sense indicated; and it is equally obvious that among normal adults there is wide variation in this ability. Some persons acquire reputations for unusually good judgment, and some others become conspicuous for the opposite. It is therefore highly proper to conceive of judgment as an acquired critical ability differing in degree among individuals.

Currently among several of the social sciences, though notably in economics, the study of decision-making and of value-choices is receiving much emphasis. Generally speaking, however, the various studies and seminars under way focus upon the outcome or the product of this process—upon ethics, logic, or some highly abstract calculus of contingencies and relative utilities; rarely do they focus upon the choosers, their identities, and the conditions under which their critical abilities develop. A thoroughly interpersonal concept of judgment, appropriate for studying its development, probably therefore must include the skill involved in getting others to be reasonable in discussion, and to handle criticism in a way that utilizes its value.

13. E.g., R. B. Raup, K. D. Benne, B. O. Smith, and G. E. Axtelle, *The Discipline of Practical Judgment in a Democratic Society*, 28th Yearbook of the National Society of College Teachers of Education (Chicago: University of Chicago Press, 1943). Also, Edward M. Glaser, *An Experiment in the Development of Critical Thinking* (New York: Bureau of Publications, Teachers College, Columbia University, 1941).

6. *Creativity.*—This component is perhaps the least amenable to precise definition and division into manageable variables which can be measured. It is ironical that the so-called tough-minded scientists and hard-headed practical people are inclined to look askance at this category as a proper object of scientific study, and yet all of these people demand appraisals of this quality in prospective associates on whom heavy responsibility for leadership and initiative will fall.

The idea of creativity is commonly associated with artistic and intellectual activities. We define it here as any demonstrated capacity for innovations in behavior or real reconstruction of any aspect of the social environment. It involves the ability to develop fresh perspectives from which to view all accepted routines and to make novel combinations of ideas and objects and so define new goals, endowing old ones with fresh meaning, and inventing means for their realization. In interpersonal relations, it is the ability to invent or improvise new roles or alternative lines of action in problematic situations, and to evoke such behavior in others. Among other things it seems to involve curiosity, self-confidence, something of the venturesomeness and risk-taking tendencies of the explorer, a flexible mind with the kind of freedom which permits the orientation of spontaneous play. While this is a none too satisfactory delineation of creativity, we can begin here and invite help in the search for a more satisfying one. In interpersonal relations, the uncreative person is continually found in dilemmas and impasses—"at his wits' end" —but the valid indices of creativity are harder to discover. Rigidity obtrudes upon attention more than flexibility, for obvious reasons, but that is not to say it deserves more scientific attention.

WHY SIX COMPONENTS OF COMPETENCE?

This brief outline of our conception of the essential components of interpersonal competence is offered with no illusions as to its adequacy or finality. If we have succeeded in giving to the reader at least a rough working idea of the content and meaning the term has for us, and have stimulated critical thinking on its contemporary relevance or implications, our purpose for the moment has been served. Perhaps such reflection will result in the discovery of other skills and qualities which should be added to this list. For the present we are unable to offer additions or corrections, and have some reasons for assuming its completeness.

Readers of George Herbert Mead[14] will recall his distinction between the "me" and "I" phases of the self in personality development and social interaction. Looking at the elements of competence, three correspond roughly to the "me" phase and three to the "I" phase:

Me: Intelligence	I: Health
Empathy	Autonomy
Judgment	Creativity

The former refer to the vested and organized experience of the community as incorporated within personal conduct; the latter, to the active, assertive, and emergent features of human behavior, not reducible to standard roles in conventional situations. But while Mead, like Dewey, relied heavily upon biological explanation for the impulsive and unpredictable character of human development, it had nonetheless been his intention to show the emergence of novel identities within the process of interaction. The concepts of interpersonal autonomy and interpersonal creativity may help to complete his task. In any social act—any episode of interaction—all six capacities are and must be employed, though their prominence varies from phase to phase.

The cultural anthropologists have offered many attempts to classify the full range of human culture. These range from the classic division into technology, social organization, and ideology, through Lowie's "universal pattern of culture" and Malinowski's six-category analysis of institutions, to the extremely elaborate Yale cross-cultural index. It seems significant that the classical tripartite scheme can be detected underlying each of its more sophisticated successors. From quite a different angle, this old division seems to gain a vague additional warrant from Morris' division of the study of meaningful verbal relationships into semantics, syntactics, and pragmatics.[15] Considering the fond-

14. George H. Mead, *Mind, Self, and Society* (Chicago: The University of Chicago Press, 1934).

15. Charles Morris, *Signs, Language and Behavior* (New York: Prentice-Hall, Inc., 1946).

ness of Western thinkers for indicating completeness by schemes of three elements and opposition by schemes of two, it is difficult to distinguish chicken from egg in trying to account for the recurrence of such schemes, i.e., do they describe reality, or is social reality not the precipitate of such linguistic constructions?

Probably neither metaphysics nor intellectual history has to be called on for defense of either the number or order of the elements of competence, however intriguing it is to speculate about their resemblance to previous schemes. Health and intelligence refer to the factual world of physical events and overt experience; both principally afford rational and efficient manipulation of the objects of the environment. Empathy and autonomy, by contrast, have to do with the relationships of selves and others, not as objects, but as human subjects with whom each person is engaged in the plots of the human drama. Judgment and creativity refer to the symbolized realm of not-present relationships, to the extent that these can be distinguished from the social and instrumental realms of immediate experience.

As mentioned at the outset of this chapter, the six elements of competence were arrived at principally through reflection upon previous research and upon the observable content of interpersonal behavior, and not from play with hyper-abstractions. If further abstraction, however, could demonstrate the completeness of a scheme that is made open-ended by the inclusion of creativity as its final element, then it would seem logical to suppose that our list of six would be lengthened by the addition only of subcategories, rather than by the addition of a seventh or eighth component.

With regard to order, the list is thought to proceed from the most given to the least given features of any interpersonal performance. Also, as will be seen in ensuing chapters, the order adopted is cognate with an order which appears not only empirically convenient in presenting types of family agencies and types of play, but also productive of further useful meditation about reciprocal implications. It would deprive the reader of some pleasant speculation to explore these exhaustively here; we prefer only to suggest the avenues which may be used to order and traverse the vast territory confronting us.

It appears to us that a community which organizes its activity so that it maximizes the number of healthy, intelligent, self-directing citizens, capable of viewing situations from perspectives other than their own, of weighing alternatives and making decisions, of defining new goals and inventing ways of achieving them, is in fact a democratic community and is producing members who can sustain it against all more pessimistic theories of human nature and the social order.

III *Hypotheses for Experimentation*

THE NOTION OF interpersonal competence is not central in current family research; indeed the term is rarely used. (This is not true of its designated components. Bibliographies on empathy, autonomy, judgment, and creativity running to several hundred titles each, have been collected at the Family Study Center.) Harry Stack Sullivan and those who utilize his interpersonal conception of psychiatry have of course oriented their theory and practice to the development of interpersonal competence, but this group has not undertaken to elaborate its rich clinical understanding and skill into a system of hypotheses.[1]

Certainly some focus for family research is needed. We have already pointed out some serious objections to adjustment as a central concept. Static functionalist theories of satisfaction or adjustment may be useful for short-run analysis in relatively stable situations, but they are almost useless when they attempt to deal with phenomena of change, which they tend to approach as pathological or dysfunctional conditions. In a society oriented to values which include the continual discovery of new values and the reformulation of old ones, theories based on static assumptions are often out of date before they can be tested.[2] The rapid postwar drop in age at marriage, plus the rise in "going steady," as against prewar theories of student dating, is a case in point.

Competent personalities in contrast to adjusted ones have the qualities, skills, and orientations which ideally enable them to

1. Articles by this group are concentrated mainly in *Psychiatry: Journal for the Study of Interpersonal Processes*, published by the William Alanson White Psychiatric Foundation.

2. For a suggestive earlier critique of the use of adjustment concepts in family research, see: William L. Kolb, "Sociologically Established Family Norms and Democratic Values," *Social Forces*, XXVI, No. 4 (May, 1948), 451–56. For another similar critique, see also: Willard Waller and Reuben Hill, "A Developmental Concept of Adjustment," *The Family* (New York: The Dryden Press, 1951), pp. 361–64.

cope with whatever confronts them, insofar as any human being can do so. And so long as people have some competence in this sense and are free to exercise it, the achievement of the basic values of our society remains a realistic possibility. Such statements cannot be made of adjustment as presently conceived.

Chapter ii contains a discussion of what we have called the components of competence for effective functioning in a democratic society. This discussion can be summarized in the form of a general hypothesis that some suitable measure of interpersonal competence is a function of suitable measures of health, intelligence, empathy, autonomy, judgment, and creativity. The testing of this general hypothesis will we hope become the focus of widespread research effort; for present purposes we shall assume the essential validity of the general hypothesis. This enables us to concentrate on the proposal of specific hypotheses bearing on the maximization of the various components of competence, leaving for another time and place further examination of the general hypothesis.

At this analytical level, we believe a productive use of research time and effort would be the formulation of hypotheses relevant to: (1) The interrelations of the components of competence. (2) The correlates of the components, with special emphasis on their distribution among families and family members according to demographic and social-cultural characteristics. (3) The study of various processes and outcomes of family behavior, e.g., marital relations, using competence or its specific components as antecedent variables. None of these three vast areas, however, are to be explored here, as important and inviting as they are.

Within our focal interest of developing new research on the family, we are primarily concerned with research that has practical relevance for the planned development of interpersonal competence. For this reason we prefer to treat each component as a variable dependent on definable antecedent conditions. As a way of visualizing the task of proposing hypotheses of this kind, we suggest the reader keep the following table in mind. That the grouping of the relevant antecedent conditions is not entirely arbitrary may be visible upon inspection.

The hypotheses, now listed serially, would if the table were large enough be contained in the various cells. In addition, the table would have depth in the sense that each cell would contain hypotheses for different developmental periods—infancy, childhood, preadolescence, adolescence, adulthood, and later maturity—and for successive phases of the family cycle—courtship, marriage, parenthood, and grandparenthood.

TABLE 1

SCHEME FOR ARRAYING HYPOTHESES

CONSEQUENT VARIABLES— COMPONENTS OF COMPETENCE	ANTECEDENT CONDITIONS					
	1 Biological	2 Economic	3 Social-Legal	4 Inter-personal	5 Educa-tional	6 Recrea-tional
1. Health..........	Infancy to later maturity	ditto				
2. Intelligence......	ditto					
3. Empathy.......						
4. Autonomy......						
5. Judgment.......						
6. Creativity.......						

The table suggests that only relatively simple relations can be hypothesized. While this limitation does not necessarily follow, the testing of simpler relations is logically the place to start; the more complex interrelationships among antecedent conditions will suggest themselves soon enough.

The rest of this chapter will present some illustrative hypotheses affecting the development of competent personalities. They are arranged so as to fall into various cells of the table. We are not able to fill all the cells with promising hypotheses of the experimental, or even the descriptive, variety. To do so would require the collaboration of many investigators, but the scheme suggested may help to stimulate others to make additions.

The ideal form of hypothesis necessary for rigorous testing contains a precise operational specification of the consequent and antecedent variables, the controlled conditions under which their relations are to be tested, and the amount and kind of co-variation to be expected under those conditions. But in all scientific fields the achievement of this level of precision is preceded by a long period of hunch statements. Vaguely perceived or guessed relations among ambiguously defined variables serve as rough guides to research, from which more precise formulations can be derived and tested. Much of what is regarded as research on the family is in this primitive state—or worse, that is, not even approaching hypothetical statement. Such a condition needs no apology provided the goal is a more rigorous level.

Few if any of the hypotheses about interpersonal competence can at the present time advance much beyond such crude first approximations. But the first step is necessary if we are ever to walk. The reader must therefore at this time tolerate a low degree of precision, rigor, and systematic elegance.

While conceding their roughness in this respect, there are nevertheless some other respects in which the statement of the following hypotheses is closely disciplined. First, it will be noted that the hypotheses selected from the infinite number possible are of course those designating conditions which, given reasonably adequate resources, are experimentally and practically reproducible.

It may also be obvious that the testing of any of these hypotheses presumes some change in behavior over time, measured by a valid index. This is a more restricted conception of what constitutes a hypothesis than the looser general usage of the term. Popular usage often includes static distributions and correlations, anticipated descriptive findings, retrospective interpretations, and even mere logical derivations. The confusion these cause makes it important to differentiate the conception of an experimental hypothesis on the development of abilities from these popular usages.

A third preliminary qualification of our selected hypotheses is that they all have to do with training rather than with selection variables. Psychological tests, to illustrate the difference, may enable an employer to pick out with some reliability employees whose performance will be good. That would be a case of prediction from selection variables, these variables having been identified through previous research as showing the highest correlations with later performance. On the other hand, an employer may find himself with a staff already on hand, whose performance he wishes to improve, not by discharging the poorer ones and rehiring better ones, but by training procedures. In that case, research, if it is to help him, must identify those conditions which will produce the desired change in employee behavior.[3]

Marriage research that relies principally on prediction of adjustment from selection variables contributes little to the understanding or control of how to produce desired changes in the capacities of mates. It thus stands to benefit from the precedent of training variables, which have been established, almost perforce, in child development research. There it has to be assumed that parents must do what they can with the children they have, rather than exchanging them for better risks. To dramatize this point somewhat more strongly, the reader, as he scans the following hypotheses, may consider in his own mind how, if validated, they could be used by husbands and wives in evaluating the conditions which they as actors create for the continuous development of each other after marriage.

Finally, because it is not immediately evident, it may be important to point out that experimental hypotheses like those to follow are not readily derived from static descriptive correlations. Because height and weight are correlated does not mean that one can grow taller by eating more. Though everyone grants that correlation is not causation, the curiosity of many is satisfied by the finding of mere associations. Some experimental hypotheses can be derived by translation from empirical regularities of this sort, but most come from theoretical propositions which cannot themselves be put to the test.

For reasons of space and the large amount of existing research, as well as the presumably greater familiarity of the reader with health and intelligence, we include only sample unit hypotheses about the conditions affecting their optimal development. Em-

3. For another effort to clarify these distinctions see Philip M. Hauser, "Social Science and Social Engineering," *Philosophy of Science*, XVI, No. 3 (July, 1949), 209–18.

pathy and autonomy are treated much more fully, partly because of the authors' special interest in these two variables. After dealing with the first four components of competence, we abandon the scheme of filling each cell of our imagined table, lest it become tedious. In the case of judgment and creativity, we have suggested a series of general conditions from which more specific hypotheses can readily be derived. The purpose of this chapter is to illustrate our thesis, in the hopes of stimulating others to further formulations; it is not to exhaust all possibilities, nor the reader.

SOME CONDITIONS FOR DEVELOPMENT OF HEALTH

Biological conditions during:

Infancy: The planned child is more likely to be born under favorable conditions of maternal health.[4]

Childhood: The health of the parents affects the child, and improvement of their health may often be more effective than direct approach to the child.

Preadolescence: Food fears run a course and abate if left alone; if alternate diets are kept at hand meanwhile, the range of taste will freely expand.

Adolescence: Developing rhythms of sleeping and eating, work and play, if disrupted arbitrarily, lead to stress reactions, but if respected, facilitate regular autonomic functioning.

Adulthood: Self-management of the body along hygienic lines depends on commitment to health as a value, and not on mere learning of practices.

Later maturity: Health histories show a cumulative feature; that is, early health predisposes to later good health, and bad health disposes to chronic illness.

Economic conditions during:

Infancy: The chances of life for each child increase with its family's rising level of living, and approach a point where chances are even.

Childhood: Since the health of each school child largely depends on the health of the other school children, where the school explicitly functions to bring community medical resources to bear in cases of need, the health of all improves.

Preadolescence: Progressive involvement in productive manual work which mobilizes energies for tasks of extended duration is conducive to good physical condition, and particularly to control of satiation.

---

4. *Ceteris paribus* is a qualification that applies to all the following hypotheses.

Adolescence: Health is favorably affected by the development of clear-cut vocational identity through ideal models and confirming groups.

Adulthood: Security of employment fosters health; assurance of permanent worth to the employment unit fosters it even more.

Later maturity: Availability of rewarding work, regardless of age, prolongs the retention of vigor and faculties.

Social-legal conditions during:

Infancy: To minimize the traditional penalties of minority status—crowding, deprivation, neglect—is to increase the chances of life for children in these restricted groups.

Childhood: If a family lives in a residential community designed for family living and for children's safety and play, then the children's health will thrive more than in an area oriented mainly to adult males.

Preadolescence: Dramatization of the public interest in the welfare of children—particularly its concern and intervention in cases of ill-treatment—causes parents to give children better protection than where the public seems indifferent.

Adolescence: Legal and moral emphasis on responsibility toward others creates an atmosphere more favorable to the growth of sexual competence than emphasis upon restraint of sexual interests.

Adulthood: As women feel accorded equal status at large, they gain in capacity for sexual response.

Later maturity: Health of the aged is directly a function of whether as a class they experience tangible evidence of respect or rejection.

Interpersonal conditions during:

Infancy: If parents are accepted as adults by parental figures, they can in turn more readily give parental care. (The famous studies of Anna Freud, Rene Spitz *et al.*—summarized by Bowlby, *op. cit.*—well cover the bearing of continuous affection upon physical and mental health, but they do not show how love might be enhanced for the unloved and the unloving.)

Childhood: The cared-for child learns to value and care for himself, by avoiding risks and following rules, when these rules are conceived as protection and not as restraint.

Preadolescence: An optimum alternation between isolation and stimulation is directly related to patterns of energy-use that fall between apathy and overstimulation.

Adolescence: Clear-cut models for sex identification improve the chances of sexual competence and reduce frigidity and impotency.

Adulthood: Control of fertility is a function of full communication and common intent between husband and wife.

Later maturity: Retaining an audience or finding new audiences, before whom one wishes to do well, is conducive to continuous health.

Educational conditions during:

Infancy: Recognition by parents and others of each gain made in the child's physical development builds up assurance and appetite for further ventures.

Childhood: Sympathetic responses of others to signs of the child's physical state help the child to recognize their meaning and importance: teaching him to report them explicitly is the basis for ultimate self-regulation.

Preadolescence: The responsibility of looking after pet animals provides a dramatic basis for learning hygiene.

Adolescence: Understanding of physiology reduces anxiety over rapid development and makes the emergence of sexual functioning a welcome attainment and thus contributes to sexual competence.

Adulthood: Full access to knowledge of sexual techniques and the range of human behavior encourages couples to explore and find various mutually acceptable patterns.

Later maturity: A sense of fruition through completion of a recognized career fosters health in later years.

Recreational conditions during:

Infancy: Space and objects for exploration induce the growth of coordination.

Childhood: Full and free expression of evening bursts of energy in play, with adult consent or participation, do more for health than their suppression.

Preadolescence: If the physical demands of sports are adjusted to slightly exceed the margin of proven competence, their effect upon growth of physical competence is maximal.

Adolescence: The rhythm and phrasing of play episodes—if the demands increase in a graded series—affect the span of potential involvement, and thereby the capacity for flexible mobilization of energy.

Adulthood: Play by its nature begs ideal performance, and by its range exercises faculties unused in work; thus play if continued maintains capacity, whilst lack of play leads to deterioration of the unused capacities.

Later maturity: Involvement in new interests looking toward future outcomes as both actor and spectator is conducive to health.

SOME   CONDITIONS   OF
INTELLIGENCE

Biological conditions during:

Infancy: Physical stimulation through handling and caressing stimulates perceptive responsiveness to the environment.

Childhood: Having other children to play with fosters intelligence; having none retards it.

Preadolescence: Regular and thorough examination and correction of deficiencies in hearing and seeing improve intelligence in children;

hearing difficulties particularly lead to attributions of lack of intelligence, and to self-conceptions as unintelligent.

Adolescence: The span of involvement in episodes of learning behavior can be steadily lengthened by progressively adjusting new tasks to the margin of ability.

Adulthood: The event of parenthood clarifies adult identity, thus reducing diffusion of intention and facilitating full mobilization of mental resources for chosen tasks.

Later maturity: Energy reluctantly expended is pathogenic, but energy expended willingly in response to stimulation, even in large amounts, is generally hygienic. Not quantity but quality of work is the gauge.

Economic conditions during:

Infancy: Objects that can be manipulated, and which disclose their principles by being disassembled and assembled, foster intelligence.

Childhood: Use of adult objects—despite cost and waste—improve the child's comprehension of its environment.

Preadolescence: If both father and mother can spend much time with their children, being responsive to their initiative, rather than doing things for them, the children's intelligence improves.

Adolescence: The opportunity to explore and experiment before being committed to a vocation makes more probable a choice which will utilize potentialities fully, thus fostering their growth.

Adulthood: Opportunity for success-experiences and for their recognition by self and others through reference to a visible product encourages intelligence.

Later maturity: To continue to have people and projects dependent upon one for support preserves motivation and faculties.

Social-legal conditions during:

Infancy: A general atmosphere of neighborhood interest in births and babies stimulates response and development.

Childhood: Subcultural emphasis on the values of learning and professionalism encourages the development of intelligence; anti-intellectualism discourages it.

Preadolescence: Cultural emphasis on the values of personal performance rather than on those of birth, race, and family connection, lifts the ceilings of motivation imposed by inherited status.

Adolescence: The complementarity of receptive and assertive approaches to knowledge and control of reality is best appreciated and employed in coeducational institutions. Thus all types of intelligence are cultivated best by coeducation.

Adulthood: As profound cultural stereotypes about the innate intellectual inferiority of particular minorities are demolished by criticism, the intelligence of these minorities rises.

Later maturity: The making of social demands upon the aged to take responsibility for themselves as a group (when put with respect and not as punishment or rejection) evokes a flow of ingenuity not obtainable when responsibility is withdrawn.

Interpersonal conditions during:

Infancy: Maternal responsiveness fosters alertness to novel elements in experience; her enjoyment in the child's discoveries intensifies his own.

Childhood: To involve the child in the pursuit of knowledge through discussion between parents, especially where there is dialectic and reasonable resolution, cultivates his intelligence.

Preadolescence: A chum with whom one can assimilate new intellectual challenges, by kindly mutual criticism and by confiding fears, is a great help in forming strategies for mastering fears.

Adolescence: Reciprocal, frank discussion of the standards of adolescent peers versus the parent-teacher generation reduces ambiguity in the self-evaluation of progress, and makes criticism bear clearly on the sources of mistakes.

Adulthood: Self-conscious recognition by a continuing critical, appreciative audience of significant others promotes disciplined attention to standards of performance.

Later maturity: Foster-home placement of aged persons stimulates their faculties when it furnishes them identification with the purposes of a younger family, and a chance to contribute to those purposes.

Educational conditions during:

Infancy: Abundant talking with the infant before he learns to talk stimulates the growth of intelligence.

Childhood: When teachers proceed explicitly, not on the notion of an original self that has to be trained, curbed, expressed, or molded, but by construing education as a joint process of discovery and mastery, they reduce resistance to learning and encourage the appetite for it.

Preadolescence: As the child is exposed to sympathetic adults of richer vocabulary, his intelligence develops more rapidly and fully.

Adolescence: Practice in group methods of problem-solving, e.g., through admission to family councils, furnishes an overt, dramatic model of careful thinking, which can be assumed individually by identification.

Adulthood: Children's questions—if welcomed and used—provide the parent with a review of his own intellectual biography and stimulate self-analysis of his resistances to learning, and so may reduce them.

Later maturity: Adult education, to evoke serious involvement when it is not to be put to vocational use, must foresee a significant audience for the products of the knowledge and skills acquired.

Recreational conditions during:

Infancy: Patient play by parents with a child as he struggles to master new phases of development creates confidence in approaching new experience.

Childhood: Observation of play furnishes clues to problems perplexing the child; spontaneous response to these problems in a friendly, spontaneous way helps in their recognition, verbalization, and control by the child.

Preadolescence: Play is both preparatory and assimilational; adequate rehearsal before and after each new accession of understanding is a means of securing it.

Adolescence: Adequate opportunity (space, time, respect for privacy) for reverie, whenever learning exceeds the rate of immediate assimilation, prevents the building-up of resistance and helps to build major themes of unified selection and composition of new experience.

Adulthood: If the parent (or teacher) in play permits his likeness as an omniscient being to be laughed at, both he and the children gain in discriminating real from false intellectual control.

Later maturity: Utopian speculation leads to discrimination of the novel and emergent, thence to fresh attacks on familiar problems.

SOME CONDITIONS FOR DEVELOP-
MENT OF EMPATHY

In chapter ii we have sketched what we mean by empathy. It is the basic response capacity on which the processes of socialization, development of a self, communication, and integration rest. Present research, meager as it is, indicates that empathic capacity can be roughly indexed and will probably be measured with as much precision as intelligence. Findings thus far suggest that there is a substantial range of variation in this capacity among individuals at a given time, and within individuals through time.

BIOLOGICAL CONDITIONS

Empathic capacity, like any other response capacity, requires a healthy organism. This type of response needs no special organ or faculty beyond the special human equipment of a highly developed cortex. Sensory acuity and capacity for accurate perception; neural and neuromuscular capacity for generalization and symbolization; capacity for covert mobilization of complex acts, symbolization of those acts, and the conduct of complex interacts at the covert level are of critical importance. We have few specific hypotheses under this heading, aside from the obvious one that when the physical basis of an organism is impaired so is the organism's capacity for empathic response.

In the field of mental illness, the testing of hypotheses on the conditions and consequences of empathy might lead to highly interesting results. In general it is widely suspected that underdevelopment or impairment of empathic capacity plays a major role in many kinds of behavior disorders, particularly in schizophrenia.

Under biological conditions also belong hypotheses concerning the effects on empathic capacity of various bodily states of extreme hunger, anger, pain, fear, excitement, intoxication, pleasure-anticipation, pain-anticipation, and similar conditions which restrict attention or reduce perception.

Additional types of hypotheses about the social psychological consequents of certain biological conditions and their effects in turn upon empathic capacity are suggested here. For example:

1. Prolonged illness increases habituation to a relationship of dependency and thus depresses empathic capacity on both sides of the relationship, but especially in the dependent member.

2. Empathic capacity is negatively correlated with repression of biological functions. (*a*) There is a negative correlation between the degree of repression of sexual functions and empathic capacity. (*b*) Thus economic, social, and educational provision for minimizing the gap between organic sexual maturity and sexual functioning will have a positive effect on empathic capacity.

3. Unwanted children are lower in empathic development than children who are desired and planned for. (*a*) Instruction in how to safely and efficiently control the number of children born, and means to exercise this control, will result in a lower proportion of rejected people in the population. (*b*) By spreading the economic burden of having and rearing children over the whole population, the probability of children being born to people who want them will be increased, with a consequent increase in average empathic capacity.

4. There is a critical point beyond which closer contact with another person will no longer lead to an increase in empathy. (*a*) Up to a certain point, intimate interaction with others increases the capacity to empathize with them. But when others are too constantly present, the organism appears to develop a protective resistance to responding to them. As the numbers of people with whom one must deal increase, it is necessary to respond to them impersonally. This is exemplified in customer, passenger, and patient relations. This limit on the capacity to

empathize should be taken into account in planning the optimal size and concentration of urban populations, as well as in planning the schools and the housing of individual families. (*b*) Families who provide time and space for privacy, and who teach children the utility and satisfaction of withdrawing for private revery, will show higher average empathic capacity than those who do not.

Economic conditions (job stability, income, conditions of work, and leisure time) become factors in the development and exercise of empathic capacity when they affect the amount of unhurried and anxiety-free time, and the facilities for stimulating activities, that parents can give to their children. Their influence is also important to empathic development to the extent that they affect contact and participation in the life of the community. In less obvious ways they influence attitudes and values, and these in turn affect empathic skill:

1. There is a negative correlation between the degree to which parents emphasize material possessions and other evidences of buying power in their evaluations of themselves and others, and their own and their children's empathic capacity.

2. To the extent that criteria of wealth predominate in the selection of associates, social life becomes restricted and unstimulating and empathic capacity atrophies.

3. Mate selection in which monetary criteria of eligibility predominate results in a higher proportion of marriages characterized by progressive deterioration of communication, companionship, and sexual compatibility. The effects on the empathic capacity of the parents and children will be correspondingly negative.

4. The assumption by children of appropriately graded responsibilities for the economic welfare of the family (as for example, regular duties and special jobs in the home, or limited jobs outside) increases empathic capacity. (Note: This is of course no argument for child labor in the old sense. But a revision of our economic, educational, and family institutional arrangements so as to make it a regular thing for all children, beginning

at junior high school age, to have a limited and safeguarded opportunity for genuine participation in the world of business, industry, and government, would probably be a desirable thing in terms of their optimal development.)

1. Members of an authoritarian, hierarchic social system will tend to develop higher empathic responsiveness to situations of superordinate-subordinate structure and lower empathic capacity for understanding other types of relations. (*a*) If the system is relatively stable and rigid, then those nearer the top exhibit the greatest empathy with persons in superior positions and the least with those in subordinate roles.

2. Family structure in such systems will tend to reflect social structure, and families are hence rendered less likely to provide the interpersonal conditions for maximizing empathic capacity.

3. In authoritarian families, the mother becomes the pivotal, mediating person, who is more able to understand both authoritarian father and subordinate children. (This may be why such characteristics as intuitiveness, sympathetic understanding, adaptability, and interest and skill in literary and artistic production have become identified as "feminine" in cultures characterized by patriarchal-authoritarian family systems.)

Age, sex, ethnic, religious, and socioeconomic differences tend to operate to inhibit the development of empathic capacity, and reduce its utilization where possessed, when these rankings serve as barriers to participation and communication.

4. Participation in activities which include members of different subcultural groups, and which are not focused on the hierarchical relations of the subcultural groups themselves but oriented to concrete solution of common problems, will increase the empathic capacity of the participants.

5. Subgroup relations characterized by anxiety and hostility are negative in their effects on the development of empathic capacity and its utilization. Families play a major role in the orientation of the child to these subgroup differences.

6. Persons from families where positive efforts are made to bridge subgroup barriers to communication and understanding

(differences in age, sex, class, ethnic origin, religion, and values) will show a higher empathic capacity than those who do not make such positive efforts.

1. There is a positive linear relation between the empathic capacity of a person at any point in his developmental career line and the extent to which his previous development has been characterized by stable, intimate communicative relations of relative equality and reciprocity with the members of his family. (*a*) For the ideal type, middle-class American family, the relative importance of the specific relationships are mother, father, siblings, in that order. (*b*) Affection is a highly important positive factor but its relative effectiveness is a function of the amount of communication sustained in the relationship. (*c*) Friction and conflict produce a negative effect to the extent that they impair communication. (*d*) The range of empathic capacity is a function of the number of different kinds of functional positions which the person has occupied in the family interaction. (By functional position of a person we mean the part played by him in a given social act, e.g., a giver or a receiver in an act of giving and receiving; leader or follower.) (*e*) Unilateral acts of parental subordination to the child's demands, or of administering rewards and punishment, minimize reciprocity and inhibit the development of empathic response. Striking the child in anger at something he has done and in other ways reacting to his acts so that he discovers that "parents too are human," is more in the direction of reciprocity and communication than the detached and impersonal application of rules of punishment and reward. The positive effect of "acting natural" is enhanced if the parent explains his reactions to the child and encourages him to consider how he would feel under similar circumstances, and then follows this by working out with the child some new line of action as an experimental solution to the problem.

2. Empathic capacity in children is positively related to the facility with which their parents learn to communicate and understand each other (though high empathic capacity does not insure marital harmony).

EDUCATIONAL CONDITIONS

Schools, secular and religious, are in a favorable situation to experiment with various ways of supplementing and facilitating the family in the development of empathic capacity. Experimental and control groups could be used without detriment to the children used as subjects, indeed, with the conscious participation of the children and parents in the experiment. Hypotheses such as the following illustrate some of the possibilities:

1. Groups of children who are given the following experiences will show more empathic capacity than comparable groups who are not given such experiences: (*a*) Taught courses in fiction, biography, and drama in which the child is instructed and is given assistance in putting himself in the roles of the various characters studied. (*b*) Taught by teachers who themselves are high in empathic capacity. (*c*) Taught by a number of teachers who represent different subcultural backgrounds. (*d*) Given explicit instruction, training, and practice in accurate portrayal of others who represent different roles in his own life situations and different subcultural identities. (*e*) Taught in situations in which the emphasis on individualistic striving for grades is replaced by emphasis on collaborative responsibility for maximizing the skill and the mastery of the subject matter by each member of the collaborating group. (*f*) Participation in group activity which involves responsibility for co-operation in planning of significant programs, resolution of real problems, and genuine discipline of members.

The design of such experiments should provide for the "non-contamination" of groups. The numbers involved should be large enough for reliable statistical comparisons. The value of the experiments would be further enhanced if the experimental sample could be further divided into groups which provide for the various relevant combinations of (i) parents: (*a*) being told and actively co-operating in designated ways; (*b*) informed, but not asked to participate further; and (*c*) not informed; (ii) experimental subjects: (*a*) informed as to objectives and participating in planning and appraisal of results; and (*b*) not informed as to objectives.

2. The general hypothesis to be tested by inclusion of the variables mentioned above is that active informed participation in the experiment will enhance the effectiveness of the antecedent variables.

In a later section dealing with planning and action agencies, we outline the way in which recreation reflects the various types of activity in our culture. Despite the demonstration there that recreation is not a separate aspect but relates to all other aspects of our life, it is appropriate here to note some of the specific relations between recreational conditions and empathic response.

1. Unilateral giving of toys with no opportunity for the child to reciprocate and to occupy the role of giver inhibits his empathic development.

2. Toys which confine the child to role of spectator limit his empathic development.

3. Abundance of mimetic and dramatic play is positively correlated with empathic development. The genuine and full participation of the parents in this play greatly enhances its effect on empathic development.

4. Reading and films, radio and television programs, which provide rich opportunity for identification with a variety of characters, increase the empathic capacity of the child.

5. Forms of play which involve discussion, planning, teamwork, and resolution of differences are productive of empathic capacity.

SOME CONDITIONS FOR DEVELOPMENT OF AUTONOMY

Autonomy has been provisionally defined as the ability to be one's self. Analytically considered, it involves and requires knowing one's self; having or finding an unambiguous identity to refer to in each situation; and being able to govern one's self in the sense of being able to choose among alternatives. The development of autonomy is not synonymous with the development of a self, though emergence of a self is indispensable. The growth of autonomy is taken as measurable and as varying within and among individuals over time. Preliminary work indicates that a satisfactory index can be devised, although the invention of such a measure requires considerable analysis of the patterns in which autonomy is exhibited, so as to differentiate these as consequents from the reproducible conditions hypothecated as their regular antecedents. The giving and receiving of characterizations of self and others not only exhibit various degrees of ease and constraint, but whether one's self-concept is ratified rather than enforced by others is often ambiguous. That human beings are characterized by the possession of selves varying in autonomy does not involve the free-will dilemma; it requires only the discernment of the differences in certain kinds of behavior expressing those selves. Experimentally, it requires that the antecedent conditions conducive to increase in autonomy be distinguishable from autonomy as a dependent variable. Because autonomy is perhaps more vulnerable than any other component of competence to being construed as a state of affairs, a trait, or a form of virtuous conduct following definite commandments, it is important to reiterate that it is here regarded as an acquired ability to handle certain aspects of problematic interpersonal situations with greater or lesser success.

BIOLOGICAL CONDITIONS

1. Health which itself is one of the components of competence, significantly conditions all the other components including autonomy. The conditions of health—nutrition, rest, hygiene —are therefore indirectly biological conditions of autonomy. But there are a few biological conditions which more directly affect autonomy than through their influence upon physical health. In marriage and family living, these concern sexual adequacy and fertility, where these enter into self-respect and sense of worth, in the estimation of self and others. To the extent that sexual adequacy and skill can be improved by knowledge, practice, or medical treatment, a contribution is made to autonomy, i.e., the person becomes more able to handle interpersonal situations making demands upon his sexual competence. The fact that there is a circular relationship here, in which autonomy significantly

affects sexual functioning, implies the reverse proposition as a corollary hypothesis worthy of investigation.

2. Fatigue as a biological variable distinguishable from health significantly conditions autonomy, and is also often the product of absence of autonomy. If practices are followed by which energy is fostered and fatigue diminished, at those times when the severest demands are made upon autonomy, autonomous capacity is itself increased.

3. Association in play exclusively with those with whom one is at a physical disadvantage, especially in the same family, leads to recurrent experiences of failure and submission which inhibit the development of autonomy. The optimal distribution of successes and failures occurs when physical opponents are evenly matched in competition.

4. The more adequate sexual satisfaction is in marriage, the less frequent is extra-marital sexual experience and consequent threats to mutually supported self-esteem.

5. Cultivation of physical appearance—complexion, weight, grace, posture, grooming—contributes to the growth of autonomy.

6. Space for physical privacy and quiet—reduction of stimulation—facilitates the integration of new conceptions of self, especially during adolescence, and thus contributes to the development of autonomy.

ECONOMIC CONDITIONS

1. Autonomy is positively correlated with children's opportunity progressively to earn money for performance of economically significant work and to gain practice in the management of their own economic affairs. (Safeguards against exploitation are assumed.)

2. Economic independence develops autonomy, while (*a*) chronic dependence undermines autonomy, (*b*) unemployment undermines autonomy.

3. Work which continually challenges the capacities of the person without taxing them beyond their limits enhances autonomy. (*a*) Continuous employment at work far below one's level of capacity reduces autonomy. (*b*) Continuous employment at

work which exceeds one's capacities and causes a chronic judgment of failure by others and self reduces autonomy.

4. Continual exposure to marked differences of reward for comparable effort reduces autonomy, whereas recognition of differences of effort by differences of reward enhances autonomy.

5. Autonomy develops in direct proportion to the experience of participation in governing the conditions of economic life.

6. Constant exposure to the inducement of wants which cannot realistically be satisfied reduces autonomy, whereas the inducement of wants within the range of realistic anticipation of achieving the means of realizing them encourages the growth of autonomy.

7. Exclusive evaluation of personal worth by monetary standards reduces autonomy, whereas making available multiple criteria of personal worth cultivates autonomy.

8. Voluntary and informed participation in the production of valued goods and services develops autonomy.

9. There is an optimal balance of work and leisure which maximizes autonomy.

SOCIAL-LEGAL CONDITIONS

1. Nonthreatening exposure to a wide range of cultural and subcultural alternatives for handling interpersonal situations enhances autonomy.

2. Repeated categorical discrimination without regard to performance damages autonomy, whereas equivalence of opportunity facilitates development of autonomy.

3. Customary community respect for individual differences enhances autonomy.

4. Persistent involvement or proffering of the opportunity for involvement in group activity, without forcing it, cultivates autonomy; persistent exclusion, ostracism, or forced participation reduces it.

5. Exclusive domination by others reduces autonomy; progressive increments of initiative and responsibility enhance it.

6. Procedures of assignment of duties and periodic reporting

are more conducive to autonomy than procedures of direct supervision.

7. Community enforcement of voluntary agreements and nullification of agreements obtained by duress encourage autonomy.

8. Marriage between persons regarding each other as social unequals reduces autonomy of both mates and children; social equality in marriage facilitates the development of autonomy in mates and children.

INTERPERSONAL CONDITIONS

1. The strength and persistence of autonomy are positively correlated with the number of respect responses received by the self from significant others in the person's life situations.

2. Possession of a family name respected by others encourages autonomy.

3. Intimate presence of adequate models which enable the growing child to form correct sex identification is indispensable for the development of autonomy.

4. Exposure to other highly autonomous persons who can serve as models for identification facilitates autonomy.

5. Recognition by significant others of progressive accomplishment encourages autonomy.

6. Correspondence between the level of performance expected by others and the capacity of the person to equal or exceed it is optimal for development of autonomy.

7. Autonomy increases as failure is met by assistance and encouragement for the next attempt rather than with derogatory personal condemnation.

8. Wherever accomplishment is competitive, matching of competitors is optimal for the development of autonomy.

9. Generally speaking, emphasis upon surpassing previous performance is more conducive to development of autonomy than is stress upon competitive standards of performance.

10. The growth of autonomy is assisted by the customary use of rituals for honoring the defeated party in situations of conflict.

11. Practice in the performance of roles conveying respect to others increases the autonomy of the self.

12. Autonomy is cultivated by participation in groups where

one receives open and direct but nonaggressive evaluation of one's self by the others.

13. Autonomy is increased as appraisals of one's self by others come from a range of perspectives, thus giving one alternative evaluations to choose from.

14. When parents praise their children individually for characteristics that differentiate them noncompetitively from their siblings, so that each can feel uniquely appreciated, autonomy is cultivated.

15. When parents permit their children to compare them objectively with other parents they cultivate the autonomy both of their children and of themselves.

EDUCATIONAL CONDITIONS

1. Rewards for expressions of curiosity and critical comparisons encourage autonomy; punishment for these reduces it.

2. Full and consistent recognition of the limitations of human knowledge, the debatability of issues, the disagreement of authorities, and the legitimacy of dissent encourage autonomy.

3. Given a broad grasp and perspective on world history, geography, and culture, one is less likely to be oppressed by the superiority or inferiority of any provincial culture or subculture.

4. Instruction and practice in scientific method foster autonomy.

5. Since teachers frequently are models for identification, they affect the autonomy of pupils favorably if they can serve as autonomous models of unambiguous sex identity.

6. If the curriculum recognizes the development of diverse skills as an objective of education this will encourage autonomy, whereas approval solely for intelligence and intellectual achievement reduces it.

7. When questions by pupils are encouraged and welcomed, the autonomy of teachers and pupils is enhanced.

8. A programming of educational experience which affords intervals of solitude for the assimilation and integration of new knowledge increases autonomy more than programs which maintain a steady barrage of work and participation.

9. Participation in the pursuit of knowledge is more productive of autonomy than mere passive receipt of knowledge.

10. Recognition and facilitation of individual intellectual interests, as they arise, encourage autonomy; enforcement of conformity reduces its development.

11. Open reciprocal criticism by fellow-students of each other's work stimulates autonomy, provided personal aggression is minimized and objectivity of standards maintained.

12. Access by parents to objective and thorough appraisal of their children's performance, if done in a way to invoke their role as audience and not their anxiety as performers themselves, aids in the growth of parental autonomy.

RECREATIONAL CONDITIONS

1. Positive encouragement and provision for play encourages autonomy; scorn, discouragement, or subordination of play to serve extrinsic interests, reduces its contribution to autonomy.

2. Games which, without threat, convey to a person appraisals of himself by others contribute to the development of autonomy.

3. Games which provide recognition of improvement on previous performance increase autonomy.

4. Progressive mastery of higher skills in play correlates positively with the growth of autonomy; if new forms of play are made available as old ones are outgrown, autonomy is encouraged.

5. Participation in play by parents or older children, serving as models for identification rather than rivals, cultivates autonomy.

6. Respect by others for privacy, reverie, and daydreaming facilitates autonomy.

7. The experience of initiative, leadership, and power in organizing play—even if artificially induced—cultivates autonomy. The device of taking turns in initiating action is an apt illustration.

8. The making and keeping of secrets and confidences develop autonomy.

9. Drama offering heroic models of identification develops autonomy.

10. Recreation which increases the range of experience increases perspective and thereby enhances autonomy.

SOME CONDITIONS FOR DEVELOP-
MENT OF JUDGMENT

Judgment in interpersonal relations refers not to the perception of differences in quantity, though a large body of gestaltist literature in psychology includes such matters under this caption. Instead, it refers to the evaluation of alternative courses of action. There is a lively current interest in critical thinking, planning, and decision-making, for which good judgment is imperative. Judgment is here conceived as very similar to the ancient concept of wisdom, as signified in the Greek word *sophia*, from which philosophy gets its name.[5] In view of the centuries of effort which have been devoted to seeking out the mysteries of its occurrence and transmission, it will inevitably seem foolhardy to some to make further tries at identifying the conditions of its development. Yet, every wise parent must continue to instill wisdom in his offspring, and there is room for hope that contemporary social science can add something toward clarifying the conditions for cultivating this long valued ability.

The operational definition of judgment must itself be the product of research; a priori definitions can at best point the way toward preliminary approximations, and distinguish judgment from some other abilities which are sometimes taken for it. Thus judgment is not another name for utility, which by an assumption common to economists, all rational choices are said to maximize. Indeed, as some of the more critical economists themselves aver, many decisions among alternative values are not commensurable through resort to some imputed quasi-monetary common denominator or intervening variable; their qualitative ordering in particular situations is not reducible to universal categories and dimensions.

The quality of judgment itself—construed as an ability to make correct decisions—must be estimated in actual situations and in reference to identified actors. What is a correct decision for one actor may be a mistake for another actor, or for the same actor at

5. Graham Wallas, *Social Judgment* (New York: Harcourt, Brace and Co., 1935). D. W. Harding, *Social Psychology and Individual Values* (London: Hutchinson's University Library, 1953). In the latter, chapter xiii, "The Average and the Excellent," is especially suggestive.

a different time. The level of judgment cannot be inferred simply from the content of decisions made; the decisions have to be gauged in their context. To take a concrete example: while as a rough guide home economists recommend that families spend no more than a fourth of their income on rent, it may be good judgment under extraordinary circumstances to spend two or three times that much. Whether the family is exercising good judgment depends on its total living situation and the other expenditure choices it makes. Thus the measurement of judgment is likely to require reference to a representative range of decisions and considerations within the history of the actor.

The interpersonal origins of judgment need heavy emphasis. A person can only be reasonable as long as the other is reasonable, and he, as one's self is reasonable. But each can help the other to acquire skill in being reasonable. On this account it might be useful to rename judgment in interpersonal relations—reasonableness or reasonability.

That measurement of judgment is ultimately feasible and may become quite reliable and exact is suggested by the fact that people are always making appraisals of the good judgment or mistakes of others and of themselves, and are interested, at least abstractly, in the steady improvement of their judgment. Arguments are popular, for instance, among parents as to how far children have progressed in the development of judgment, how far they can be trusted to exercise responsibility for themselves and others. Although it is generally recognized that children increase or improve in judgment as they grow older, laws are continually debated as to the age at which teen-agers may drive cars, choose their own movies and reading matter, govern their own morals, spend money wisely, and depart from parental counsel. The practical bearing and importance of the optimal development of judgment on marital choice and the rearing of children seems obvious.

But judgment does not necessarily reach a plateau at the age of twenty-one, or a peak at any other age. Its growth is not an inevitable concomitant of aging, since it can be readily arrested, and can even degenerate and decline. When paternalistic husbands restrict the responsibility of their wives, for example, their wives' judgment deteriorates in consequence, leading to further restrictions of their responsibility. Neither is there any upper limit to judgment; it can develop progressively like the other elements of interpersonal competence.

Judgment is to creativity as criticism is to creation. The ability to evaluate a situation, to define the problem which it presents, is antecedent to the projection of a positive response or resolution. But after the creative response has been made, its adequacy must in turn be evaluated; in this respect criticism is also subsequent to creation. A major problem in the definition of creativity is to determine the degree to which the adequacy or quality of a novel product needs to be taken into account in assessing the creativity of an actor. The solution of this question has to be left to future research; for present purposes, judgment is conceived as the ability to evaluate the available alternative responses in problematic interpersonal situations. Whether these alternatives are novel or traditional, they must be plural for judgment to operate. Creativity can supply additional alternatives; and in this hypothetical respect, creativity itself becomes a condition conducive to judgment, while clearly distinguishable from judgment.

The hypotheses that follow assume potential alternative responses to problematic interpersonal situations. They refer to the antecedent conditions which, through time and repeated interpersonal experiences, are probably conducive to the improvement of judgment.

1. If sufficient time is allowed for the completion of each sequence of decision-making, each experience can be assimilated with previous experience, and learning can occur in the sense of greater integration and efficiency in the process of judgment.

Conversely, pressure of time which forbids completion of the process is disruptive of particular instances of decision-making and inhibitory of the progressive improvement of judgment. (Generous allotments of time for making up one's mind may seem easier to obtain than the patience to utilize the time in careful weighing of alternatives, where in the past patience has been punished by parental figures.)

2. The greater one's experience as a decision-maker, the better judgment becomes.

Experience varies in both range and intensity. It may include both performance as a judge of outcomes as well as a mediator among potential alternatives, in the role of actor as well as that of critic. Age does not automatically lead to experience in decision-making. Experience in decision-making is not only to run the risk of mistakes with costly consequences, but to make the mistakes and bear the consequences.

3. If the exercise of judgment is practiced in a playful and symbolic manner, competence in the judgment of real-life situations increases.

Judgment can be practiced in such forms of play as team debating, rhetoric, mock trials, window and catalogue shopping, and academic discussions. Symbolic practice in judgment can be obtained through vicarious participation in the solution of real or prototype problems by leaders or other representatives. Explicit training furnishes concentrated practice. Practice is increased by systematically taking the roles of others, e.g., changing sides in debate.

4. Judgment improves if responsibilities widen with the growth of judgment. Withdrawal of—or from—responsibility inhibits the growth of judgment.

There appears to be a need here for the enlargement of responsibilities in a graded series at an optimal rate of increase, so the person is continually challenged and stimulated, but not overloaded and made anxious. Others must dare to trust one's judgment if it is to grow, and must be willing to share the necessary cost of mistakes, keeping them at a reasonably low maximum but not excluding their real possibility.

5. One's judgment improves as one acquires a vocabulary for articulating the criteria of judgment.

Self-conscious scrutiny of the judgment process, utilizing explicit criteria for identifying the points at which mistakes occur, is as important as the verbalization of the standards applied in making particular choices. Being called upon to voice opinions or defend decisions accentuates self-conscious attention to both the process of judgment and the elaboration of criteria. Freedom to criticize and to dissent is most conducive to the competent exercise of judgment when fully institutionalized in the custom and structure of the groups concerned. Counsel by others is a form of criticism easy to assimilate and conducive to judgment if freely rejectable. Explicit and systematic means for checking mistakes and errors, for comparing expected with actual outcomes, are an objective form of criticism which removes it from anxiety-provoking surveillance by others.

6. As it becomes possible to note improvement in judgment, to measure its fluctuations under varying conditions and compare it with changes in others, judgment tends to improve further.

Not only do success and failure predispose to more of the same, but confirmation by others tends to stabilize important changes. Ratification of progress in some dramatic or ritual way by a sympathetic audience is an especially effective means of retaining and stimulating gains.

7. As provocations to diffuse anxiety are lessened, judgment improves.

The disruptive effects of anxiety upon the exercise of judgment and its growth can be considered as negative conditions to be removed, whilst self-confidence and trust in the ability to judge can be cultivated positively. Common negative conditions are extreme sanctions against failure or error in judgment, fear of punishment or stripping of responsibility for mistakes, hostile criticism or outright aggression by opponents, excessive partisanship which forbids compromise, and the treatment of values as sacred or absolute. Positive tactics include the steady widening of the values open for discussion, limited pilot commitments for trial decisions, redefinition of ultimate values as instrumental, inducements to rest and refreshment, recesses in deliberation, breakdown into smaller units of discussion, postponement of decision, and the injection of humor and play. Assurance of face-saving for defeated parties is a less honored but indispensable means, along with the rhetoric of compromise, which—like sportsmanship—promises losers another chance.

8. As the right to exercise judgment is recognized and excellence in its practice is honored among members of a group, its possession by members is enhanced. Recognition of the possibility of sound, impartial judgment is a necessary condition of its exercise.

In part, this is to say that autonomy is a condition of judgment. More particularly, it means a climate hospitable to "third parties," to the *via media*, to the secure and independent status of judge and mediator. The historical identification of legal justice with equality and reciprocity finds warrant in interpersonal relations. In this atmosphere, the victor does not gloat and the vanquished is a "good loser." Triadic concepts dissolve the irreconcilable antinomies of a more hierarchical order.

9. Exposure to highly competent decision-makers facilitates identification with them, and thereby the acquisition of their skills, and confidence in the exercise of judgment.

While exposure to just judges and inspiring critics does not guarantee identification with their example, isolation from challenging models may quite effectively thwart the growth of judgment. Furthermore, exposure to persons as models, even when only vicariously witnessed, helps to furnish persons with solutions of problems in judgment which may be valuable in future situations. For example, famous legal decisions are unlikely to be literally transferable to new cases, yet they may stimulate efforts to achieve equal wisdom. Good managers of household income, or domestic crises, set standards of judgment for their children to emulate.

10. The greater the quantity and reliability of relevant knowledge available to participants in problematic interpersonal situations, the more likely is improvement in their judgment.

Intelligent awareness of the consequences of alternatives affects the making of decisions in numerous ways, but knowledge is not a substitute for judgment in situations presenting genuine problems; neither can general rules be devised to apply strictly and mechanically to all cases. The bearing of knowledge upon action has been an ancient philosophical problem, but it is possible that research can illuminate the relationship in new ways. Knowledge tends to accumulate with experience, and is thus one of the features of age which contributes to wisdom; again, however, it is only one necessary element in the process of judgment, and a limited influence in the growth of judgment.

11. Judgment develops optimally among group members who

hold some values or standards in common while admitting a moderate margin for interpretation and change. Without some rules, situations become wholly arbitrary, fluid, and chaotic. Yet if rules are applied to situations mechanically without deviation or change, there is no room for judgment, which cannot develop without exercise. The optimal function of rules is thus analogous to that of grammar in language—they limit and facilitate, without dictating what statements will be composed by users. This margin of freedom for responsible decision also accounts for a sense of uncertainty, for which there is an optimal degree at various developmental levels. Problems of judgment which may terrify a child may challenge an adolescent whilst boring an adult. A group whose ultimate standards are too diverse may be unable to reach decisions; if too homogeneous, actions may become monotonous; there is an optimal ratio of variety and consensus, of innovation and assimilation. Without some rules held in common, it is unlikely that judgment could be measured, since there would be no standpoint from which decisions could be evaluated as correct or mistaken, either by actors or observers.

SOME CONDITIONS FOR DEVELOPMENT OF CREATIVITY

Creativity in interpersonal relations refers to the actor's capacity to free himself from established routines of perception and action, and to redefine situations and act in the new roles called for by the new situations—in short, it means inventiveness in interpersonal relationships. Of all the components of competence we have considered, creativity is perhaps the most difficult to specify and to investigate. Nevertheless it is evident that competence in interpersonal relations requires some such group of qualities and skills. It therefore becomes necessary to develop research on the conditions for their optimal development and utilization.

The following are general hypotheses from which we believe specific testable propositions can be drawn for the various classes of antecedent conditions noted in Table 1.

1. Participation in social relations which are permissive rather

than repressive, equalitarian rather than hierarchical and authoritarian, mutual and reciprocal rather than unilateral, is favorable to creativity.

2. Rotation of functional positions among the participants in a social relationship is a source of new experience, providing a broadening base for creativity and increasing the probability of its development. Role-reversal in role-playing is an almost universally usable substitute device when more extended rotation of roles is not feasible, as with children and parents.

3. Participation in social relations where diversity and individuality are valued above uniformity and conformity increases the probability of creativity.

4. Extensive and obligatory routine is unfavorable to creativity. Routine in a particular activity may be favorable to creativity insofar as it frees the individual's attention, energy, and other resources for creative activity in another area. A balance between established routine, preferably flexible, varied, and of limited range and duration, and opportunity for deviation from routine is optimal for creativity. Some areas of the individual's experience and activity must always be subject to routine, but procedures which encourage the variation of routine activities increase the probability of creativity.

5. Situations which provide challenges that exceed the individual's previous achievement without exceeding his ability are favorable to the occurrence of creativity. Even if the challenge exceeds his usual conception of his ability, a condition favorable to creativity exists, provided true ability is not overchallenged, and particularly if the support of significant others can be introduced to bolster unrealistically modest judgment of ability. The suspension of his own judgment regarding his ability is important in such a case. Resultant spontaneity may permit the individual to go ahead and act creatively, even though his usual conception of his ability would lead him to appraise the situation as threatening and demanding withdrawal.

6. Experiences increasing self-esteem will increase the probability of creativity. A distinction between self-esteem and self-satisfaction (a seeking for stability, permanence, perpetuation of the status quo of the self) is necessary. Self-esteem is conceived

as a positive self-valuation operating independently from changes in other areas of the self-system. Involved in self-esteem is a kind of detachment which permits a person's appraisal of his general worth to stand independent from particular success and failure events; critical appraisal of products is thus not seen as directed against the performer.

7. If experiences are provided affecting the individual's self-organization and symbolic processes, so that his "threshold of stimulation" is lowered and he becomes able to be more fully responsive to the stimulation of other people and interpersonal events, the probability of creativity is increased. A playful and sociable atmosphere—as created by the capable host—is the best example.

8. Practice in make-believe and utilization of imaginary, absent, or hypothetical audiences, when real or socially present audiences are inimical or inhibitory, increases the probability of creativity. Respect for one's own voluntary fantasy and ability to withdraw are the principal cases in point; these must of course be distinguished from compulsory fantasy and worry.

9. Effecting self-organization and symbolic processes which enable the individual to be self-rewarding and self-validating, i.e., able to provide his own consensual validation and social reward, increases the probability of creativity. Comparisons with historical models known through reading and drama are familiar examples.

10. Increasing the variety and range of a person's experience increases his potentiality for creativity, providing a richer fund of materials and a broader base for creativity. The greater the variety of interpersonal experiences, the greater the probability of a cumulative growth of creativity. Extensive experiences in reading, travel, parties, games, discussion groups, interclass and intercultural exploration, and other sources of variety in interpersonal experience—both direct and vicarious—increase the development of creativity, particularly through the metaphors they provide for reinterpreting present activity.

11. The availability of privacy and the positive valuation of its use for reverie, self-exploration, and self-experimentation increase the probability of creativity growth.

12. Creativity operates under a law of increasing returns, in that each episode of creativity increases the potentiality for future creativity. Providing people with experiences of creativity on a small scale increases the probability of more extensive creativity on a larger scale in the future.

13. Interpersonal activities and orientations which are genuinely playful are favorable to creativity. Competition and conflict (where competitors are matched and consequences limited and not serious), satire, parody, and burlesque of cherished values; humor; the playful juxtaposition of incongruities; the playful cultivation of illogicality, fantasy, and the mixture of the real and the unreal are among the kinds of playfulness favorable to creativity. There is a serendipity of play where creativity, whilst unsought for, may emerge from useless pleasure-seeking activity.

14. Cultivation of an aesthetic orientation toward activity ("do it because it pleases you") as opposed to a utilitarian practical orientation ("do it because it is good for you") increases the probability of creativity. The sense of performance before an audience, where performance is valued apart from its consequences, expands potential for creativity.

One is tempted at this point to look back over the above hypotheses from several points of view. For example, certain independent variables recur under each of the six components of competence. Does this mean that the six components do not vary independently, or does it mean that conditions conducive to the growth of one will contribute to the others? Any efforts to develop competence imply some theory of learning and human development; might this not be made explicit? Might it not, for example, be well to generalize that there is a triadic movement in interpersonal learning: 1) one sees in others what they can less well see in themselves, and learns abstractly how to vary the conditions of their development, 2) one thereby teaches the other how to create the same favorable conditions for the development of one's self, and 3) by identification with the other who becomes so significant, one learns (by taking the role of the other toward himself) how to create for himself those conditions favorable for his development. Applied more generally, one sees broad implications for any group which acts on the proposition that each member's behavior is a vital condition for the development of every other. Such speculation has always been important to progress in research, but there is not space here to indulge in it further.

To conclude, regardless of how the suggested hypotheses are appraised by the reader, at the very least he should seriously consider the case for a new approach in family research which is satisfied with nothing less than explicit, testable experimental hypotheses. These should state in if-then form the conditions thought to be causally effective in producing a change in the development of those abilities required for successful handling of interpersonal situations, especially those found in families. If and when research can then go on to validate such hypotheses, then —and only then—will there really be scientific justification for publishing the procedures by which research findings can actually be applied.

The authors make no pretense of having presented an exhaustive system of hypotheses, nor of being able to do so. Nor are we prepared to argue that the hypotheses we have listed are the best ones and should necessarily be given top priority in research on competence. But we do contend that competence as we have defined it is a top priority research problem; that the hypotheses proposed here are not mere offhand illustrations but merit serious attention; and that elaboration of significant hypotheses in all of the cells provided for, and the design and conduct of research to test them, will give to family research a unity, coherence, and impact it has not yet enjoyed. If we are wrong in our evaluation, then it is of the utmost importance that a more acceptable structuring of the problem be proposed without delay.

IV   *Developmental Perspective on Family-serving Agencies*

IF THE FAMILY IS the fulcrum, then the family agency is the lever of professional intervention for the development of interpersonal competence. If family research is to shift the center of its thinking from the idea of adjustment to that of competence this will have important implications for family agencies. And the outlook of these agencies in turn has important bearing on the family research problems that are likely to arise. The final step in testing hypotheses such as those in the previous chapter is to see how they work out in practice, and how they influence the behavior of the staff and clients of family agencies.

Of the hypotheses listed in chapter iii family agencies should select those that apply to their particular needs. And what these needs are can only be discerned by examining the historical development of the agencies.

The question of whether it is legitimate to intervene in family affairs when the family's own resources no longer suffice rather than leaving it to relatives and friends is not to be debated here. The book takes it for granted that the modern family requires the continued service of a range of agencies. Some of these will be described in this chapter.

There probably never was such a phenomenon as a self-sufficient family, securely equipped with resources for meeting all its needs and crises. It is useful theoretically to imagine such an ideal type, as a guide-line from which to calculate varying degrees of change, but it constitutes a hypothetical extreme which could only be approached and never attained in reality. It would be strange to conclude that the further back one goes in history, the more competent each family was to meet the needs of its members. It is true that in earlier times larger families and omnipresent neighbors gave the individual family member constant support. However, many couples nowadays get along quite well

95

without dependence on either of these. Furthermore, techniques and resources are more plentiful now than they ever have been.

If the self-sufficient family is taken as one extreme, the opposite would of course be the situation where all the former functions of the family had been transferred to other, specialized institutions. It is often said that in the early twenties certain communist thinkers and leaders in the Soviet Union actually sought to establish such a state of affairs; the evidence indicates that they moved in that direction, but not quite that far.[1] Their later reversal of direction suggests the probability that this extreme, like its opposite, while a concept useful in theory, is not a goal achievable in practice.

In practice, the functions of the family fluctuate within a considerably more narrow range than these extremes. It is doubtful if any function of the family has been wholly or permanently transferred to other institutions. If one looks at the family historically, it may appear as if the transfer of functions to and from the family has on the whole been unfavorable to the family, but some functions have occasionally been returned to the family, and almost any of them may be. The conspicuous current example is of course the rise of home television at the expense of the movie theaters. It must be kept in mind that what are usually termed the functions of the family are but names for large categories of concrete behavior, and that the content of these categories is continually changing.

It is important to emphasize that transfer of function can and does occur in both directions. In Professor Ogburn's[2] analysis of the changing functions of the family there is the perturbing implication that the spectacular recent decline in family functions is inevitable and irreversible. Some of the commentators who have elaborated upon his analysis accept these pessimistic implications. Others declare that while now the family is largely deprived of its economic, protective, educational, recreational, and religious functions, it can concentrate better on its remaining tasks of child-rearing and affectional response. If this is not mere-

1. Rudolf Schlesinger (ed.), *Changing Attitudes in Soviet Russia: The Family in the U.S.S.R.* (London: Routledge and Kegan Paul, Ltd., 1949).

2. William F. Ogburn, *Recent Social Trends in the United States* (New York: McGraw-Hill Book Co., 1933), pp. 661–708.

ly a wishful play on words, it is at best a groping conclusion. To get a firmer grasp of the realities we must come down from such a level of abstraction.

First it must be asked why the conspicuous recent transfers of functions have occurred, and also, why they have gone no further than they have. Clearly, questions of values are involved here. Next we will consider how the unanticipated consequences of deliberate changes have made repeated reappraisals necessary. And finally it is proposed that the continued acceleration of this process of change must ultimately precipitate concerted effort toward defining goals, even if in the course of time these goals have to be redefined. Not only the structure and processes of family life but the other institutions of the community would thus cease to be regarded as natural and inevitable givens, but as the instruments, embodiments, and consequences of values held and changed through common experience.

Why transfers of function occur.—The functionalist type of analysis, which starts with the postulation of an array of human needs and proceeds from there to delineate the necessary character of any social system which is deemed to satisfy these needs, is perhaps a useful model for the description of a community, its members, and their institutions at a given moment. It cannot, however, account for change or conflict within that community except through making auxiliary postulates about the natural, organic unity of the social system and the occurrence of dysfunctions or external interferences impeding the system's healthy, natural operation. Thus the many variants of functionalist analysis all share the idea that the goal of human striving is social and personal equilibrium or adjustment. Some of these theorists utilize an analogy to Newtonian physics, in which the components of a field acquire their relations through a balance of forces; others utilize an analogy to homeostasis or the healing process in the living organism, whereby the organism restores the status quo ante external deprivation or injury. Our retention of the concept of function should not be taken to imply acceptance of any such debatable explanations. On the contrary, we have discarded adjustment as the imputed and desired end of activity, and we consider it indispensable to account as realistically as possible for each of the recent historical changes in the family, and for conflicts over those to come. To do so, the concept of values must keep precedence over the concept of functions.

It might be supposed that family agencies have come into existence only to repair deficiencies in the structure and functioning of the family. There is some truth to this observation but it is a limited truth. When subject to disaster or disability, families in the past have often turned for help to kin and neighbors, that is, to other families. On the other hand, quite unprovoked by calamity or deprivation, they have often combined to create new institutions which by concentrating on a limited task could perform some function better than the family itself. Even if it is only to make up for deficiencies, a new institution must prove its superiority over potential competitors or over informal aid by other families. The family as an institution or any particular family does not simply try to discharge its function but it seeks to maximize its values which are ever in flux—being clarified, criticized, harmonized, added to, subtracted from, and limited by what is believed or found to be possible.

If it were correct to assume the existence of given needs and their necessary satisfaction, then at any given time, if these needs were not met, the individual would perish. While this is true of a person's organism, each person is more than a mere organism. If a person as a self-conscious personality does not sufficiently and intelligently value his organism, he will let it perish; his organism is his servant, not his master. A person wants not only survival but many other satisfactions as well, the nature of which cannot be deduced from his organism. He wants optimal satisfaction of these wants also. Moreover, he must in practice balance the satisfaction of these many wants—which accumulate by discovery and ramify with experience—against each other. He must constantly evaluate. He must set up categories and standards of judgment for organizing his behavior. These are his values. His values are constantly being corrected, ratified, intensified, extended, and systematized through the sharing of experience with others. For this process of interaction in which he is immersed from birth, language and other signs furnish the necessary concepts and rankings. Communication is the *sine qua non* of objectification of values, for the investigated as for the investigator.

If we may then define functions as the tasks or necessary actions for realizing taken values rather than given needs, the explanation for the transfer of function from the family to other institutions becomes, looking backward, almost obvious. Looking forward, it becomes problematic, contingent upon how current programs work out compared to expectations, and contingent upon continuous reformulation of what is desirable and possible. We thus seek to anticipate the emergence of changes and polarization of conflicts from within the system, rather than blindly awaiting disturbances from without.

Within the space of this report it is not possible to do more than give a brief indication of the various types of agencies which serve as supplementary resources for the family, and to offer a perspective for evaluating their operation. In reviewing the resources of family agencies it is necessary to keep two things in mind. First, many functions previously performed within the family have been taken over by institutions not currently regarded as family agencies. Hence, in terms of realization of values almost any agency could broadly be regarded as a family agency.[3] Second, some institutions have developed that explicitly assume responsibility for the welfare of family members. Only these will here be called family agencies. Even with this limitation, it is clear that there is a vast proliferation of institutional machinery allegedly concerned with aiding the family, either directly as a unit, or indirectly through help to individual family members.

Family functions have often been transferred to other institutions, not because of the failure of the family to do its duty, but because another institution could realize the values involved even more fully. Recreation is an example of this. Occasionally a transfer of function has had the unwanted effect of weakening the family for the performance of some of its remaining tasks. Homes for the aged, for instance, cannot conserve the emotional

3. In social work circles, the term "family agency" is used only for the member agencies of the Family Service Association of America. In view of our interest in five other types of agencies in addition to the counseling agencies, we must impose a much broader definition, which includes but goes beyond this professional usage.

value of grandparent-grandchild relations. Such cases raise the question whether retransfer, though desirable, is possible in certain instances. This problem, for example, is reflected in discussions about the use of foster-homes rather than institutional care for the aged. The personnel of certain institutions, which began by being able to offer superior realization of certain family values, have so vigorously sought to enhance their institutions by usurping additional family functions that they have at times endangered other values of the family. Thus higher education may alienate children from parents, just as commercial services can weaken the housewife's *raison d'être*. This sort of thing has happened more often under the stimulus of commercial than professional considerations, yet certain agencies, which were originally set up to help families in need, have sometimes unduly prolonged the families' dependence on outside help. In short, agency programs whilst intending rehabilitation or improvement have nonetheless at times produced unintended negative (and positive) side effects.

The ambiguous consequences of professionalization.—The growth of specialized agencies for remedying deficiencies in family functioning is a potent condition for the evolution of professional technique and the scientific analysis and codification of the factors at work in family life situations. The same process operates here as can be witnessed throughout all other institutions of industrial, urban society: the more refined the division of labor, the more likely the generalization of subtle differences and associations, with consequent innovation in practice and understanding. Here lies no doubt the major positive benefit to be derived from the transfer of functions from families to family agencies.

On the other hand, as already suggested, such transfers may come to seem not only inevitable under certain historical conditions, but irreversible, due to the fact that the layman can never hope to appropriate the knowledge and skill of the professional. Probably the majority of family-serving professionals hold this point of view, either unreflectively or deliberately. Only a minority relish the notion of prolonging or enlarging the dependence of their clients; the majority take the rueful view that the transfer of functions to professionals, despite its liabilities, is a net gain for family welfare, and thus justified. Moreover, it is easy to point out that not all transfers of function have been to responsible agencies devoted to family welfare; if transfers there must be, it is better that they should be to professional rather than commercial hands.

The process of professionalization need not halt, however, with the emergence of the certified family-serving professions. It can move on to encompass the commercial and the irresponsible, raising their standards of ethics and performance. More important still, it can work backward to professionalize the layman, in terms of his knowledge and self-conscious standards of application. Every agency and profession can readily adopt the objective of building the confidence and competence of its clients as family members. Some family agencies already disavow a vested interest in client dependency; a few are actively seeking to professionalize their clients in the sense just outlined. These we call the planning agencies.

Historically, the development of family agencies can be schematized, with the usual gains and losses of simplification, into three stages: charity, therapy, and planning.[4] At each stage there have been corresponding private and public forms, the one supported by voluntary contributions or dues, the other by taxation. Thus at the stage of charity there is private aid to the afflicted by specialized persons and groups other than kin or neighbors, and public aid in the form of county farms and state institutions. In the second stage there are the various voluntary benevolent and charitable associations dispensing aid in an organized and professional but still rather uneven manner; and on the public side, the conduct of regular, wide-scale services like home relief. Emphasis at this stage tends to be upon professionalization and rehabilitation through treatment of individuals. In the third stage, the emphasis shifts still further from the alleviation of distress and emergencies arising in families unequipped to cope with them, to the concerted achievement of more positive goals for organized publics, or for the community as a whole. Not boards of philanthropists but the affected people themselves form volun-

4. Adapted from Alva Myrdal, *Nation and Family* (London: Kegan Paul, French, Trubner and Co., 1945), pp. 151–53.

tary associations of various kinds, where their members participate directly in the planning and execution of programs. Such
voluntary associations may be self-help agencies like insurance
societies and co-operatives, or the public affected by the operation of some government executive agency, like the Farm Bureau
in relation to the Department of Agriculture.

Taking a rough average, most family agencies in the United
States may be said to have evolved to a point somewhere between the second and third stages. Some of the newest, however,
are only commencing at the first stage; some, like the public
school systems in a number of states, have reached very advanced
forms of planning, and furnish standards for judging others.
At this third stage, it becomes less and less possible to distinguish
family agencies from the other institutions of the community,
because they are all embraced in a conscious, collective responsibility for the welfare of families and family members in the
community. Yet charity and therapy may continue to be required indefinitely, though in changing proportions.

Just as the inadequacies of charity have led to therapy, so the
inadequacies of therapy are leading to planning. These inadequacies are relative to the increasing scope of the problems, and
to the increasing scope of the opportunities for improvement as
the evolution of the community continues. Where once, for example, cases of mental breakdown were simply confined in a
county asylum (often run in conjunction with the poorhouse),
there have since then developed a number of family agencies
offering psychiatric care aimed at rehabilitation; but the volume
of mental breakdown, despite psychiatric progress, still runs far
ahead of the volume of cures. This has forced attention on the
need for the prevention and early detection of mental breakdown. Many thinkers have also become aware of the need for
broad positive programs of social change which would create a
more definitely beneficial psychological environment for the
entire population.[5] Some commentators on the problems of mental health have become fixated, to borrow one of their own concepts, at the stage of psychiatric cure, and seem to desire nothing

5. Patrick Mullahy (ed.), *A Study of Interpersonal Relations* (New York:
Hermitage House, 1949), Introduction, p. xxxi.

better than the multiplication of therapists, clinics, and mental hospitals. It would appear invidious to quote an example of this view, because its advocates are many. While it is perhaps most common among those who are explicitly concerned with psychotherapy, it dogs all other family agencies. It is closely allied with the functionalist view which aims to regain or restore some putatively healthy status quo ante. The extreme case may be those decentralists who would restore everyone to the family farm of the nineteenth century.

The torrent of changes affecting the family as a consequence of science and industrialization during the past century is like the flood unleashed by the sorcerer's apprentice. The effects of the transfer of the production of goods from the home to the factory, which converted children from assets to financial liabilities, have far from run their course. The resulting decline of fertility has meant that there are more people with no children to support them in age or infirmity, and older people find it more difficult to support themselves since there are no longer family enterprises to which they can make a contribution. At the same time, from the point of view of the community as a whole, lengthened life expectancy and lower fertility have meant a declining number of working people is maintaining an increasing number of nonworking older people.[6] Because the smaller family is less and less able to care for its aged, pension systems, both public and private, have been spreading quite spectacularly, and these in turn have the effect of further diminishing the function and responsibility of the family in caring for aged parents. Each sequence of change has inevitably forced another, and no resting place appears in sight. It is not to be wondered at that some people, including a number of serious thinkers, are beginning to experience the same mounting anxiety that gripped the desperate little apprentice, and like him are praying for the sorcerer to give them respite.[7]

Though they may get sorcerers, they will get no respite. Those who are fearful of the unanticipated consequences of purposive

6. Myrdal, *op. cit.*, chap. v, "Forecasting the Future," pp. 77–89.
7. Ralph Linton (ed.), *The Science of Man in the World Crisis* (New York: Columbia University Press, 1945), pp. 201–21.

social action may succeed in handing over their responsibility to someone who promises order and stability, but they are not likely thereby to escape other consequences which may be both less easy to anticipate and more fearful to contemplate. The promise which the situation holds out to them is wiser anticipation and greater competence in making their hopes prevail.

If a father left the family farm to work in a factory or office, it was probably to achieve a higher standard of living for his family. If old people live longer, it is because everyone wants it that way. If child labor outside the home is forbidden, it is because of long campaigns of moral reform against it. If children are fewer per family, this is manifestly the choice of parents, abetted somewhat by landlords and proponents of the sales tax. These historic developments were responses to previous problematic situations, but they were never the only possible responses. And if things do not always turn out as expected, there is no reason to suppose people will be less competent to handle any new problem than they were to handle the prior situation which instigated it. Nor does the future offer fewer alternatives among which creatively to form a pattern of choice; indeed, it does just the opposite.

The balancing of values in, by, and for the family.—A rather useful neologism has recently been added to economics. It is reprivatization. If the operation of the post office were detached from government control and put into the hands of the Railway Express Company, this would be an example of reprivatization. In contesting the notion of an inevitable drift to socialism, without gainsaying the desirability under some conditions of certain kinds of public enterprise, some writers seek to find a balance between private and public, appropriate to the situation faced. From time to time this could require reprivatization, as it might nationalization at other times. This concept is directly applicable to the division of function and responsibility between private and public family agencies. And the insight it affords into the value problem entailed helps to illuminate the question of the transfer of functions, back and forth, between the family and the other institutions of the community. While transfer of some duty from a private family agency to a public body calls for a formal group decision, the shift of family responsibilities to private agencies and institutions is more often the result of thousands of unco-ordinated individual decisions. Nevertheless, either type of decision is tentative, conditional, reversible.

Of course the effect of a given instance of reprivatization may be costly, but that has to be calculated against other costs, before a balance can be struck which will indicate the proper course of action. Suppose it were proven that an exceedingly valuable part of the development of a child was furthered by his participating in some form of work. Although the goods produced might in dollar-and-cent terms cost his parents more than if they went to the store and bought them, the net result might nonetheless be far more worth while; the same may be true of adult do-it-yourself.

This example, of course, immediately suggests that the values which must be balanced in the management of a family are not reducible to dollars and cents. An economist may count the cost of developing the competence of a child, but a parent is hard put when he has to calculate its value, as against competing values. Who has yet plumbed the mysterious calculus of human motivation which operates when parents must decide whether they can "afford" another child?[8] At least in parenthood one thing is certain—the decline in standard of living which will result from having an extra mouth to feed. But it must be left to social psychologists not yet with us to discern what goes on in courtship, when the man becomes sure that she is the maid to ask, and he, the man for her to accept. Despite the efforts of certain thinkers to impute to this tangled welter of subjective transactions some homogeneous, metaphysical medium of exchange analogous to money—libido, tension, energy, utility—the values which direct people's actions remain incommensurable. No "classical economics of the psyche" has survived its author. And for that matter, has anything conclusive been recorded by economists about the process of value formation? For the present, the best we can do is to confine ourselves to a qualitative and perhaps genetic account of values, and take for granted the fact that through as yet little understood and not conspicuously rational processes of

8. Myrdal, *op. cit.*, chap. iv, "The Changing Family: Parenthood," pp. 48–76.

thought and discussion, people balance and conciliate the seemingly incommensurable, and thus direct their own actions.

In tracing the evolution of the many kinds of family agencies from philanthropy through therapy to organized self-help, this balancing of values among the parties concerned will be kept in the foreground as our principal mode of explanation. In this review, we shall follow a six-category classification of family agencies which is more or less cognate with the previous categories of conditions affecting the development of competence: (*a*) medical agencies, (*b*) economic agencies, (*c*) protective agencies, (*d*) counseling agencies, (*e*) educational agencies, (*f*) recreational agencies. Each class of agencies is thus presumed to be mainly engaged in affecting respective categories, but it should be evident that it affects other categories as well, and thus has some effect on all components of competence.

A community committed to the optimal development of all its citizens will usually find—unless it is very small—that it has an array of all six types of agencies, both public and private. At the national level these are mostly grouped in the new Department of Health, Education and Welfare; at the local level, the city departments (plus some units of county and state) tend to cover the range, though very unevenly, and so do the councils of social agencies on the private side. Together they make up an impressive complement of personnel and machinery. From the administrative standpoint, not more machinery but its co-ordination to serve the family as a unit, appears to be the most pressing demand.[9] From the standpoint of the citizen and the family, however, the salient point is the effect achieved by the expenditure of resources; what matters is whether the agencies encourage dependency or foster development. Expressed in terms of values rather than functions, does the family agency attempt to define and achieve an optimal family, or does it avoid such responsibility, and merely seek to supply the most obvious and agreed-on deficiencies, as if these deficiencies were objective facts, not subject to different interpretations?

9. Bradley Buell and Associates, *Community Planning for Human Services* (New York: Columbia University Press, 1952), pp. 411 ff.

MEDICAL AGENCIES

In most parts of the United States, the hospital rather than the home is the place where babies are born and where patients with the more acute illnesses are cared for. Professional nurses and subordinate aides have largely displaced kind relatives and helpful neighbors.

Yet while the hospitals have been taking over certain medical functions from the home, the biological scientists have been urging that greater responsibilities for nutrition, sanitation, and mental hygiene should fall upon the family itself. The vast and burdensome scale of mental disease in particular, which cannot possibly be reversed solely by psychiatric treatment at the point of breakdown, as well as an increased consciousness of the contribution of disturbed mental states to physical illness, have led physicians to expect more from the family than in the past. Nursing education steadily includes more social science. Likewise, the modern knowledge of bacterial and other origins of disease, and the biochemistry of healthful nutrition, have led to the elaboration of genuinely new functions, whereby the family may contribute to the physical competence of its members. Even if desirable, it would not be possible to have a psychiatrist, a bacteriologist, and a dietition stand over every living unit of the community. If there is to be a rise in health along these lines, the members of each living unit must co-operate in supervising their own hygiene. It is not easy to think of a better institution for performing these functions than the competent family.[10]

There is a conspicuous problem for present families who attempt to cultivate the physical competence of their members. This is not really a medical problem at all but an economic one. It is the problem of hospital and doctor bills, and of spreading the risks of chronic or catastrophic illness. The three-stage schema, outlined for the evolution of family agencies in general, also applies here. At first the problem was treated by extending a helping private or public hand to the few with the lowest in-

10. Notwithstanding this jarring statistic: "Home accidents in 1940 caused nearly as many deaths (33,000) as traffic accidents (34,500)." (From *The American Family—A Factual Background*, U.S. Inter-Agency Committee, National Conference on Family Life, 1948, p. 214.)

come or the most extreme misfortune. This called for charity by philanthropic individuals and associations, or assistance through government relief offices.

At the second stage there were privately organized bodies such as the National Foundation for Infantile Paralysis and special clinics maintained by subscription for such purposes as cancer detection. On the public side there were organized preventive agencies such as the health departments, and state institutions like mental and tuberculosis hospitals.

The third stage has only arrived for scattered segments of the population, and only partially for most of these, despite the vast interest of the American public in health as a value, an interest which is reflected in advertising and every other medium. Most notable of the private agencies at this stage are the voluntary group insurance plans fostered by the various state medical and hospital societies (Blue Shield and Blue Cross), whose combined coverage is now said to be above fifty million persons. There are a multitude of other risk-sharing agencies, which are sponsored by companies, unions, fraternal organizations, and, of course, private insurance companies. On the public side, the only agencies which could be called co-operative are Workmen's Compensation bureaus at the state level, and Veterans Administration provisions at the national level. And even in these, the recipients' participation in policy-making is slight and only possible through the awkward medium of labor and veterans' pressure groups.

The famous Ewing report (*The Nation's Health—A Ten-Year Program*, Federal Security Agency, 1948) outlines a model structure for citizens' participation at all levels of health planning, but the plan only exists on paper. Moreover, it is impossible to anticipate what effect a continued rise and wide distribution of real per capita incomes will have upon the adoption of such a scheme. Schemes of this kind raise a real problem as to how desirable it is to shift the economic responsibility for proper medical care further away from the family. Perhaps families can be adequately equipped to discharge this function through lesser expedients than national health insurance, which was the part of the Ewing program which aroused most opposition. In any case, both advocates of a federal program such as the Committee for the Nation's Health, and opponents of it such as the American Medical Association, seem to agree that the problem in financing adequate medical care is the limited financial resources of middle-income families. Well-to-do families have adequate resources to meet all their medical costs; dependent families, though suffering a higher incidence of sickness, receive considerable, if as yet inadequate, care through the various private and public relief agencies. Yet between these two segments of the population there is a large group who fall far short of the level of medical care they could receive through a comprehensive program. The grounds of judgment as to appropriate action here are patently debatable, as also are the latest proposals for the reinsurance of companies offering private plans for entire families. Whatever decisions emerge, Americans can well take pride in the vigor and rational nature of the present discussion of national policy. Whether the ultimate decision is for a private or a public plan, it seems that meanwhile the stage of concerted action is spreading rapidly and embracing more than a mere segment of the population.

A number of medical agencies, while maintaining a vigorous interest in their therapeutic and preventive functions, have moved beyond these stages to a concern for planning for more general values of maximum physical and mental health. This is most conspicuous in the field of medical research, where one can indeed speak of positive programs and of genuine, even spectacular progress. Medical research has long moved beyond the etiology of disease to fundamental theoretical research in a great array of fields such as physiology, biochemistry, bacteriology, and the like. Medical research is now in a position to give authoritative guidance on the hygienic conditions optimal for the physical competence of the nation's family members. The bulk of such research is now conducted by salaried investigators in public institutions, or through tax-exempt foundations and nonprofit corporations such as universities, within which the commercial incentive, as distinguished from the professional incentive, is subordinate if not absent. A parallel development in the commercial field is the excellent research done under the sponsorship of certain pharmaceutical houses. The interpenetration of medical problems, like social problems, as well as the cost, makes researchers turn for support to the whole community. In the United States Public Health Service, appropriations for the research divisions are now a substantial part of the appropriations for the disease control divisions.[11]

Another field of positive planning is the health programs of the schools. Where these are most fully developed, they include periodical physical examinations and recommendations to parents, instruction in hygiene and sex, physical training, and planned school lunches. While these programs ostensibly only cover school children, much of what the children learn is passed on to their parents. The controversial problems that arise in the school health programs such as diet, sex instruction, or immunization again bring up the issue of the extent to which the school should claim functions previously or potentially the responsibility of the family. Most of this controversy is conducted in terms of moral and religious beliefs, without much thought for the allocation of resources between school and family which would result in the development of each child's maximum competence.

A third promising trend is in pediatrics, where there is a movement toward child development in the positive sense, as exemplified in such growing institutions as well-baby clinics. Well-baby clinics are gradually perfecting measures of child development and procedures for training parents in matter-of-fact and reliable methods for fostering optimal development, but they still have far to go. Obstetric programs also are giving increasing pre-parental instruction to mothers and fathers, on both delivery and infant care. As such schemes evolve, they will seem less like medical agencies and more like schools. "Social hygiene" has come to mean "training for personal and family living." Planned parenthood clinics are turning toward the correction of infertility in the sedentary classes, to nonmedical counseling, and to preparing young couples for marriage in other respects. Public health nursing and health education have become distinct professions.

Apart from the gains being made through biological research,

11. *Annual Report of the Federal Security Agency, Public Health Service, 1953* (Washington: United States Government Printing Office, 1954).

programs to advance the health and physical competence of the people in the positive sense will in the future be conducted as much through economic, social service, counseling, educational, and recreational agencies, as directly through the medical agencies themselves. And the medical professions, as they intensify their concern with prevention of ill health and with public health generally, are not only finding themselves linked with other professions, but with their clients. Their clients as fellow-citizens become partners in organizing the conditions for the growth of competence.

ECONOMIC AGENCIES

The transfer of production from the home to the factory is the principal cause for the existence of the family agencies we call economic. Since the Industrial Revolution and until recently there has been a definite distinction between agencies explicitly concerned with the financial or economic welfare of the family and the other general industrial and economic institutions of the community. This distinction has held good except in the case of family farms and businesses. In these, production—even if only for direct consumption—has always been subordinate and instrumental to the welfare of the families who carried it on.

The same cannot be said of the new institutions to which most of the productive functions of the family have been transferred. These institutions—corporations in the main—have taken on only limited responsibility for their customers and employees. They pay for goods or services rendered and in turn supply goods and services in return for payment. If it is asserted that the efficiency of corporations ultimately leads to the greater welfare of families, it has also been asserted that the welfare of families, at least of employees, has often been subordinated to the efficiency of corporations. Empirically, the gains and losses to families have to be calculated not just in economic terms, but in such noneconomic values as health, education, recreation, and family solidarity. As mentioned earlier, the task of economic family agencies is largely to make up for deficiencies in family resources caused by industrialization.

The major problem, of course, has been the maintenance of

income. The extreme division of labor and the commercialization of economic activity has made each family extremely dependent on the continuous and regular receipt of income. The paycheck of the family wage-earner is the nexus between the family and most of the other institutions of the community. If this vital tie is broken, the results are potentially disastrous. And because it is frequently broken, due to age, unemployment, layoff, sickness, accident, or business failure, many family agencies have arisen to repair the break or remedy some of the consequences.

The development of family agencies devoted to income maintenance closely follows our three stages of social policy, but it can usefully be elaborated into five: (1) the situation in which family resources are inadequate to meet sporadic severe demands on income, and where the family through banking and lending agencies, engages in saving and borrowing to level out the peaks and valleys of income receipt; (2) the situation in which reciprocity on either a neighborly or commercial basis is inadequate, and necessary minimum aid is given unilaterally and more or less philanthropically by charitable agencies; (3) the situation in which agencies make efforts to rehabilitate the earning power in individual cases of economic breakdown; (4) the situation in which a degree of reciprocity and co-operative self-help is restored through insurance schemes; and (5) the situation in which comprehensive community action so organizes economic relations that the continuous receipt of an adequate income is assured to all families, save the most disabled. In this elaboration, the first and last stages of our earlier three-stage sequence have been broken down into two stages.

While the social policy on family income maintenance has evolved in these five stages, all these stages have in some form endured to the present. These stages could thus alternatively be construed as types of family agencies which grew in response to different family situations and needs. At the fifth stage, what action there has been thus far has largely been limited to a selected public. The incomes of some groups have been raised through a redistribution of income among workers and employers. On the private side, of course, this has meant such agencies as unions and producer co-operatives; on the public side, it has led to minimum wage legislation like the Fair Labor Standards Act of the federal government, or the minimum wage orders affecting service industries in certain states. The five-year General Motors–United Auto Workers contract represented recognition of the corporation's responsibility for the maintenance and steady enhancement of the standard of living of employee families, and of the union's responsibility for a continuous contribution to the productivity of the corporation.

So far measures for the enhancement of income have been carried on independently of measures for its stabilization at a minimum level; minimum income levels have been considered a palliative rather than an ideal. Corporation-union contracts, for example, furnish few examples as yet of full acceptance of responsibility for continuity of employment or income. The most impressive exception is the postwar establishment of employee pensions in industry. Nonetheless, stability at a high level (the guaranteed annual wage) has been stated as a future objective, if not an immediate goal. Moreover, without fanfare or formal acceptance of responsibility, every economic institution is steadily transferring a higher proportion of its personnel to a salaried status. If and when the majority of family breadwinners achieve the security and predictability of salaried positions, they will not only have left behind much of the necessity for present-day ameliorative schemes for assuring minimum income during adversity, but they will have entered upon an economic way of life superior by far to the security offered by the most self-sufficient of family farms. If and when that state of affairs comes to be, then our current distinction between family agencies and nonresponsible other economic institutions will have become in part irrelevant.

On the other hand, each year that passes more fully deprives the traditional family of a major function that as yet no other agency fills with assurance; that is its role in vocational guidance and training. On the family farm or in small business, the normal course was for the heirs of the family to carry it on. Their vocational choice was so gradually assumed from earliest years that they had no sense of a lack of freedom; they could observe and learn all the habits and ways of work with minimum effort. But now inheritance of an occupation is the privilege of a decreasing minority, and even these frequently feel a sense of conflict about stepping into paternal shoes. Preparation for a career involves the development of a vocational identity, a commitment and an education. This calls for much more than is supplied by employment exchanges and guidance bureaus. No simple counseling or job referrals can handle the problem; it is a task for social engineering. As a psychological problem, the sense of worth derived from a vocation has found a far from secure basis outside the family, save for the few who gain confirmation of their vocational identities in the most advanced professional associations. Here is an instance where no notion of remedy in a therapeutic sense seems reasonable; only the development of positive means for assuring a conscious choice of careers seems appropriate to the situation. The family itself, beyond instilling the basic habits of work, has more than ever before the duty to prepare its members for the interpersonal competence and the sociability that are required for most modern employment; its function in occupational transmission has not only been partly curtailed but also transformed.

This brief glance at economic agencies serving families has touched on the first two of the traditional economic categories— production and consumption. Given that sufficient and dependable money income can be earned by American families, is there any reason to suppose that families under urban, industrial conditions need to be assisted or need to co-operate through agencies related to consumption?

If the answer to this were assumed to be in the negative, then it would be hard to account for the considerable number and variety of existing family agencies, whose efforts are directed toward the protection and improvement of family consumption. If we consider each of the main components of family expenditure, we find a remarkable degree of specialization among economic agencies focussing on the consumer. Some of course are concerned with the provision of minimum amounts of essentials to needy segments of the population, but generally these may be considered as agencies serving to maintain income, even though, in many cases, they furnish goods and service in kind rather than cash, e.g., county homes for the aged.

The subsidization of certain items of consumption for certain segments of the population, as in the school lunch program, might also be considered under the heading of increments to income. The volume of goods and services purchased from tax funds, and communally distributed in this way, has been steadily rising in recent years—especially in such fields as health, education, and recreation. While in one sense such services are always consumed in accordance with need, e.g., families without children receive no direct benefit from public schools, it is illuminating to distinguish between public services distributed to the whole community and those received only by the needy.[12]

Meanwhile it is also of some importance to note how many aspects there are to consumption beyond the mere provision of the means of consumption. Thus we have agencies concerned with the regulation of prices and rents, not only the wartime agencies, but the permanent commissions regulating what consumers have to pay for public utilities and transportation. On the private side, consumer co-operatives may be said to carry on similar functions of trying to hold down consumer costs. Then there are agencies, from municipal to federal, concerned with guarding and raising the quality and purity not only of goods offered for sale, but even of the advertising, labeling, and weighing and measuring done by their sellers. Private organizations of this sort are meagerly developed—perhaps because this truly is a matter of public concern. A long-standing proposal would turn even the functions of the best-known consumer organization—the Consumers Union—over to a government agency such as the United States Bureau of Standards. Since agencies concerned with the more efficient and tasteful utilization of income are largely educational, a discussion of these will be included under educational agencies.

Of all the items in family budgets, housing above all others has called forth a host of private and public agencies for supplementing the efforts of the individual consuming family. The range of

12. For a careful analysis, see: Hazel Kyrk, *The Family in the American Economy* (Chicago: The University of Chicago Press, 1953).

tasks such consumer agencies carry on includes fire protection, extending credit, design and construction, sanitation, zoning, raising community standards, city planning, and style leadership.

While some of the work of these consumer agencies is to correct conditions which the consumer cannot rectify himself, much of their work makes possible for families things which in the past were out of their reach. For example, families can now enjoy with complete safety an unsurpassed range of variety in their diet. For the common man, as once only for nobility, eating has become an aesthetic experience, full of the joys of invention and the excitement of discovery. Fear of strange foods has become a mark no longer of prudence but of provinciality.

It is plausible to speak of some functions of the family having to do with consumption as having been transferred to other institutions and agencies, but note has to be made of the addition and elaboration of other functions, even of something like "reprivatization." If family servants be thought of as an institution, one may in a sense speak of the restoration of their function to many families. Household appliances and kitchen gadgets, which Americans crave, are gradually taking the place of the servant class in our society. Shopping and budgeting are examples of recently elaborated family functions. These are activities nowadays usually shared by all but the youngest members of the family; they involve discussion and the balancing of values and make every family a microcosmic forum in which the character of demand in the whole economy is debated and formulated.

As family incomes rise, a family does not merely eat and drink more, nor add a useless frill or gadget; it may choose instead to put more into services, spacious housing, health, education, entertaining, recreation, travel, and community participation, in other words, into obtaining those resources and experiences which have potentialities for developing their personalities. The easy generalization of critics that the growth of American wealth leads to materialism is found on investigation to be superficial. High culture—once the property of a leisure class—becomes the possession of all families when the increase of wealth is well distributed. Families achieve material comfort only to move beyond the primary concern with physical existence. Paradoxically, economic activity becomes most clearly instrumental to the highest development of individual personality, just at the point where enjoyment of self by means of existing resources becomes preferable to denial of self in order to obtain increases of income.[13]

The competence of the producer himself may be conceived as a channel of investment. There is a spiral relation in which income spent on personal development contributes ultimately to further productivity, through the improvement of human resources. We may thus expand the suggestion of Mrs. Myrdal[14] that programs for the family, to gain the degree of favorable opinion and financial support necessary for large aims, must appeal to the investment motive. Investment in the competence of the nation's manpower by careful engineering can appeal to a powerful investment motive—a person's interest in advancing his own career or his child's, while improving the most strategic of all factors of production, labor.

It is proper to seek the rehabilitation of the handicapped, but if the attention of family agencies goes no further than to release the handicapped from dependency, then the agencies still deserve to be described as fixated at the therapeutic stage. Even the Swedish family policy, aimed only at preventing or arresting the economic consequences of a declining population, stops short of the goal of national action implicit in American ideas. If we think of this nation as a household, and manage it as a set of conditions for the cultivation of competence, we can hope to complete a benevolent circle, from more production to higher income to better consumption and the optimal development of human resources, and thence back again to production.

PROTECTIVE AGENCIES

Generally speaking, the original so-called protective functions of the family as an institution are in modern times discharged by legal and political agencies. Beyond basic physical protection

13. For an expansion of this point, see Nelson N. Foote, "The Autonomy of the Consumer," *Consumer Behavior*, ed. by Lincoln Clark (New York: New York University Press, 1954), pp. 15–24.

14. Myrdal, *op. cit.*, pp. 152–53. See also Nelson N. Foote and Paul K. Hatt, "Social Mobility and Economic Advancement," *American Economic Review*, XLIII, No. 2 (May, 1953), 362–78.

against human and nonhuman enemies, such institutions as police departments, child welfare agencies, marriage license bureaus, legal aid bureaus, inspection and regulation bureaus, traveler's aid for desertees and the runaway child, and courts of every kind, are principally devoted to guarding the rights and safety of citizens.

In the past, these functions have been construed as largely negative or corrective. That is, when someone encroached upon another, or deviated from given rules or standards, it became the duty of one of these protective agencies to set matters right. In more recent times these bodies have tended to take a more affirmative approach. There are no clearly marked stages in the transition, and new functions have often been simply superimposed on old ones.

This steady transformation of family legal agencies, though quite in accord with the ancient principle of equality before the law, nonetheless involves a conspicuous paradox if not a contradiction. For, of all institutions, the family is traditionally the most addicted to conserving inequality, among, if not within, families. Many critics of the family have seen it primarily as a means for transmitting advantages from one generation to the next. The rewriting of family law, e.g., on inheritance, has repeatedly run across the grain of this profound impulse of people to favor their own kin.

Nepotism is a term of discredit in the United States. Legal responsibility for misdoing is uniformly fastened on the individual, not upon his family. The near-legend of the Hatfields and the McCoys gains its popular interest largely from the extraordinary uniqueness of interfamily feuds in this society. Surnames, instead of being treated as facts of nature, are continually being changed by immigrants, members of minority groups, and by people who, like entertainers, appear before the public. Antagonism to vestiges of primogeniture is as vehement among younger sons and daughters today as it was in the breast of Jefferson; heirs must share alike, estates be broken up, and dynasties be avoided. Sons of great men find a thousand knives sharpened to whittle them down to size. Evidence like this could be multiplied to exhibit unmistakably the clash between our majority sentiment of individualism and philosophies of feudalistic or neofeudalistic familism.

In spite of some opposition by a minority, pursuit of that idealized state of affairs, in which the person's standing in the community is entirely a product of his own character and not at all the result of his family connections, appears to be waxing, not waning. It has at least the vitality it had in Jefferson's day and probably more. This ideal, however, would be absurd prima facie if it failed to recognize the overwhelming influence of the family in the formation of individual character. Perhaps this fact was unrecognized in Jefferson's day; perhaps he and his allies thought that the leveling off of the extrinsic advantages and disadvantages of inherited property was the most important step toward equality. Anyhow, it is recognized today by students of the family that there are other advantages and disadvantages, just as important as those of inherited wealth and poverty, which must be dealt with, before every American child can truly assert that he enjoys equality of opportunity.[15]

There are extrinsic conditions for the development of competent personalities other than the kind of income possessed, and there are conditions intrinsic to family structure which may give even children within the same family differing starts in life. If individuals are to enjoy equal opportunity for the development of competent personalities, and this is limited by the resources of their families, then the objective of a community sharing such an ideal must be to provide these families, if not unlimited availability, at least some fair minimum of such resources. In general this has been a guiding principle, though sometimes none too consciously, for the development of the agencies concerned. We shall thus survey legal and political agencies and try to discern and evaluate their contribution to the protection of rights and the establishment of equality of opportunity. Finally, we shall consider the functions of legal agencies in making it possible for the citizen to take his part in determining public policy.

Equality before the law has been, of course, the bedrock prin-

15. E.g., W. Lloyd Warner, Robert J. Havighurst, and Martin B. Loeb, *Who Shall Be Educated?: The Challenge of Unequal Opportunity* (New York: Harper and Brothers, 1944).

ciple upon which all these protective activities have been founded. Pursuit of this ideal virtually required the state to take over and monopolize the function of securing justice for individuals when they were injured or threatened by other individuals, rather than leaving retribution to private feuds. The state taking over the elementary protection of life, liberty, and property could thus be regarded as the earliest and most irrevocable of transfers to another institution of a family function.

There is, however, a function centered on family life which was in the hands of another institution even earlier than that, although it is not a function which the family itself ever possessed. That is the legitimation in the eyes of the community, through ritual and certain binding commitments, of marriage and parenthood. While the enforcement of these responsibilities has long since been concentrated in the state, in a society such as ours where there are so many faiths and churches the element of ritual with which these monogamic commitments are solemnly chartered by the community still remains conspicuous. The ritual testifies to the view that from its beginning any family is as much the creation and concern of the community as of its principals. In addition to formal legitimation of marriage (and of course of its rupture through divorce), there is a large area of family law, e.g., inheritance of estates, administered through the appropriate legal institutions. The legal responsibility of a husband for the economic support of his wife, his children up to certain ages, and even his parents and siblings, remains in effect, though some of the economic burden has been taken over by family agencies. Specific provisions vary widely among the states. Proposals for change in family law are more often concerned with codification on a national basis than with release of family members from their responsibilities. Indeed the notion, however fallacious, that by stringent limitation of divorce, family stability is somehow conserved, has served to arrest the liberalization that might narrow the gap between profession and practice; while efforts to move into a therapeutic phase, e.g., family courts, have been largely resisted.[16]

16. See Max Rheinstein, "Our Dual Law of Divorce: The Law in Action versus the Law of the Books," *The Law School, The University of Chicago, Conference on Divorce*, Conference Series No. 9 (February 29, 1952), pp. 39–47.

There is, however, a noticeable trend in the family law which deals with the authority of husband over wife, and of parents over children. The trend, of course, is toward greater freedom and equality for wives and children, and greater restriction upon the authority of husband or parents to dispose of the person or property of dependents. Compulsory education laws, laws restricting employment of minors, laws limiting the degree of physical violence which may be practiced upon one's closest kin, often monitored by private humane societies, are of quite recent emergence, and are still being extended, along with appropriate inspection and enforcement agencies such as state licensing of boarding homes, nursery schools, and camps. For those to whom the family means patriarchy, the picture is one of steady encroachment by legislatures. For those to whom the family is a means to personal development, new horizons of emancipation remain to be achieved. Greater freedom and equality for women and children, moreover, reach outside the immediate family circle into the community, where extension of suffrage to women is being followed by a reduction of the voting age. Political efforts to pass laws to protect working women from special occupational hazards have been followed by agitation to dissolve the remaining barriers to their entering any occupation of their choice.

Intimately related to the hereditarian conception of familism which has been steadily weakened in past decades is the much less rapidly crumbling restriction of caste inferiority which is imposed upon large sections of the population. Both brands of hereditarianism are based upon a normative, hierarchical conception of the family and society, which has similarity to feudal notions where each person was supposed to be content in the place to which he had been born. Certain family agencies have clearly recognized this connection. Unions, for example, concerned with discrimination in employment of women and ethnic minorities, treat both as facets of the same problem. Some interesting questions for research in this area are suggested by the pregnant hypothesis of Horkheimer and Fromm[17] that the pattern of authority in the family is extended to society at large and vice versa.

17. Max Horkheimer (ed.), *Autorität und Familie: Studien aus dem Institut für Socialforschung* (Paris: Librairie Felix Alcan, 1936).

Some latter-day Freudians of conservative persuasion, on the other hand, find psychological reasons for discouraging women from taking up men's occupations.

A less psychological and more historical approach to equality of opportunity might start with an account of how America was primarily settled by religious dissenters, who eventually were able to establish as official policy the separation of church and state, and a private attitude of live-and-let-live among the multitudinous dissenting groups. The later waves of immigration from Europe had much the same effect as sectarianism, for they perpetuated a multiplicity of subcultures and subcommunities within the larger whole. While both religious and ethnic differentiation continue, though in diminished degree, there has been a steady increase in the differentiation of subcultures based upon occupational stratification and on similarities of interest—recreational, educational, avocational, and political.

Due to the pioneer necessity of co-operative self-help, voluntary associations of all kinds have always been a conspicuous feature of American life, but vastly improved communications have made the formation of such groups much easier and increased leisure has made more people eager to join them. The decline of sectarianism and the success of "Americanization" thus have not diminished the heterogeneity of American communities. Contrary to those who profess to see, especially in occupational differentiation, a trend toward hierarchical strata, a persuasive case can be made for the thesis that American society is more unified and equalitarian than ever. For the American theory and practice of equality has never set a dead-level homogeneity as an ideal, but rather mutual respect for qualitative differences which constitute neither superiority nor inferiority. No doubt a hierarchy can be observed among those who share a particular value; moreover, some values such as wealth, education, and prestige are often gathered in families longest in a community. Nevertheless, the vital point is that in their pursuit of happiness the American people are committed to no single, central, supreme value. They pursue a multitude of values, which they have in most cases found to be distinctly separable, not to say often inconsistent or contradictory, even at times for a single personality. Equality in the American sense is not a leveling with respect to some fixed category or value; on the contrary, concentration of values into some preferred hierarchy leads almost inevitably to some repressive or even totalitarian scheme of social structure. The best guarantee of equality is a multiplicity of ends pursued, and freedom to elaborate and actualize new ones. Multiple ends lead to multiple forms of organization, multiple organizations mean no one organization can expect to gain a permanent majority. The criss-crossing of memberships in these many groups creates bonds of identification not possible in a society where activities cutting across strata and subcultures are discouraged if not forbidden.[18]

Directories of family agencies of all types are testimony to the variety of ways in which interested people attack what they conceive to be the problems of the family. While proposals are heard from time to time that these many family agencies ought to be co-ordinated, such proposals have to be carefully scrutinized before they can be properly evaluated. On the one hand, it could mean subordination to some authoritatively ordained set of ends; on the other hand, it could mean further freeing the channels of communication among agencies, so that experience could be more fully shared and consensus widened, with decisions involving all arrived at through compromise or synthesis of recognized, conflicting interests. The adoption of the annual budget of a community chest or council of social agencies is an excellent model of such decision-making. It involves politics, strife, compromise, and restless revision of goals and means, but it does create a kind of working unity—even the common understanding of respected differences—which is faithfully believed by Americans to be superior to the superficial appearance of harmony found in an organization dominated by a supreme value and a ruling elite which professes to embody it.

Whether it is the society that moulds the family, or whether it is the other way around, there is much evidence for supposing the same correlation between the democratic family and democratic society as between the authoritarian family and authoritarian society. Full and free participation by wife and children—to

18. Henry A. Myers, *Are Men Equal?* (New York: G. P. Putnam's Sons, 1945).

the limits of their capabilities—in the discussions and decisions affecting the whole family makes the family members willing to dissent and prepares them to respect dissent in others. Sympathetic consensus and agreement to disagree are essential to our characteristic voluntary associations.

Certain recent writers have sought to add to Ogburn's analysis of the changing functions of the family two other functions besides those he named: status placement and cultural continuity. By this they mean identification of the person through his family with the social class into which he was born or hopes to rise, and indoctrination in the subculture of that class. To accept such concepts seems to imply acceptance of the family as a permanent device for insuring that advantages and disadvantages will be passed on from one generation to the next. That families have so behaved is manifest; to assume that such behavior is inevitable and necessary is neither manifest nor helpful analytically. Rules against nepotism are broken, but they are also kept, and social mobility is almost demanded of the next generation.

The ideal of equality of opportunity has furnished the basis for our review of the development of legal and political family agencies. At the first stage of their development, it might be said that political and legal agencies, apart from providing police protection, were mainly concerned with the redress of particular grievances. Orphans received guardians; abused children were put in foster homes. Injured mates could take their partners to court and receive divorces or separate maintenance. On the whole, however, the efforts of family agencies at this stage were primarily directed at obtaining conformity with law and seeing that family responsibilities were fulfilled. The assumption was that if families did their duty, individuals would be protected in their access to opportunity. At their second stage of development, it is recognized that not merely occasional individuals, but considerable segments of the community, are recurrently subject to special hazards and ailments which require treatment. Thus to family courts are added counseling bureaus, whose job is to guarantee the welfare of dependent children. Parole and probation work is added to the methods of dealing with offenders. Perhaps more so than any other class of family agencies, legal and political agencies have been slow in reaching this therapeutic stage. As for moving into preventive and positive stages of evolution, examples among these agencies are quite scarce. The best example of the therapeutic approach is perhaps the juvenile court, and programs for the prevention of juvenile delinquency have made headway in some places. Group therapy among prisoners, probationers, and parolees is still very much in the experimental state. Scattered youth commissions try to combine mental hygiene clinics with sports programs. Indeed, the paucity of positively oriented family protective agencies may account for the limited vision of just what they could be. Some citizenship educators and teachers of social studies have a fairly clear vision of positive aims, though their efforts fall under the heading of educational agencies, and their methods apply to the individual outside his family setting.[19]

Yet the type of experience which leads to social skill is that which positively oriented legal and political family agencies could help bring to family members. In the large family of the past, individuals had much more opportunity than at present to develop their capacities for participation in group decisions and activities. Today, if such skills are to develop, it must be through supplementing the family's efforts, through life-like practice and at least vicarious exposure to wide experience.

Generally speaking, the development of social competence is a matter of learning by doing. If one family member has the opportunity to meet strangers, to plan and conduct parties, to speak before audiences, to obtain the co-operation of others in group activities which he leads, he develops social competence. He learns not only how to avoid giving offense to others, but how to elicit their approval, sympathy, and collaboration—"how to win friends and influence people." If such experience is not available to him, his potentialities for social growth remain undeveloped. Moreover, his social ineptitude is not merely an embarrassing handicap or distressing lack to him; it is a serious impediment to the equal exercise of his right as a citizen to participate in group matters involving his welfare. Inequalities of this

19. I. James Quillen and Lavone A. Hanna, *Education for Social Competence: Curriculum and Instruction in Secondary-School Social Studies* (Chicago: Scott, Foresman and Co., 1948).

character are hazards to the genuine enjoyment of that political equality which is supposedly guaranteed by law.

As long as individuals were relatively independent and government was minimal, the one-man-one-vote principle displayed on election days may well have been sufficient evidence of political and legal equality. But now with the increasing requirement for individuals to participate daily in large organizations, something more than the mere opportunity to vote in periodic elections becomes more conspicuously necessary—namely, the power and ability to exercise one's voice in governing the conduct from day to day of those enveloping organizations. Otherwise, as critics of Anglo-American political democracy contend,[20] membership in the community for large numbers of presumed citizens becomes formal and empty, conveying no sense of sharing in its control.

It has always been recognized that experience in forming and operating voluntary associations has been the best training ground for responsible citizenship outside the family itself. In this sense at least, all voluntary associations, whatever their concrete aims, might be termed family agencies for the development of the necessary competence. For this reason, it is impossible to list here as legal and political agencies all the countless voluntary associations which exist. Instead, when we come to consider potential changes in the operation of the various other types of family agencies, the function of equipping individuals for active citizenship will have to be considered as distributed among all of them.

The emphasis of historians and other observers of American society upon our characteristic plethora of voluntary associations may be well deserved. Nevertheless, numerous as the many forms of association are, membership in them is confined to a relatively small segment of each community (one-third is a generous estimate), and activity to an even smaller segment. Where members of one family may belong and hold office in half a dozen organizations, another half-dozen families belong to none at all. In almost every community, the cry goes up constantly that leadership, activity, and influence are concentrated in a few hands, and

20. E.g., the works of Edward Hallett Carr, *Conditions of Peace* (New York: Macmillan, 1940); *The Soviet Impact on the Western World* (New York: Macmillan, 1947); *The New Society* (London: Macmillan, 1951).

among the older rather than the young people. This cry goes up no more often as a complaint from critics than as a plea from the leaders themselves. In public as well as in private forms of association, the complaint is chronic that far too few people exercise their rights to vote, to petition representatives, to keep informed on issues and to exert influence upon their outcome. Perhaps these persistent exhortations and condemnations are but the negative expression of our national ideal of full and equal citizenship; perhaps they point to a grievous deficiency which demands remedy; in either case there is a need for a considerable development of competence if there is to be successful working with others in accomplishing common ends. From this standpoint alone we can presume to suggest that ways are needed whereby family agencies can contribute a great deal more to universalizing such competence. From this standpoint also, it seems fair to point to legal and political agencies as the type of family agencies which have done the least to go beyond the mere redress or correction of grievances, into the therapeutic and positive planning stages of development.

COUNSELING AGENCIES

Counseling of family members by persons and agencies outside their family is very old, probably as old as humanity. Nevertheless, the process of differentiation, specialization, and professionalization which has brought into being agencies staffed by full-time counseling personnel is decidedly recent. And the application of the concepts and findings of social science to counseling is more recent still. Since counseling agencies were started a few decades ago their methods and philosophy have only become systematized in some areas of their work. The rapidity and unevenness of their growth—further confused by conflicting schools of thought—makes generalization risky, but for any appraisal of their place in the institutions affecting American families some rough summary of their emergence is necessary.

The development of family counseling agencies can be schematized in several ways. When their characteristic techniques in successive periods are considered, it may be said that they proceeded from moral exhortation and sanction, through individual guidance or therapy, to procedures adapted to work with groups. Some of these group methods are oriented to conventional individual psychology, others stress interactional conceptions. When the doctrines rather than the techniques of the agencies are considered, it appears that successive periods saw emphasis on religion and morals, then on individual psychology or psychiatry, and finally on social psychology or sociology. As mentioned before, these phases of development have overlapped and still do. Also, certain family agencies primarily devoted to activities like medical care or economic rehabilitation carry on family counseling, although it is not their main duty. Every family-serving professional, whether lawyer, clergyman, teacher, or even architect, can rarely avoid being asked to advise on matters for which the psychiatrist, social worker, and clinical psychologist are especially trained. The quest for guidance goes far beyond a mere demand for information. Similarly, many agencies listed as primarily engaged in counseling do not always limit their work to guidance, advice, and insight, but may offer such services as recreation, participation in clubs, or education.

After this brief glance at the development of counseling agencies, it is necessary to get down to finer points and qualifications. From the standpoint of their personnel, it might be fairer to survey and evaluate counseling agencies according to their success in reaching goals they have set for themselves. However, in the following survey counseling agencies are considered in relation to the goals of those agencies which have evolved furthest along the line of our three-point schema.

In what follows only those agencies will be called counseling agencies where the personality problems are the primary concern and responsibility of the agency. This excludes those counseling agencies which act primarily as directories or clearing-houses for information about the availability and whereabouts of resources and services dispensed by other agencies. As the roster of government offices and social agencies and public service institutions has grown, this directory function has grown in usefulness and importance for all citizens. Nevertheless, it is not exactly what is meant here by counseling. The main focus of attention of counselors in the strict sense intended is the personalities of their clients. To be sure, questions of vocational guidance or family budgeting frequently involve personality questions, and cannot be avoided or isolated in a doctrinaire manner from economic concerns. It is only when personality problems are paramount in the concern and responsibility of the agency, however, that it will be called a counseling agency.

Of all types of family agencies, the counseling agencies are most conspicuously bunched at the second or therapeutic phase. They show an especially lively interest and experimental attitude to group therapy. A number of mental hospitals are actively experimenting with various forms of milieu and play therapy as major tools for providing large numbers of patients not merely with custody but with psychiatric care. Crime prevention bureaus in certain cities are exploring the value of clubs for delinquents modeled after Alcoholics Anonymous, and some experiments in group rehabilitation are actually going on within correctional institutions.[21] While much of the development through official and professional channels is still handicapped by an individualistic approach, some agencies in theory and procedure are adopting a much more interactional outlook. Yet even where community organizers have set up community councils and conducted community self-surveys, the therapeutic motive has in the end predominated, and tended to lead to clinics and casework. Inevitably such observations appear disparaging, yet the intent is not to criticize or condemn but merely to note the direction these developments have taken.

The feeling that progress is not as rapid as originally hoped, and that some sort of ceiling is soon reached by efforts aimed only at correction of evils, has pervaded several studies of social work. In Koos' analysis[22] of families in trouble, for example, he found that various kinds of families had characteristic persons or groups to which they turned when in trouble. In the same way, each family counseling agency appears to attract a characteristic clientele. When an agency has recruited as its clientele all that segment of the community which habitually turns with its kind

21. F. L. Bixby and L. W. McCorkle, "Guided Group Interaction in Correctional Work," *American Sociological Review*, XVI, No. 4 (August, 1951), 455–61.

22. E. L. Koos, *Families in Trouble* (New York: King's Crown Press, 1946).

of problem to that kind of agency, its operations are likely to settle into a routine procedure. Its progress then becomes measured mainly in terms of technique, such as its interview methods or efficiency in spending its means. Only where it can set before citizens a creative succession of new and positive goals does it have a fair chance to avoid such a ceiling of routinization.

There are still immense areas and many strata of communities in the United States which barely enjoy the philanthropic or charitable phase of development of counseling agencies; there are many more which have yet to reach professional standards at the therapeutic phase; and there are only a handful who have made the step from individual casework to group work. It may thus seem premature to suggest inadequacies in the therapeutic approach. Yet there is no apparent reason, other than the failure to conceive goals beyond adjustment, to prevent the adoption of a positive, planning approach to the functions of counseling agencies.

From the standpoint of the counselor who finds his role ambiguous, it seems more than likely that exploration of a developmental perspective would help resolve the conflicts implicit in his professionalization. For the psychotherapist who thinks of himself as a physician who cures sickness, or who avoids this and speaks only of the "difficulties of living," there may appear to be no conflict in his role. He may be satisfied to reduce symptoms of disorder, to solve the problem presented and to think of himself primarily as someone who relieves distress, without defining his goals beyond that. But apparently more and more thoughtful counselors do not think they can stop there, or do any permanent good, unless they leave their patients better able to cope with later problems and future strains. Some even feel as mentioned in chapter ii, that it is their job to plan for the optimal development of their clients, or to organize clients to plan for their own.

The ambiguous feelings of the professional who presumes to assist in the personal problems of family members may be all to the good if these are construed in a framework of family relations which includes himself. The concept of transference goes only part way. The client in the course of the counselor-client

interaction frequently construes the counselor as a figure representative of previous others, with whom relations have been unresolved but are thus worked out through the interviews. The
difficulty, however, from the client's standpoint, is that no matter how versatile his counselor may be, and no matter how facile
or fantastic his own imagination, the range of persons with whom
a person needs intimate discourse in order to achieve his optimal
development of self far exceeds the resources of this single relationship. Moreover, there is the fact that the client must pay in
cold cash for the kind of communication which the best families
afford on a basis of affectional reciprocity; thus the most sacred
disclosures hover at times on the verge of something equivalent
to prostitution. Regardless of ethics and their enforcement by the
counselor's colleagues, any such relationship is severely qualified
by professional insistence upon its eventual termination, and the
limitation of reciprocity to monetary reward; in a word, the
elaboration of this relationship leads nowhere. The best hope for
fruition of any gains that accrue is that they serve as a bridge to
the regeneration of the client's involvement in a quasi-family
constellation which includes near-rivals and critics, models and
admirers, other ages and the other sex, in both work and play.
Only through others can one obtain the continual characterizations of self essential to valid knowledge of self.

Research and experience have already shown that the human
being, from birth until death, almost to the degree that the fish
requires water, thrives only in social interaction. Neglect, isolation, loneliness, solitary confinement, are deteriorative influences
very hard to endure, even though every physical condition of
survival is met. And among all kinds of interaction, the most potent of all for personal development are those characterized by
the unconditional acceptance of family relations. Only here is the
listener who always finds more in the person than he presents in
his actual behavior. Only here is the audience that never grows
tired. Only here is the person of similar background, for whom
every aspect of the culture—of class and ethnic experience—reso-
nates with comparable meaning. That a counselor could ever
aspire to duplicate these functions of the optimal family is beyond the hope of those who have thought and written about it.

In a sense this analysis of the implicit or potential demands on the counselor's role both justifies and specifies a therapeutic approach. It also shows that his role must be transcended by more adequate institutions for providing each client with a stable constellation of significant others, who can be the precisely appropriate self-definers at each critical stage in his personal development. For the person whose actual family has failed him the solution suggested by this analysis is the invention of effective quasi-families.

The process by which each person contributes to the self-knowledge of others, and others contribute to his knowledge of himself, is immanent in human society. Where self-knowledge and self-control are deficient relative either to norms or ideals, the best means for reversing these deficiencies is effective utilization of all available knowledge of how selves originate, operate, and co-operate. Recognition that some tasks are beyond the powers of the unaided individual does not mean that society must be divided into two classes, therapists and their patients. It means, or at least can be made to mean, joint action to perform these tasks. Such an approach is as relevant and applicable to the tasks of counseling agencies as to the other types of family agencies.

The simple theoretical analysis of the evolution of family agencies into three phases appears to be corroborated by the growth in all six types of agencies of what may indeed be called quasi-families—that is, small groups of persons similarly affected by some distinctive problem, condition or interest, who come together voluntarily to solve, correct, or pursue it by concerted action, meanwhile providing each other with a degree of understanding, encouragement, and support which they have not found elsewhere in the community. Most of these have only arisen within the past two or three decades. While they are predominantly found in urban areas, since only in such centers are there enough persons of any one type or category, e.g., parents of feeble-minded children, to form a substantial group, certain kinds can be found in quite small towns, e.g., the Townsend Clubs, which considerably outlived the depression. While some of these quasi-families have been the products of invention and experiment by therapists, so many have sprung up apparently quite spontaneously (e.g., child study groups attached to co-operative nursery schools) as to suggest that they are a particularly fitting response to current situations confronted by members of the community. Their fraternal rather than patriarchal structure does not negate the value of construing them as quasi-families; indeed, to recognize their correspondence with the more fraternal character of contemporary families improves the analogy.

The desire of many public and private agencies to foster participation "at the grass roots" is most successful when the grass roots consist of strong, intimate, small groups, not collections of strangers. Under urban conditions, such groups do not as a rule get constituted on a neighborhood basis, but out of common interests; they may primarily focus on these interests, yet they frequently have corrective and therapeutic effects on their members.

While the characteristic quasi-family has a fairly homogeneous membership, drawn from some limited segment of a community, this does not mean that one has to regard them as simply the result of an ever more refined division of labor or fragmentation of interests. An urban quasi-family often recruits only one member of a family, which makes it quite different from those farm organizations whose local units aim to provide some engrossing activity for every member of a family. Yet every quasi-family so rapidly takes on and elaborates other functions, that few persons would ever need or want to belong to more than two or three quasi-families at most. Every member can remain as convinced of his own individuality within a quasi-family as within his actual family. In fact, scrutiny reveals a number of respects in which membership in quasi-families offers certain advantages which real families cannot. Involvement in these groups, however highly committed and intense it may be, is more like becoming a member of a club or a team in a game. Family commitments, by contrast, have still an inescapable character posing the gravest consequences for the unwilling participant.

It is unlikely that individual counseling can or should be dispensed with. Yet, the theoretical shift to recognition of the family origin and interpersonal nature of personality difficulties, justifies the support counseling activity gives to voluntary group procedures. Sociologists long ago recognized the threat to individual psychological existence in the breakdown of ancient primary group supports. Though the rural village, like Humpty Dumpty, cannot be put back together again, the incessant reorganizing of the various institutions of the urban community can well take account of the means whereby citizens continually reintegrate their selves.

If it is granted that small, intimate groups of significant others play a vital part in supporting every self, it is probable that groups formed solely for the sake of such mutual support will be less durable and successful than those which accomplish this in the process of pursuing other ends. It is improbable, therefore, that individual counseling agencies could produce a full solution even under ideal conditions, since the problem involves the whole structure of the community as this bears upon personality. We have outlined the setting, and some favorable trends. What the best solutions will be is known to no one, and will only be approached through imaginative experiments of many kinds.

EDUCATIONAL AGENCIES

The public school system in which the United States takes pride is one of the most paradoxical if not self-contradictory institutions in American life.

On the one hand, it is completely socialized. No family pays directly for the education of those of its children who attend it; each family pays taxes more or less according to its ability, receives according to its need. All the children in the school share its services, except where segregation and discrimination occur. The public high school in particular is the most cosmopolitan and equalitarian congregation of people in any community. Education is not merely available to all children, but compulsory during certain ages in each state. No child can be rejected as a pupil, save for reason of severe defect. The entire staff of the school—administrative, professional, and maintenance—is salaried. The whole roster of citizens in each community is eligible to participate in selecting members of its board of education and in affecting their policies.

On the other hand, in the actual conduct of teaching and learning, conventional procedure is the incarnation of competitive individualism. The assignment of pupils to grades, rooms, and seats usually ignores the social ties among them. The marking system ranks each on the basis of rivalry with all. Beyond this marking system is the swarm of psychological tests devised on the premise of an individualistic psychology to which few theorists remain willing to commit themselves. The tasks imposed on pupils are for the most part individual tasks, with no group decisions and no group responsibilities. To the extent that the problem of motivation is consciously considered at all, it is generally assumed sufficient to rely on the stimulation of rivalry for grades, and on parental interest in fostering the art of getting on in the world. Yet realistically, the spectacle is one of a majority sentenced to unfavorable comparisons and burdensome compulsions, from which they escape daily and yearly as fast as they can—50 per cent dropouts in the high school years is still the rough national average.

It would be redundant to recite here the long struggle between those who want the school to concentrate upon putting vocationally useful knowledge into children's heads, and those who have declared their aim as the development of the entire personalities of children. The liberal educationalists tend to be those who emphasize the school's function in developing people for their responsibilities of citizenship; the vocationalists, those who emphasize training for economic competition. Nevertheless, there occur numerous crossings of these lines. For example, if one considers the method of examination employed in purely vocational schools run on a commercial basis, the pupil is usually passed on the achievement of a standard level of objective competence, rather than upon the calculation of a minimum numerical average maintained in competition with other pupils. As the scope of formal education comes to include adults and the very young, it is notable also that this new population in nursery schools and adult programs is not subjected to the usual competitive apparatus. Methods in adult education especially, where participation is completely voluntary, rely largely on noncompetitive motivation such as: group recognition, recruitment through friends, sociability, a degree of student choice of subject matter, choice of instructors, and design of methods. Forums, workshops, round tables, committees, conferences, and seminars characterize adult methods. In public school extracurricular activities, it is obvious that only voluntary methods seem appropriate to induce participation, that motivation depends primarily upon the membership standing of a person in a group. Any teacher in a high school can give examples of seemingly dull, resistant, apathetic youths, who suddenly come alive in extracurricular activities, and exhibit prodigies of ability, energy, and ingenuity when given a responsible share in the tasks of a voluntary group. Not as many teachers have grasped the possibility of finding ways in which channels of motivation can be put to the service of serious learning. Since much of the best learning occurs in extracurricular activities, how could this be made to include more of the ordinary curriculum subject matter, thus making the child's learning a part of his active involvement with his fellows?

The evolution of policy within the school falls readily into our familiar three stages, although this may not be as readily apparent as with other types of family agencies. At the first stage, the intervals of spontaneous activity by pupils—recess, playground periods, assemblies, and singing—are regarded as concessions, as ways for children to let off steam, so they can return more seriously to the work of learning. At the second stage, extracurricular activities are recognized as having some values on their own account, more facilities and encouragement are provided, and these activities become more definitely and extensively organized on a group basis, but with a substantial element of adult guidance; counseling services grow, starting with health and going on to home visits and intensive testing. At the third stage, which is far from being realized, the responsible self-governing group which is characteristic of many extracurricular activities permeates school activities, less as a concession to recreational demands, or as an attempt to supply social graces to children from limited home environments, but as a positive program of complete education.

The parent-teacher associations connected with public schools are potentially the bodies through which all adult citizens may participate directly in the planning and evaluation of the educational programs in their communities. At present, however, the boards of education are too remote from ordinary citizens on the one hand, and the parent-teacher associations are too frail on the other. School boards, consisting of a handful of unpaid citizens elected for several years on a normally nonpartisan basis, tend to leave initiative and leadership to the salaried administrators. They are less governing boards than boards of audit and review. Their members are often so busy and aged that they have less intimate day-by-day knowledge of what goes on in the schoolrooms than do the parents of school children. Yet, in the hands of boards of education rests the ultimate power to modify what goes on in the schoolrooms day by day. Lacking any such power, parent-teacher associations normally operate (save in certain small school districts) under the handicap of seeming to be purely "social" organizations, where acquaintances may be made, tea drunk, and speeches heard. Biennial elections of school boards, and, in smaller places, annual school meetings to hear and accept reports, are usually pale and bloodless versions of what might be possible if the powers and functions of boards of education and parent-teacher associations could be fused in some workable manner. A few boards have made groping efforts in this direction by appointing parents' advisory committees. This dilemma, of course, is not peculiar to public school systems. It is the characteristic shortcoming of local government in general. The frequently heard suggestions for a revival of town meetings or their equivalent fail to appreciate the peculiarly modern nature of the problem—the frustration of citizenship in the city. So far no inventor of social procedures has suggested a solution which has worked as well as town meetings are reputed to have worked in their time.

It is an ironical fact that the school after audaciously taking over so many functions of the family now is beginning to provide instruction on how to conduct family life itself. Across the country during the past few years, high school or college students in hundreds of institutions have asked for courses in marriage and family living. When their demand is granted, as it usually is, no one is likely to consider this a revolutionary event.

Nor is the so-called family life educator very likely to be regarded as a great innovator. All this shows how basic assumptions have changed.

To be sure, when family life education is confused with sex education (as when the course is assigned to a biology teacher), and when parental anxieties about public discussion of sex are aroused, there may be a temporary hullaballoo. It seems surprising that some adults strongly oppose the matter-of-fact presentation of the facts of life to high school or college students, facts known to the usual farm child before he reaches kindergarten age. Nevertheless such anxieties persist in considerable segments of American communities. Family life educators, while disappointing young people, have often made it easier for parents to accept them, by distinguishing carefully between sex education and education for marriage and family living. To do so is not merely a matter of practical diplomacy; it makes sense theoretically. Not only is the student likely to know the basic physiology of reproduction, thanks to the mass media if not to the parents, but of course the most important content of family life education is in the realm of interpersonal relations. The major studies of sexual adjustment over the past generation have all converged on the finding that sexual difficulties in marriage have their origins primarily in personality, not in physiology.

The arts of achieving and maintaining intimacy, communication, and consensus are learned, not inborn. Moreover, they are learned much better by children in some families than in others. The child of parents low in social skill has in the past been most likely, statistically speaking, to fail in marriage. He or she is a poor risk as a potential partner, because in a very real sense he carries on the tradition of his family. As everyone dealing with problem families knows, not only may a person's character difficulties be traceable to those of his parents, but their difficulties, to their parents, and so on, as far back perhaps as the biblical seven generations. Recent researchers, instead of falling into fatalistic acceptance of the chains of transmission by which the habit of frustration and failure becomes virtually immortalized, have pondered means of breaking these chains.[23] Yet to announce such

23. E.g., Buell *et al.*, *op. cit.*, pp. 411–40.

an aim is almost to say that the expert will counter the influence of parents. What the family life educators are doing is searching around for means by which deficits in social skill, passed on to children like debts of their parents, may be made up by the schools. In a groping and confused way, this objective probably informs the impulse which leads young people to ask for courses in marriage and family living. Some of them say quite explicitly that they do not want their marriages to be like those of their parents, or that they do not want to bring up their children as they were brought up. Others, less condemnatory but still critical, imagine that family living could be better than it is at present. And some of course, strongly attracted to marriage and parenthood on their own account, want to improve their technique for practicing them as arts. This demand for greater knowledge about family living poses a more serious problem than opposition by groups who fear encroachment of the schools on the prerogatives of home and church: it raises the problem of whether the schools can claim to possess the knowledge and means for instruction.

Social science can help, of course, but is well advised not to promise too much too soon. On the other hand, scientific caution cannot be used as a warrant for refusing to do as much as can be done; to offer functionless theory and stale description to students who sincerely put answerable questions is to give them a stone when they ask for bread. Practical educators, pressed by importunate queries and pleas, are greatly tempted to supply answers and prescriptions which have not been validated. This in a way is the characteristic position of the practical administrator of any agency; he cannot wait for certainty but must make decisions and go ahead on the basis of the best knowledge available. He needs from the social scientist not the promise of an unspecified utopian future, in which unassailable truths will ultimately be available, but rather a means of rating the reliability of his current predictions about various lines of action. The researcher in family relations who can bring his investigations to bear at this point may seem to offer less to the family life teacher than either the latter had hoped for, or he himself had aspired to, but the aid will be real, not indefinitely potential. It can avoid those painful episodes in which a tentative finding of research is converted into a sweeping dictum by a teacher or popularizer, with consequent scorn by the scientist. Such scorn is the futile reciprocal of the scorn of the practical man for useless theory.

Many of the materials and methods now employed in family life education—textbooks, pamphlets, movies, lectures—consist of popularized research findings, interlarded with invalid opinions and prescriptions, not even suggested by previous research.[24] It is not a counsel of perfection to suggest that closer ties between teachers and researchers have fewer hazards for either than their alienation from each other. If teaching and research are to discipline each other there must be a closer association between teachers and researchers. The fact that teaching and research are often done by the same person has not in the past automatically produced the sort of research that can be applied to family living.

The steady growth of scientific evaluation procedures in education already indicates the proper channel for such collaboration. If the over-all objective of education is conceived as the production of desired changes in behavior (or potential behavior), then the evaluation of whether and how those desired changes can be produced becomes a matter of scientific measurement and understanding. And the teaching of a course can be seen as an experiment. Of all the subjects in the curriculum of a high school, it would seem that family living most lends itself to the latter construction.[25] Those who speak of functional family life courses mean courses in behavioral change, not merely courses that reproduce information. Few courses now given on the family are demonstrably functional in this sense.

The average family life teacher today may claim that his purpose is to improve the quality of family life in his community.

24. Nelson N. Foote, "Playing the Part of Family Expert," *Marriage and Family Living*, XV, No. 1 (February, 1953), 3–4.

25. For one of the best worked out formulations of this point of view, see Eugene R. Smith, Ralph W. Tyler, and the Evaluation Staff, *Appraising and Recording Student Progress*, Vol. III, *Adventure in American Education* (New York: Harper and Brothers, 1942). For an account of some actual attempts at evaluation, see: Muriel W. Brown, *With Focus on Family Living* (Washington: United States Government Printing Office, 1953). Eugene Litwak of the Family Study Center has compiled an extensive bibliography of evaluation studies in family life education.

Even if he supposes he is doing this only by transmitting knowledge, and not by training his pupils in greater social skill, unless the result can finally be measured in terms of changed patterns of behavior, his methods can only be defended by wishful thinking. To the extent that he is indeed assuming some responsibility for improving the quality of family living through the school, he is quite radically challenging the traditional assumption that each family is adequate to prepare its offspring for competent marriage and parenthood. The small size of modern families, the rate of change between generations, afford immediate grounds for supposing that the contemporary family is less adequate to impart social skills than older families were; and numerous less direct arguments could be adduced for the same conclusion. The more important question is whether the school is more adequate, and beyond that, whether the school—at least through the medium of the next generation—can make the family more adequate.

From the standpoint of parents all this may seem a little bit more than they bargained for. Unless they are progressively involved in such developments, and become committed at each important decision along the way, it is to be expected that they will react against the school's new roles. The process of exploration into the possibilities of what the school can offer to raise the standard of family living in the community requires a reciprocal relationship between citizens and their public institutions. An increasing number of studies show that children's performance is intimately related to their family situation. It is thus clear that parents cannot throw total responsibility for the performance of their children upon the schools. In order to share that responsibility most effectively, the parents' family situation may have to be looked at in the light of what can be learned from family research and educational psychology. It is by these avenues of reciprocity, rather than by any simple transfer of putative functions, that the schools may contribute to raising the standard of family life in the community, while the improvement of family life in turn can facilitate the performance of children in schools. A program so conceived is likely to produce results without the cross-purposes and mutual frustrations which result when the family life educator creates the impression that he is threatening the most venerable of institutions.[26]

It is paradoxical that Americans at large should have ambivalent feelings toward their schools. Not only has this country carried free public education further than elsewhere in the world, but it is constantly extending its range; higher education will soon be claimed as a common right, judging by the increasing public support for colleges and universities. Yet alongside this attitude lies a fear that the school may lead pupils too far from the beliefs of their parents, or fail to develop traditional habits. The notion that education is a solvent for most ills counterbalances the fear of experiment. And the tendency to depend on the school for many functions where the family does not suffice conflicts with the reaction against usurpation.

This paradox, however, may not be strange, if viewed in terms of family development. The professional who comes between parent and child can expect to be regarded with suspicion. Each parent, moreover, was himself a child, and the many who disliked their school experiences may account for much of the hostility that emerges in a number of ways, in spite of the manifest honor that is paid to teachers and learning, to books and writers. The identification with their child's development is likely to tempt parents into encouraging the personal rivalry that countless teachers have fought to assuage, and demanding a show of relative ranking, instead of judging performance against potential. If the paradox yields to this explanation, then educational policy may gain in effectiveness if it is guided by a similar analysis. What would follow if the classroom were explicitly conceived as an extended projection of family relations?

If the entire curriculum over the ten-to-twenty-year school experience were organized as a continuous venture in family living, the results to be obtained from single courses on the family would pale by comparison. If classes were conceived as quasi-families, they would have to be kept small and stable. Teachers would have to be chosen more rigorously as models for identification.

26. Kenneth D. Benne, and Bozidar Muntyan, *Human Relations in Curriculum Change*, Illinois Secondary School Curriculum Program Bulletin Number 7 (Springfield: Superintendent of Public Instruction, 1949).

Experiment could soon establish how valuable it would be to put each class in charge of a pair of teachers, a man and a woman, one observing interaction while the other conducts the program. The optimal audience and timing for performance by each pupil could likewise be determined by trial and observation. A wide vista of possibilities is opened up by taking this view (which should not be confused with what is advanced as the life adjustment curriculum, despite some similarities).

Of course, research and experiment represent the furthest expression of the planning stage of agency development. Perhaps the paucity of private educational agencies in America, below the college and university level, accounts for there being less research and experiment than there might otherwise be. Some of the private schools are the least progressive, and some the most. The exploratory temper of an agency's clientele seems to be a more important condition than whether it is private or public. State teachers' colleges may tend, as often charged, toward uniformity, yet state colleges of home economics, through their extension services, have the most inviting opportunity in sight for getting involved in the rapid developments in family living occurring in the suburbs and schools of American cities. While sociology tends to predominate in the study of families at the college level, home economics is far ahead in answering the appetite of high-school youth for courses in marital preparation. And the suburban high school, as a community center, involves parents far more than do country town or metropolitan schools. The high schools because of their coverage are also the soundest hope for producing a whole generation competent for family living. On the whole, therefore, the evidence seems abundant that hopes invested in the public school are justified.

And as for adults, to the degree they are involved as participants in experimentation first as pupils, and then as parents, the ambiguities in their reactions to the professional educator may perhaps diminish. The atmosphere of public interest in family relations as shown in the commercial media, libraries, and churches is already quite intense. The rising enrollments in volunteer courses and child study groups, the attendance at forums and the purchases of books on marriage and parenthood, attest convincingly to the demand for educational aid in the adult years. Taken as a whole, therefore, the educational agencies serving the family, whatever the resistance they still encounter, are no doubt further ahead in terms of development than any of the other five types of family agency.

RECREATIONAL AGENCIES

The picture of recreation in the United States is impressively novel, and novel in a variety of ways. In contrast to most other countries, leisure here is not the possession of a privileged class but of the mass of citizens. Its development has been little influenced by the tradition which scorns work and fosters the cultivation of aristocratic pleasures. On the contrary, American recreation has made its way against a tradition which held work a virtue and play—if not a vice—a secondary and residual activity, a tradition which still persistently seeks to impose upon recreation some criterion of moral worth or practical gain. Yet for all these lingering puritanical inhibitions, probably no people has been more abundantly blessed with leisure time and recreational facilities than Americans in recent times.

Enriched by the cosmopolitan extraction of its people, watered by the volume of ideas transmitted through its unparalleled channels of communication, the field of play has effloresced in unequalled variety and profusion. Idealistic emphasis on the civic virtues engendered through sportsmanship has reinforced commercial incentives to promote recreation. The multiplication of jobs consisting of routine drudgery has for many depreciated the value of work and enhanced the appeal of avocations. And the reduction of the average working week to five days of eight hours each has created a vacuum of leisure which ingenuity has not been slow to fill. The result has been an elaboration of playful pursuits almost beyond comprehensive grasp.

In only a very limited sense is it true to speak of a transfer of recreational functions from the family to other institutions; most of such activity simply did not occur previously. And since this is a new situation that has only existed previously in embryo, we are ill stocked with generalizations for describing and explaining its character. As the oak tree cannot be deduced from the acorn, earlier thinkers, though familiar with limited forms of play, could not have discussed its modern growth and differentiation. If current students have not yet made it the subject of substantial research, perhaps the degree of its novelty excuses them. But social scientists can no longer scorn its importance.

What follows does not attempt to be a discussion of the wide range of recreational forms, but only a rough classification of the various kinds of recreation.

1. There is a wide range of activities which are primarily physical play. These we shall group as sports, and under this rubric include all those activities which simply explore and exercise the faculties and capabilities of the body, for motion, function, or sensation. They may utilize physical instruments, but not for the sake of manipulating and changing the environment.

The range of physical play could also be classified in terms of elaboration from the simple individual exercise of some organ of the body through increasing degrees of complexity until it reaches the institutional size of the World Series. The facets in this sequence of elaboration include: number of faculties employed at one time; elaboration of forms; number of persons involved; increase of skill, strength, speed, endurance, accuracy, dexterity, facilities, competition; rules; chance; formation of teams, and growth of team work; competition among matched teams; formation of permanent fostering organizations; spectators; adoption of the sport by regular publics, and the season for its play becoming recognized in the calendar of the community.

Equipped with a somewhat more precise analysis than this brief schema, it is more than possible that someone may sit down and invent an ideal sport which could overnight become more popular than baseball. Baseball itself was just such an invention; it was one of the first team games to become popular in this country, which for its first few centuries possessed very few team games. Social historians could make much, in terms of cultural change, out of the shift in interest late in the last century from contests to games. Contests and games both conspicuously include the element of competition, but whereas the contest emphasizes displays of strength and skill, the game includes a large mixture of chance. Matching maximizes this tension of skill and chance, and so the game can be played again immediately. The contest if repeated at once would turn out exactly as before, though of course there are marginal forms like boxing, which are neither clearly a game nor a contest. In the evolution of sports, a step beyond the team game might be said to occur with professionalization, and its arduous practice, coaching, and even development of abstract theory.

Whether individual or group, simple exercise or elaborate game, a competitive or concerted effort, physical play in its various forms creates the opportunity for its participants to explore and develop the powers of their bodies in compensatory, and normally salutary, ways beyond those permitted or called for by routine physical work.

The drama of success and failure, the prestige of demonstrated superiority, even the delights of graceful or dexterous movement, can be shared by spectators, though only the participants share in the enhancement of health and physical competence. Every sport recapitulates and idealizes the everyday bodily experiences. But in evaluating the ultimate contribution of recreational institutions to interpersonal competence, it is vital to note how physical sports can foster other elements of competence besides health. The vicarious feature of all kinds of play is visible here on closer look.

2. The spirit of play can and does invade every department of culture. Every kind of work has its counterpart in play. Crafts include recreational forms which represent the categories of serious economic activity all the way from hunting and fishing, which have their counterparts in extractive industries, through fabrication and construction, distribution and communication, to services and consumption. Although such activities, as distinguished from the work they represent, are engaged in for their own sake, they all involve practice in the intelligent adaptation of physical means to envisaged ends.

Thus "industrial" play is distinguished from physical play in being directed toward the exploration and manipulation of the physical environment rather than toward the exercise of the body. While some product or service of economic value may result from engaging in crafts, this is not its primary objective.

The distinction between work and play is perhaps less obvious where crafts are concerned than any other type of play. Also, any hobby which is pursued as recreation may also be undertaken as a livelihood, just as every hobby is in a direct sense an imitation of a serious occupation.

Even though work merges into play and there are no hard and fast margins between the two, it is yet useful to make some polar contrasts between them. Work seems to be performed in response to routine obligations. In the economic sense it provides the goods and services to maintain a customary standard of living. Play—including economic play—is a break in routine. It is free, not required. It explores new possibilities and potentialities, so that invention and discovery bear the closest relation to it. Treating familiar pursuits as play permits their idealization. Work is most fully work when it evokes no free release of energy and when it is all drudgery and chores, making demands for a minimum, not an optimum performance. Play is most fully play when it is spontaneous, unrestrained, and unforced. To look upon play as a childish preparation for adult activity is therefore to run the risk of making it work. The ambiguities of play are at their liveliest in crafts, which makes sketchy resort to common sense in defining them a less futile strategy than attempts to define them with more precision.

In economic activity, as in sport, chance can according to taste play a great or a small part; or economic activity can entirely be reduced to pure chance, as in gambling. Likewise with competition, though of course competition in economic life is different from competition in sport. Competition in sport is most zestful and fair when it occurs between equals, or when rules and devices, such as handicapping, are employed to simulate equality between competitors. Rivalry between teams is perpetuated through this balancing of powers. In business, by contrast, the effort of each competitor is to enlarge rather than to diminish the advantages he possesses, with the ultimate effect of eliminating competitors. To be sure, there are many similarities between the two kinds of competition, for example, competition between business institutions is often, as in sport, invoked simply as an added stimulus to effort. Certain large organizations in particular, which have largely lost their external competitors, encourage a nondestructive sort of sporting competition among their internal units for the sake of the gains in motivation it brings. Perhaps it is not too crude a simplification of economic evolution to suggest that as the one type of competition in business runs its course, the other which emphasizes competition within, rather than between, organizations may take its place.

A significant distinction is made by farmers between regular kinds of work known as chores and the work that differs from day to day. The latter kind is for many farmers very close to play, just as the work of some professions gives such scope and variety to the expression of capacities that they continue to be absorbing. It is evident that the skilled practitioner of every kind of play can change from amateur to professional status, and that many people have found their vocations by this route. Happy is the man who can make his living by getting paid for what he loves to do. In no other kind of play is the shift from amateur to professional status of such broad social significance as in crafts, because in the possibility of conducting industry as the crafts are conducted lies—as thinkers like William Morris foresaw long ago—the means of restoring joy to work, and of ending the alienation from work which plagues so many contemporary occupations.

The democratic revolution which has been abolishing the division of society into leisure and working classes may be completed when work and play, vocation and avocation, are merged in economic activity itself. Their extreme polarization in conceptual analysis may therefore frustrate the full understanding of their interrelation.

3. A third grouping consists of activities which are engaged in primarily for sociability—these range from casual joking or petting a dog to highly formalized collective expressions of sociability such as parades and banquets. Sociability is more often found mixed with other types of activity than by itself. Nevertheless, there are enough concrete kinds of association for sociability alone, to justify classifying them by this separate category.

Though sociability for some may be but a supplementary and entwining motive, it is just as true that for others collaboration is only an excuse for sociability.

Ritual, for example, may involve as much effort as the conduct of work; and much work is ritual, a kind of pageantry, not aimed at production but at fulfilling the duty of group solidarity.

In a society guided by ideals of work, sociability was not only taken as residual, properly confined to evenings and Sundays, but led to guilt and condemnation except when seen as seriously supporting group existence. To speak of funerals as recreation seems sacrilegious, yet steadily reunions and celebrations have lost their grim aspect of sacred obligation. As a result many forms of sociability are not only recognized as legitimate play, but since their release from old inhibitions, have effloresced with remarkable speed and profusion. Conversation about people, once uneasily viewed as gossip, has become something akin to friendly analysis. Dating has become fully differentiated from courtship, and can be enjoyed on both sides without serious intentions. The giving of gifts and sending of cards has grown in proportion as it has been treated as a form of expression, not merely as a requisite sign of affection. Where children were once excluded from attention when families visited others, they are now favorite conversation pieces, often in their presence, and with their contribution. Just to watch them is a favorite parental joy. As with sex, one can speak of family living as play.[27] Little girls not only entertain other "mothers," but discuss their dolls in terms of personality. And boys like their fathers speak of holding a "convention." Conference-going within a half-dozen years has burgeoned as a new national industry, though expense accounts still exclude the family, who only dine out as honestly avowed recreation. The growth of vacations, on the other hand, is going forward on the family plan. These types of example may serve to show the freedom and range of sociable play. This movement runs parallel with the development of serious associations as group purpose has become less confined to loyal obedience and the performance of sacred duty.

27. Nelson N. Foote, "Sex as Play," *Social Problems*, I, No. 4 (April, 1954), 159–63.

4. Our fourth classification is reverie (daydreaming, meditation, wondering, and speculation) which as play may be differentiated from the disciplined purposeful fantasy which is thinking of the critical-creative kind. Reverie continually assimilates new experience within the self, but not with respect to a foreseen end. It must also be differentiated from compulsive fantasy, such as worry, remorse, and grief (although the last of these may have an integrating function, if mourning is enacted without restraint).

Reverie appears in children at the age of two or three, and unless discouraged continues throughout life. If the past and the future of the person are to be knitted together by consistent purposes and conscious values, if the identity of the self is to become clear and autonomous, reverie has to be protected and engendered.

Like other forms of play, reverie, save as prayer, has also come under the ban of puritanism, and has only recently received due appreciation. Americans have given it so little explicit attention that their vocabulary for dealing with it is limited. Such terms as they possess bear for the most part disparaging, archaic, or foreign connotations—terms like talking-to-one's-self, solitude, intuition, or soliloquy. American law fortifies private property but does much less to restrict attention-getters who disturb the privacy of the person.

If each person told the circumstances under which he most freely explored his self—as in watching a fire, taking lonely walks, lying abed daytime, or just sitting—these settings would not be a classification of the forms of subjective play. Of all types of play, reverie is the most formless, while the most creative of new forms. Springing from unsatisfied longings and vague apprehensions, it is yet an activity which more than any other contributes to consistency of wants and integration of personality. Like other types of play, in being playful only when unforced, it is often least available to those who crave and need it most. At the same time there are souls who are so alarmed at the prospect of confronting themselves with detached objectivity that their response is properly called a flight into activity.

Counselors occasionally regard categorically withdrawal from others as a symptom of maladjustment, yet it is the person who cannot endure separation at all who is truly maladjusted. Loneliness has become almost a national problem, not merely an interest of family researchers. The development of interpersonal competence not only renews sociability; it makes solitude and reverie a form of recreation. The recreative power of solitude is a kind of therapy, when alternated with periods of intensive intimacy. It was a psychiatrist who noted that:

"The role of card games in a prevailingly juvenile society can be far greater in importance than a relatively non-competitive person would guess. People who have but very limited ability for human intimacy can assuage loneliness through these instrumentalities, without any risk of troublesome interpersonal developments."[28]

It is no longer considered helpful for a distraught and distracted person to have his future planned for him; that kind of counseling may only add another pressure or tension. But to provide recesses in time and space, where such a person can catch up on his deficit in the unceasing labor of organizing his behavior with foresight and insight, this is the kind of positive planning which imposes on the integrity of no one. Yet planning to leave people alone may be the hardest kind of planning.

5. Intellectual play includes those interests which have as a primary focus the exercise of mental skills and the pursuit of knowledge for its own sake (puzzles, card games, debating, reading, collecting, sightseeing). They have much similarity to sports and crafts, save that they are directed only to exploring and knowing the world, not manipulating it, except symbolically. Like crafts, they recapitulate the whole range of serious intellectual pursuits; like sports, the various individual forms test all the intellectual powers such as: memory, imagination, problem-solving, dissimulation, and anticipation of others. On this account, intellectual play is readily professionalized, and conversely, serious intellectual pursuits can readily be motivated by the fun involved.

28. Harry Stack Sullivan, *Conceptions of Modern Psychiatry* (Washington: The William Alanson White Psychiatric Foundation, 1947), p. 110. From lectures given in 1940.

The constant elements of intellectual play are these underlying aspects of curiosity—about the nature of the world, and of other men, and of one's own powers for grasping them. When such abilities are compared with those of others, there is a nonphysical contest or game. Guessing the moves of others appears to have far more attraction than mere comparisons of mental ability, undoubtedly because the element of chance is involved. In American culture, however, the attraction of intellectual contests and games seems underdeveloped; some other civilizations in the past seem to have gone further in this direction. The volume of reading, and use of other media of communication and education—apart from the arts—are steadily mounting and probably differentiating into new forms. As education becomes fun instead of duty, through the decline of the sense that it must be profitable before it can please, the student of popular culture at the middlebrow level will probably find a vast efflorescence of intellectual play.

6. Our sixth and final grouping is artistic play—that is, the arts. From the order in which we have arranged our classification, it is apparent that the arts recapitulate the range of human activity, just as other forms of recreation are re-creations of workday tasks. Thus dancing can be seen as an abstraction and idealization of sports; the applied arts, as representations of crafts; storytelling and drama, of sociability; graphic and plastic arts, of intellectual interests; poetry, of reverie (as in Wordsworth: "poetry is emotion recollected in tranquillity"). Music is the most distilled of all the arts, an evoker of all the forms and feelings of experience, of images suggestive of all the senses, a medium falling not short of words but transcending poetry in its power of abstraction. In pure music, the spirit is free of every toilsome entanglement; music is thus the apotheosis of play, the singer, the paragon of all players.

While the practice of artistry may be either by individuals or groups (orchestra, chorus, dramatic companies), and there is some development of artistic contests, there are no games consisting of artistry. Other types of recreation acquire spectators and auditors, but none invite them to quite the degree that artistry does. The way in which the element of chance enters into the artistic situation is largely in terms of the size and composition of the audience it draws. Audience reception is vital to most artists, suggesting that in this type of recreation something occurs between artist and public which is uniquely social. What that something is—the expansion of experience or its unification, the affirmation of human brotherhood or the criticism of life—must still be left to philosophers to ponder, but that such a relation exists seems as true for the amateur milliner as for the professional painter.

The phenomenon of style as localized in time, space, and segments of society also testifies to the intensely social aspects of artistry, to the sharing of artistic experience, and its intensification by sharing. The elusive phenomenon of taste is at once a most individual and a most social experience; critics testify to the unceasing dialectic of expression and communication in artistic production; art historians, to the efforts of publics to discriminate the ephemeral from the eternal.

Like other forms of recreation, it is unquestionable that artistry adds new elements and dimensions to experience; at the same time, art always bears a definite and necessary relation to the realities which it represents, it is an idealization or selection of the actual; decoration is always decoration of something; this something is not the design itself but a feature of existence which would be necessary with or without decoration. It is this subtle relationship to the more strictly purposeful and obligatory that puts art and artistry into the realm of play, however intense the seriousness with which they may be themselves pursued.

Now what has all this to do with families? Why should recreational agencies be considered as family agencies?

If the family is viewed only in traditional terms, as an institution to be preserved, the connection adduced between family welfare and contemporary recreation must appear trifling, or even inimical. If, on the other hand, the measure of a family is taken as its effect in developing competent personalities among its members, the provision of recreational opportunity assumes an importance compounded of functions performed by all the other types of family agencies.

It is evident that sports contribute to the development of physical health; crafts, to purposeful choice of a vocational identity and the acquisition of manipulative understanding; sociability, to practice in empathy; reverie, to the integration of self-conceptions; intellectual interests, to the stimulation of intelligence and the improvement of judgment; and the arts, to creativity. Furthermore, beyond these direct contributions to competence lie all the overlapping, complementing, and mutually reinforcing contributions of each type of recreation to the other aspects of competence, as for example, when experience on a baseball team brings out leadership ability, which is then usable in a government job.

The evolution of recreational agencies to the present has occurred in less time than the invention of the concrete forms of recreation. It should therefore not be surprising that the current procedures of recreational agencies only faintly foreshadow the shape of their future responsibilities toward the family, and the changes of method which will be necessary to discharge them. Fortunately a number of contemporary thinkers are working on these problems.[29]

Americans have resorted to recreation as an escape from the boredom of enforced leisure before they have ceased to think of play as an escape from the drudgery of work. While writings about recreation are scarce, there is some literature on leisure, and it seems significant that much of this was produced during the depression of the thirties, when so much of traditional social philosophy was being reassessed. As employment resumed, leisure came to be talked of less as a problem and more as a positive value to be pursued.

Neither family agencies nor anyone else has yet devised community-wide, positive programs to fill the vacuum of leisure with recreation. Since play ceases to be play when it is not undertaken for its own sake, an insistence on wholesomeness frequently destroys the appeal of a play program. Yet the family agency which exists simply to promote recreation is rare; so far the agencies which have sought to provide recreation to families have

29. Buell *et al.*, *op. cit.*, chaps. xvii–xxi. Also, Gertrude Wilson and Gladys Ryland, *Social Group Work Practice* (Boston: Houghton Mifflin, 1949).

justified their actions by reference to some ulterior, utilitarian purpose. Recreation unquestionably has all the values attributed to it, but these must be trusted to accrue spontaneously; they cannot be forced or directly seized. Only programs which accord recreation a *raison d'être* of its own can truly be called positive; only agencies set up to create the optimum conditions for its growth among the whole community have grasped its relevance for the whole of society as well as for the whole of the culture.

These considerations make the three-phase scheme for describing the evolution of recreational agencies as apt here as elsewhere. In their primitive phase, recreational agencies have aimed, through charitable and philanthropic means, to relieve the discomforts of individuals which were assumed to arise from lack of leisure or recreation. Poor children, overworked employees, youths in need of "character-building," were the special recipients of such attention. One not inconsiderable social problem was solved by occasionally relieving parents of their children. No disparagement is implied; the achievements of agencies so oriented have been substantial, as visibly demonstrated by thousands of playgrounds, parks, Boy Scout camps and YMCA's, built under both public and private auspices. Of course, the form of recreation is not necessarily synonymous with the form of agency which provides it, though often it may be inferred, and the same forms of recreation may be provided with diverse intentions.

At the second phase of agency evolution, we come to those who can hardly speak of play without calling it "play therapy." Music and painting as such are unaffected by the Salvation Army band leader who is motivated by the slogan that "the boy who blows a horn will never blow a safe," or the settlement house aide who feels that finger-painting will help her unhappy charges to "work out their conflicts." But the question is raised whether music and painting are as likely to engross their intended beneficiaries under such conditions. If not, the end desired will be defeated by the means employed.[30]

30. Adaptations of the therapeutic point of view can be quite enlightened, e.g., Ruth E. Hartley *et al.*, *Understanding Children's Play* (New York: Columbia University Press, 1952).

The fatigue of a worker may be increased by a sense of obligation to participate "on his own time" in a company sports program supposedly set up for his benefit. Compulsory sociability, prescribed as a medicine, has been the poison of persons and even large groups. In the evolution of recreational agencies, it probably cannot be maintained that the therapeutic approach is in any way an improvement over the charitable approach. Its very purposefulness too often betrays it. Not a few such programs for curbing juvenile delinquency by recreation have turned out to be, at least in the eyes of their recipients, programs for curbing juvenile delinquents. As we come to the third phase in the development of recreational agencies, therefore, the sharpest kind of distinction needs to be made between programs for providing recreational opportunities and programs of recreation. It is not precise enough to speak simply of providing recreation. The program for providing recreational opportunities can probably be that of any agency: the program of recreation can only be that of the participants, otherwise it ceases to be recreation.

It is but a short step from the voluntary associations for recreation for which Americans show such genius to the phase of planning, in which the participants themselves take responsibility for providing their own opportunities and facilities to engage in common avocations. Some of these voluntary associations are the finest examples of democratic planning. The rod and gun clubs have taken the initiative at every point in widening the interest in their craft, in encouraging skill, in establishing codes of fair play, in creating state conservation departments and passing conservation laws, and in being watchdogs on the expenditure of license fees. No better example of popular participation in the actual execution of planned programs exists than the wholehearted, voluntary work of rod and gun club members in restocking streams. Here also an executive agency of the government has acted in its least paternalistic yet most advanced planning role. These clubs may serve as a guide to other agencies who wish to maximize participation.

Most agencies, apart from those that provide recreational opportunities for children and certain specially disadvantaged parts of the population, tend to be governed by the participants in their activities. Even with children, there is frequent strife over adult domination; the young participants want control, even though they are not financially capable of providing their own facilities as a group. From the standpoint of Erikson's theory of play[31] as the achievement of ego-mastery, control of the process of rule-making would seem integral to play. The notable exceptions to agencies controlled by their clientele are, of course, commercial amusements, and, to a certain extent, public institutions like parks and museums.[32]

Commercial amusement institutions especially, but many non-commercial public and private recreation agencies as well, constitute a vast new industry, or series of industries. In addition to the enormous sums spent each year by spectators for admission to hear and see professional performers of every kind, there is tremendous expenditure for purchase or rent of equipment to be used by amateurs in every category of recreation. Much of the trade of hotels, restaurants, and their derivatives depends on customers bent on recreation rather than business; the same can be said for travel facilities.

If it can be shown that recreation is not only a needed medicine for an industrial people, but that it contributes positively to their over-all competence, it makes an economic contribution which ultimately leads to greater productivity. If, as seems probable, creativity is enhanced through recreation, and this creativity leads to innovations in the conduct of the work of society, then the cost of recreation may be rewarded geometrically. If in the end it turns out that play is neither an escape from work nor a method for therapeutic restoration to working conditions, but that it is an avenue for profitably investing in the human resources of a society, then a culminating irony will crown our already paradoxical evolution in the uses of leisure. Work will not have been deposed from its place of honor as the creator of wealth, but play will have been raised above it.

31. Erik H. Erikson, *Childhood and Society* (New York: W. W. Norton and Co., 1950), chap. vi.
32. For a searching critique of vested interests in client dependency, see: David Riesman, "Recreation and the Recreationist," *Marriage and Family Living*, XVI, No. 1 (February, 1954), 21–26.

CONCLUSION

The United States has no family policy. Many American students of the family, as shown by their reactions to this phrase, do not know what it means. In the absence of an explicit family policy, they not only find it difficult to imagine what one might be, but are inclined to question if one would be desirable. Perhaps the absence of a declared policy is typical of the pragmatic American temper. Yet whether this question is thought about by the public at large or not, both family researchers and professional practitioners in family agencies can postpone at peril of sterile futility the effort to state an over-all policy to guide their activities. What the researcher needs if his findings are to prove relevant is the designation of dependent variables of vital interest to the subjects of his study; what the practitioner needs if he is to evaluate the effect and efficiency of his efforts is the specification of definite goals.

It may be argued that a family policy is already discernible in implicit form. It may also be argued that nothing would be gained by striving to articulate its essentials; indeed something might be lost in the way of future flexibility by trying to fix on paper the nature of such a labile entity. This view though plausible in the abstract does not hold up when tested against the benefits of knowing what one is doing. Nor is it correct to charge that when purposes are made explicit they become less easy to alter. To state the objectives of research and of action makes them easier to criticize and modify on the basis of experience than when they remain behind the veil of sacred assumptions. In particular instances outcomes can be legitimately judged only in relation to defined intentions.

A national policy for the American family, though derived from implicit views and common practices, would have to be discussed and agreed upon before it could become official. One could surmise its main outlines, since these are embodied in occasional statements of goals like those alluded to in chapter i. Interpreters differ the closer they approach the concrete instance. It would be presumptuous, therefore, to do more than suggest that the concept of interpersonal competence, which allows for an open-ended view of personality, could stand for the optimal product of family performance. Yet there can be no doubt that the development of the individual member would hold first place among the goals of a family policy.

A family policy includes not only general goals but specifies appropriate means for their realization. The typical family agencies of the American urban community are the nearest we have to self-conscious instruments of a coherent family policy. But as we have found in examining them, all six types are hesitant to avow a positive program for constructing some optimal pattern of family living for American communities. Whether taken separately or in combination, they seem to abjure any responsibility for family development more inclusive than current clienteles and their recognized problems. In part this diffidence seems to be based upon the specializations among the multiple, segmented agencies, though this fact of proliferation could also be used as an argument for a coherent policy. In part the tendency to limit responsibility seems also to derive from the therapeutic approach. As will be shown, the two explanations are interrelated, since agencies historically have arisen to deal with discrete problems.

To put the question of a family policy in another form, should all the families in a community be considered as agency clients? Should even the entire complement of agencies claim as its province a program so broad as family development?

If we look at the new Department of Health, Education and Welfare, this appears to be the public agency at the national level which most fully comprises the six types of service to families described above. Its main units are the Public Health Service, the Social Security Administration, and the Office of Education. The Children's Bureau falls under Social Security, along with certain services to the aged and disabled. The only other protective agency in the government, directly concerned with families, is the Women's Bureau in the Department of Labor. Though suggested for many years by professional bodies, there is no Office of Recreation. Counseling agencies find a minor link with the National Institute of Mental Health, a research unit in the Public Health Service, but on the whole mental health responsibilities are left for the states to discharge through institutional care of the mentally disabled. Although the Department of Health, Education and Welfare tries to rationalize the miscellany of its components by referring to their common thread of family service, neither its structure nor its programs exhibit a comprehensive family policy.

On the private side at the national level there is even less evidence of any organized instrument for expressing or implementing a family policy. The National Council on Family Relations, though it aims to bring together all members of the disciplines and professions which deal with families, is puny in its effect; its journal, *Marriage and Family Living*, is of unsure viewpoint and meager circulation. The Family Service Association of America, though oriented mainly to social casework, has a considerable interest in family life education and recreation, but its viewpoint remains almost exclusively therapeutic. The American Home Economics Association is a professional society interested mainly in the advancement of that profession. As a single example of how narrowly it conceives its responsibility toward families in the community, it is a fact that its association with the field of social work is almost nil. The National Conference on Social Work co-ordinates annual meetings of numerous professional social work bodies, but speaks with less voice than the National Social Welfare Assembly, and the latter speaks only for social welfare agencies in a fairly narrow sense. These organizations almost complete the picture. The many minor private agencies at the national level are even more specialized and oriented to professional problems. The National Conference on Family Life, held in Washington in 1948, under the sponsorship of a great many government and private bodies, was comprehensive in scope but ephemeral. Its reports, moreover, offered less substance in lieu of family policy than the White House Conference on Children and Youth held two years later.[33] The latter undoubtedly remains the nearest approach on record to stating a family policy for the United States. How little it is known or talked about, however, suggests the degree to which it has mobilized support.

33. Helen Leland Witmer and Ruth Kotinsky (eds.), *Personality in the Making: The Fact-finding Report of the Midcentury White House Conference on Children and Youth* (New York: Harper and Brothers, 1952).

Within the states, their health, education, and welfare departments are principally concerned with the care of the indigent. The peculiar divisions of responsibility between state and federal levels, in both public and private agencies, make it unlikely that any state will institute a positive family policy. A much more feasible possibility is its institution at the local level, particularly in metropolitan communities. Because it is only at this level that practitioners come into direct contact with families themselves, and thus potentially can lead families into programs of voluntary action, these are the agencies on which we have concentrated our attention. Yet only to glance at the hundreds of agencies which belong to the welfare council of any large city, and to know how little their programs are unified by common objectives, is to confront in conspicuous form the absence of a family policy. The public agencies, that is, the departments of municipal government, hardly offer a more hopeful spectacle, however much can be said for the public school systems in particular cities. To jump to the conclusion that what is now needed is co-ordination on bureaucratic lines is a remedy made dubious by the observation that public agencies, no less than private, can multiply and operate chaotically when not informed by unifying purposes. The erection of hierarchies and jurisdictional monopolies is no substitute for a family policy, though it consume ten times the effort required to arrive at the latter.

Let us imagine that a council of all six types of family agency in a community, both public and private, wants to break out of the bonds of the therapeutic approach and assert joint responsibility for positive family development. Quite apart from the virtues of ending their preoccupation with the elaboration of specialized treatment of discrete ailments among their overlapping clienteles, it follows logically that attention would shift from the disabled to the normal majority of the community. During the past decade or two, the whole trend has been toward the reduction of the extremes of wealth and poverty. Public agencies at the national level in particular, through use of the taxing power and the assurance of minima of consumption, have reduced the proportion of indigent members in every community. For some private agencies at the local level this has meant a shrinkage of their clientele, and a few are already looking around for new services they might offer. But to the extent that they still think of clients as persons in need, whose needs must be met by professional assistance, their strategy appears to net them meager response, with perhaps one exception. The counseling agencies have been finding a striking growth in the number of clients from the middle- and upper-income groups of each community, persons well able to pay for the aid they seek. This particular example, however, does not refute but supports our major contention: If family agencies are to foster optimal family development, in the community at large, they can only succeed by adopting a policy that attempts to create new values, not by offering to remedy unfulfilled needs.

Instead of conceiving themselves as intermediaries between donors and recipients of professional services, each of whom constitutes a minority of the community, family agency personnel by this perspective would become expert in invoking the participation of the middle majority of normal people, by holding forth goals for family development that would require planning and joint effort for achievement. Their expertness, moreover, might eventually consist in applying the findings of research to the conditions where desired outcomes would be expected to occur.

Instead of referring their efforts to the restoration of some mythical status quo ante, usually entitled adjustment, they would logically assume a condition of continuous change and development, with goals of action phrased in terms of directions of movement, rather than some terminal state.

This recommended developmental approach to family-serving agencies does not imply elimination of therapeutic agencies such as hospitals, for which need will remain. But it does mean reducing that need as fast and as far as possible, and transcending the goal of mere adjustment to some minimum norm by opening up a range of as yet unachieved possibilities in family living.

What are some examples of values that might be proffered by a policy directed toward the optimal development of families in an American community? In abandoning the functionalist notion of definite needs, we open up a limitless horizon of emerging values, but lest it seem vacant of concrete goals for the immediate future, we shall outline a few extensions of current values, following the captions of agency types:

a) Medical agencies: Demographers have long spoken of population quantity and quality as the obvious variables in any population policy. As a nation, unlike many others in the world today, the United States has no population policy. Births are neither fostered nor discouraged. Yet it is quite evident that any explicit family policy at present is bound to recognize not only the appeal of babies to families who can afford them, but the diffuse public interest in child health and rearing. Family size as a function of rational choice by the family itself is a value yet far from realization. Parent education in the hygiene of optimal child-rearing has grown so prodigiously that there can be no doubt of its continued appeal and extension.

Beyond childhood, health is no longer thought of only as the absence of disease, but in terms of weight, appearance, energy, vivacity, longevity, and the joy of competent performance, sexual performance being included. Diet is undergoing unlimited elaboration according to standards of aesthetics, novelty, interest, and etiquette, and the same is true of sex life. On the strictly physical side, the mobilization of family agencies to pursue health as a value seems more clear-cut and unified than almost any other element of our implicit or explicit family policy. It is at the margins where mental states produce physical symptoms that the organization of the community to promote positive health in a unified manner is more questionable. The fatigued housewife with nothing to do is a numerous example; by proper organization of community resources, her leisure could be rewarding instead of unhygienic.

b) Economic agencies: Any common-sense assumption that values in the economic sphere are simply reducible to the idea of more would fail to recognize what has been happening in American families, at least to those of the middle majority. Until very recently, it has been almost universally taken for granted that progress was to be measured by the steady liberation of our citizens from conditions of necessity. However, a long succession of triumphs in turning conditions into means and scarcity of means into fullness, though gratifying in retrospect and provoking envy abroad, has brought us to the threshold of a peculiarly novel problem. The goal of progressively overcoming natural limitations was always a value. Since it motivated all alike, it awakened no problem of values. But as the further conquest of limiting conditions more and more loses its importance, through success and becoming the routine of specialists, the problem of values strikes with full force.

If we turn to the economic situation of the fortunate majority of American families, we find that despite the great variety among them, a common predicament of choice among values confronts us. The problem is not how can I produce enough to live, but what career shall I undertake? Not how can I pay for necessities, but, shall I take the job that pays most, or the one I shall enjoy most? Not the living wage, but the wage regarded as fair in relation to the incomes of those with whom comparisons count. Not to keep the wolf from the door, but to keep up with some set of Jones' in their pattern of consumption, or leisure, or kinds of friends. The outstanding necessity is the necessity of choice, of selecting alternatives and sticking to them. On the side of consumption, the perspective for the extension of positive values can perhaps be summarized in the notion of development of personal style. The economic agency that can organize the procedure by which consumers can become effective critics of their own consumption will be advancing this value.

On the side of distribution, it is obvious that incomes in the United States are still very unequally distributed, though their per capita average has been rising steadily. Likewise leisure is unequal. Another value respecting income, in the pursuit of which American families welcome leadership, is that of further stabilization, including duration after retirement.

On the side of production and employment, it is almost astonishing how definitely and widely Americans have come to prefer a salaried career in their favored occupations. The very concept of a career has come to express a complex value, which includes education, status, security, and satisfaction from one's work, the nature and rewards of which evolve in an orderly way over the lifetime. Preparation of family members for pursuing careers is a transformed function of the family, and expansion of access to careers is a growing function of family agencies in this sphere.

c) Protective agencies: The function of protection has long since been transformed into a concern for preventing exploitation, for safeguarding equal rights to opportunity, and lately for expansion of opportunity for free movement of men, goods, and ideas. Although it is not three generations since human slavery was abolished in America, the artificial barriers which have restricted achievement by minorities are progressively being leveled. The value of political and social equality bids to endow every minority with full citizenship. Yet when we observe the way in which people have neglected to exercise their freedom to associate in co-operative enterprises of all kinds, we note that many find choice difficult, and multitudes participate hardly at all, save in the sense of passive drift. The value of participation has moved only a fraction of those who now possess opportunity for its realization. Nonvoters exceed those denied suffrage. Yet as adequate examples show, people's appetite for participation can easily be stimulated to such heights that assumptions of their native apathy are reversed.

d) Counseling agencies: In the past, the personality of each individual was inherited very much as if it were a fact of nature. The widespread idea that it was of hereditary origin only amplified and confirmed the conviction of its intrinsic and unchangeable nature. Since nothing could be done about it, personality was not a problem and received little attention as an object of scientific study. The rise of experimental education and of social psychology has opened the doors of self-determination to a degree which renders obsolete the tragic conception of a man's character as fated. Yet instead of a nobler conception of responsibility for the self, through organizing the conditions which determine the self, our theater offers the pathetic spectacle of drifting characters who are unable to establish their identity, and who regard the conditions of existence not as potential means but as excuses. People who enjoy what would once have been considered fortunate circumstances, having few external barriers to overcome, still invent imaginary psychic ills, or in a daze of pointless futility adhere to the values of their parents, or conform with a mass of suggestible others in following ephemeral fads. Although the remedy is certainly not a return to harsh patriarchal discipline, it seems not too strong a statement to describe a whole new generation as suffering from overprotection. Having freedom to choose, they have no criteria for choice. As suggested by David Riesman in *The Lonely Crowd*,[34] millions seem to occupy a limbo between values indoctrinated in them by parents and values freely chosen by themselves. Without commitments to past or future, they are rudderless, other-directed, unable to design and organize a style of life which can in any determinative sense be termed a personality. Without leadership by family agencies in the creation of positive values for personality, the new freedom from paternal domination can readily be replaced by a new tyranny in which more lonely crowds seek father figures.[35] The pursuit of identity is a positive value without limit, the subjective side of any philosophy of self-government.

e) Educational agencies: The extent of American success in the long struggle against scarcity has not been grasped by those segments of the public who still think of education as only a process of inculcating the fundamentals for getting along in the world, or merely as the transmission of an established culture. The interpretation of education as enrichment of the appetite for new experience sets a task for schools far greater than that of traditional educational strategy. Of all the potential avenues of new experience, which one shall the student choose? Though for some, the problem is still how to get a basic education, for most it has become a matter of choosing between the many pursuits open, how to select and integrate their selection from the vast chaos of impressions which modern means of communication convey to them. How many have stuck to a wrong choice rather than renew the agonies of choosing again? Perhaps earlier than most family agencies, some public schools have recognized the peculiar current need for career guidance, but the guidance movement is still groping for an authoritative while nonauthoritarian

34. Riesman, *op. cit.*
35. Erich Fromm, *Escape from Freedom* (New York: Rinehart and Co., 1941).

rationale. Higher education for careers is on its way to becoming universal, before many students know why they want it.

f) Recreational agencies: Formerly, time for recreation was won with difficulty from the onerous demands of work, and no questions arose over the desirability of leisure. Ways of utilizing leisure seemed endless, its maximization, an unquestioned good, not a problem. Yet today for many Americans the extension of leisure has created a vacuum (an abyss, Riesman ominously calls it) which they are perplexed to fill. People can be as much at a loss for something to do with themselves when surrounded with opportunities for recreation as when lacking them. For some time to come, there will continue to be the community problem of providing certain kinds of recreational facilities, yet complete success along these lines will yet fall short of solving the emerging crisis of mass boredom. Boredom, Robert M. Hutchins has declared, is as great a threat to American society as the atom bomb. Boredom is lack of involvement.

Recreation, as our classification of its forms suggests, still bears a mysterious representational relation to all the binding concerns of life. The various kinds of recreation seem worth while according to how much they correspond to these concerns of life. When the serious concerns lose their value, recreation also begins to pall. Thus the mere pursuit of fun is no guarantee of relief from boredom, which may derive from a basic lack of involvement in serious pursuits. Even in play, human beings find it necessary to invent and devise ends, even though they may be purely symbolic. On the other hand, as mentioned earlier, the deliberate effort to have fun—to make fun the end itself, and to pursue it directly—often stultifies the possibility of having it. By contrast, the person who is able to give himself fully and freely to any serious pursuit is likely to have fun without requiring—though he may periodically enjoy—standard forms of recreation. Theories of leisure and recreation are still very tentative, and any interpretation is risky. Nonetheless, it seems safe to conclude that the major emergent problem of recreational agencies, as of all other types of family agencies, is no longer that of further expanding leisure and recreational facilities—though such expansion will continue—but of leading in the creation of recreational values in which families may become deeply involved and committed. To a large degree, of course, such a program calls for the organization of recreational groups which will generate or expand their own specific values and morale.

This may be the place to propose a general recreational value, lest the preceding words seem to lack reference or to contradict each other. The concept of self-transcendence describes such a value. It lacks the misleading connotations of the popular term "growth," which raises questions of the organic analogy, naturally predetermined sequences, and quantitative accretion without differentiation. Self-transcendence implies only that exploration and extension of capacities will occur, but does not specify the forms their exercise will take. Self-transcendence is possible at all ages, but not in all directions at all ages. In adulthood, it goes beyond pretense and vicariousness to exercise movement from potentiality to actuality. As a principal value to be sought and found in recreation, the concept of transcendence is congenial with several major theories of recreation which have been proposed so far—Groos' practice theory, Piaget's theory of representative activity, Erikson's idea of ego-mastery, Huizinga's notion of "stepping out of common reality into a higher order."[36] Play furnishes the perfect model for free involvement and commitment. As such, approached with discrimination, it offers some promise to the contemporary person who wishes to "declare his own values," i.e., who recognizes that he needs rules to live by, yet wishes not to be inescapably bound by them. A person can if he lets himself become deeply involved in a game, yet know it for only a game; he may be fully committed to his role, but for only the duration of an agreed upon period. Precise sociological and psychological analyses of the processes of progressive involvement and commitment (phrases which have been significantly used to define courtship and marriage) may thus help to define the means for solving the widespread problem of aimlessness in society.

36. Karl Groos, *The Play of Man* (New York: D. Appleton and Co., 1914); Erikson, *op. cit.*; Jean Piaget, *Play, Dreams and Imitation in Childhood* (New York: W. W. Norton and Co., 1951); Jan Huizinga, *Homo Ludens* (New York: Roy Publishers, 1950).

When it was taken for granted that what was needed was simply more health, more economic means, more opportunity for participation, more freedom for self-development, more education, more leisure and recreation, the old situation looked simple by contrast with the present. In spite of all its bad memories of the depression, and the uncertainties of war-imposed separation, the coming generation is in the uneasy position of being the heir to a fortune. Being forced to do nothing and free to do anything, the young person finds that he does not integrate unless he can become a valued part of some activity with others which makes demands on him; that he cannot esteem himself unless he finds a way to win the esteem of others by contributing productively to a goal which he shares with them. Countless parents today, in releasing their children (and in some cases, wives or husbands) from all obligations of effort, rob them of their chances to achieve social worth and self-esteem. In place of crude necessity they should introduce some chosen values, values shared by a company of others who will support these values and reinforce the child's conception of who he is when his parents can do so no more. With the best of intentions, that is, the most loving parents may accomplish the worst of consequences, through a mistaken, obsolete interpretation of the wants of youth, for example, by refusing to give any negative or positive criticism when asked for appraisal of performance.

In summary then, we take it to be the unique new task of the contemporary American family and its official helpers to prepare each member for continual reinvolvement and resocialization as a member of the various changing institutions in which he participates outside his family. The aim which must accordingly run across all family research and all action by family agencies is to endow every family member with competence for genuine participation, the ability to develop shared commitments to some defined and defining values in every sector of his life activity.

It used to be taken for granted that one's family, social-psychologically speaking, would automatically be identical with one's biologic kin. There have always been exceptions to this correspondence, however, and in the perspective of the present it is conspicuously evident that there may be the widest divergence between one's circle of intimates—one's quasi-family of significant others—and one's actual parents, relatives, mate, or children. The period of adolescence is the classical example of this divergence. The classical picture of the adolescent in revolt against parents seeking still to control him as if he were a child, however, has been superseded in subtle but crucial ways. In the transition of the past few decades from patriarchalism toward liberal, equalitarian relations between parents and children, a transition which Professor E. W. Burgess has persuasively documented,[37] children have received greater leeway for developing individuality and self-direction than in the past. They have less need to revolt, or perhaps it could be said that their revolt has been successful. At any rate, restrictions upon development of a personal style of life and a set of companions to support it have diminished. Yet it is doubtful if parents and children have been brought closer to each other, or, on the other hand, if the children have found the degree of unquestioning support from nonfamily intimates that in the past they expected and got from their families. The gap between generations, so wide in America because of the rapid rate of social change and the relatively provincial origins of parents, has if anything continued to widen, despite the countervailing influence of mass media of communication. It is almost commonplace to expect that children will see things differently from their parents. But the dilemma is that if they are going to see things differently from their parents, how are they going to see them, and what other groups of identification are going to fortify their views? In becoming detached from the values of their parents, millions have not become reattached and committed to alternative, more timely, values. Those in this condition may be compared to a ship which has neither anchor nor rudder nor sails. It would undoubtedly be futile for parents, assuming they themselves hold firm to definite values, to attempt to fasten these on their children, yet nothing can give, or should give, parents more concern than the belief that their children are merely drifting. Moreover, more and more parents themselves seem to have no stable values, and when the obligations of marriage and parent-

37. Ernest W. Burgess and Harvey J. Locke, *The Family: From Institution to Companionship* (New York: American Book Company, 1945).

hood are not strengthened through mutual commitment to common values, requiring faithful collaboration through the years, they are seriously weakened. If, therefore, the problem of the guidance of youth is solved, it is likely that it will be solved for whole families at once, and not just for their adolescent members.

It would be fatuous to wish for a return of hardship. Yet for the millions of young Americans, especially for those from middle-class homes, the problem seems to be that of finding some powerful purpose in life. Merely to find a job, raise a family, and feed their children seems insufficient for them. It is too easy; it calls for no courage, no great struggle, no sacrifice, no threat of failure, no test of self. And it leaves vast potentials unused. To attempt to divert these unused human resources to unplanned recreation—to kill time by having fun—does not do it, or does it only in part, as in the deliberate seeking of danger. Certain thoughtful union and industry leaders are groping for a more challenging conception of "more," not more in the sense of material gain, but more use of the talents of the man who works.

Probably the average student in the liberal arts college at the present time is typical. The most favored of American youth, he yet often is the least happy, because happiness comes from the realization of values, and his values are inchoate or not really his.

Many parents today seem unable to divine the nature of the problem facing their children. Some quite frankly admit to being baffled. "What more can we do?" they say. Like the theorists of adjustment, they only imagine fulfilling wants. What might be more effective is the exact reverse. The creation of wants may seem absurd, until one witnesses the frequent resentment of young adults when their parents solve all their problems for them, thus preventing them from doing things for themselves. Success in struggle is very satisfying. The levity and flippancy now so characteristic of youth only poorly conceals a craving for challenging purposes. If family agencies can transcend the outlook of the older generation and articulate these values, then the potential energies of youth will be directed to new and promising uses. If moreover, not youth alone, but parents also, can be imbued with these emergent values and involved in their attainment, the rent between generations could be narrowed. The problems of adolescence (which might justly be called "problems of obsolescence of parental norms") might then become memorials of that turning point in industrial society when, freed at last from the bonds of scarcity, and recognizing their freedom, human beings began to re-create themselves through their children in a more ideal and versatile image than as slaves of nature.

If family agencies construe their tasks in terms most appropriate to the present, they will take the responsibilities of community leadership by attending to emergent values and organizing action for their realization, and in getting the involvement and participation of families and quasi-families. To foster such involvements means to start with the child in the family, for it is here that his identity and capacity for further identification are cultivated or discouraged. It is also necessary to think of leadership in nonauthoritarian terms and in a way that is most evocative of spontaneous self-expression. The bulk of the current professional literature on strengthening the family, about the widespread longing for love and commitment, and about the meaning of the small group, revolves around this matter of identification. In Jung's felicitous phrase, what many students are observing is "modern man in search of a soul," that is, in secular terms, in search of an identity to which he can be firmly committed.

The family is the ideal type of all social bonds. Marriage is the ideal type of formal commitment to a tie of common identity. Courtship is the ideal type of experimentation in finding others to whom full commitment appears promising. Parenthood is the ideal type of identification with the welfare of posterity. The solidarity of the whole community cannot surpass the solidarity of these its nuclear constituents.

The family will be solid as long as there are values for which it may function; its members will unite with others in the community as their families endow them with competence for sharing the orientation of others. If a child can make such commitments, no parent need worry about sending him out into the world; without them—or the capacity for making them—the child most removed from want is still in peril, even while in the custody of his parents. In the case of husband and wife, also, since personality is never formed but always in the process of being formed regardless of age, it is likewise true that only as there exists the capacity for widening and deepening involvements will the marriage progress. The salvation of the family, of the person, and of the community, in today's dynamic world, is through continual reinvolvements, adventures in scaling the heights of social responsibility for the optimal development of each.

V The Planning Process

ALL AGENCIES PLAN, AS DO all persons and families; planning in the generic sense distinguishes us as humans from creatures who cannot transcend the immediate. But planning in the specific sense of highly modern attainments in social organization is what we mean when we speak of the planning stage in family agencies. In the long history of man's ascent toward rationality in social affairs, conscious awareness of the planning process in action agencies ranks as a major invention. The image of the competent man is out of place except in the context of modern planning.

The generalized outline of the democratic planning process which follows should not be taken as a recommendation that every family agency should immediately plunge into the planning stage. The model presented in this chapter is put forward simply as a rough guide by which family agencies can determine such questions as how near or far they are from the planning phase of their evolution; or, if they are already engaged in planning, how thorough and effective a job they are doing.

Planning by a family agency is not unlike the planning by a person of his career. When the aim of an agency is personal development, there are many reasons why its planning method should self-consciously follow a model which permits the agency to transform itself by its own operations.

Since Cooley in 1902,[1] if not long before, many thinkers have held that human nature and the social order reflect each other. There have been divergent opinions whether the line of causation runs from personality to community ("human nature writ large"), or whether the person as microcosm incorporates as habit the regular recurrences which constitute the institutional fabric of society. The developmental view conceives a spiral of interaction between the careers of persons and of institutions.

1. Charles H. Cooley, *Human Nature and the Social Order* (New York: Charles Scribner's Sons, 1902).

It is the obligation of the family agency that adopts the aim of optimal development to maintain this nexus in a dynamic sense. To keep the parallel always in mind can cumulatively influence multitudes of decisions.

In concrete terms, the action of agencies, families, and individuals is not a constant flow; it is episodic, organized in fairly regular, qualitatively distinguishable sequences. As a unit of reference, the behavior of each of the three can usefully be brought together in a conceptual analysis of the planning process that is applicable to all three levels of abstraction. To study the phases of the planning process, as seen in the furthest advanced of the family agencies, is to see in enlarged detail what in family or personal living may be only implicit or rudimentary. But from this enlargement of the social act one can then derive clues and questions which are relevant when observing the smallest sequence of interpersonal behavior.

The model of the planning process as here presented is adapted in its broad outlines from Professor John Dewey's original delineation of the steps in problem-solving, published in *How We Think*, in 1910. The five phases into which we have divided the planning process are: (1) the definition of problems; (2) the formulation of proposals; (3) the decision on policies; (4) the execution of programs; and (5) periodic appraisals. Students of Dewey and other American experimentalists will note further echoes of pragmatic philosophy. Many elements, however—for which credit can only be given partially in references—are due to quite different thinkers, including American critics of Dewey, like Professor Frank Knight of Chicago, as well as writers in England and Sweden. Agency practice, when fully evolved, seems to be empirically represented by the model, if in the absence of a systematic survey the impressions of experienced observers are accepted as reasonable.[2]

1. *Definition of problems.*—Before there is an agency, or planning, or the possibility of planning, there must be a public with a problem. The public and the problem are defined in reference to

2. For a partially successful effort to verify the phase hypothesis, see: Robert F. Bales and Fred L. Strodtbeck, "Phases in Group Problem Solving," in Cartwright and Zander, *Group Dynamics: Research and Theory* (Evanston: Row, Peterson and Company, 1953), pp. 386–400.

each other. They never stand alone, and cannot be defined
alone.[3] A problem always belongs to some group of people, and
generally speaking any group comes into existence as a group
because its members feel that they are confronted by a common
problem or problems. But an outside expert cannot always determine what constitutes the problem of a group. And yet the
problem exists and arguments may abound as to how to define it.
Alternatively, a certain state of affairs may be a problem to an
observer without being regarded as a problem to those whom it
seems to affect. If a state of affairs affecting a number of people
is also to become the problem of a group, then the members of
the group must participate in defining the problem. Otherwise it
is not their problem and they are not likely to feel responsible for
its solution. The expert may assist in the recognition and clarification of a problem, but must be prepared for his interpretations
to be rejected.

Each phase of the planning process, when fully developed in a
community or a large institution, employs a characteristic type
of document. In this first or problem phase, such a document
functions primarily to call attention to a problem and to convince
the public involved that something ought to be done about it.
The definition of what ought to be done occurs in later phases
of the planning process, and yet in the successful attention-get-
ting and definition of the problem, the outlines of later phases
vaguely emerge. On this account, the importance of the problem
phase of planning is often underestimated; that is, action goes off
without adequate preparation. Even more often, the importance
of getting the public involved and committed to solution of the
problem is underestimated. Yet it is the arousal of concern, and
participation in the definition of the problem as their problem,
which motivates the public to act.

Generally speaking, these documents are often the work of a
single person skilled in persuasion. He may utilize the researches
of many others, and his work may overflow with tables, charts,
maps, and pictures, but these are not expected to be exhaustive

3. John Dewey, *The Public and Its Problems: An Essay in Political Inquiry*
(Chicago: Gateway Books, 1946), especially chap. vi, "The Problems of
Method."

or conclusive. They have to be chosen primarily for their effect in securing attention and deepening the involvement of the reader or listener. For example, five issues of the Federal Budget 1941–45 would mean less in the concrete experience of the average citizen than the dramatic comparison of the cost of one day of World War II with the entire cost of the TVA system. The expert who is skilled in getting attention, provoking discussion, and dramatizing problems plays an indispensable role in the planning process, and deserves perhaps more honor than he gets, since too often he is treated as one who troubles the sleep of others. Poets and prophets may be indispensable as movers of opinion and intolerable as team mates.

The unquestioning assurance with which we habitually assume that everyone knows what is meant by a social problem attests that we are dealing here with one of the valid preconceptions of our culture. Yet our and other cultures show that what is problematical to some people is not so to others. In our culture, circumstances such as the condition of the weather and the coming of death are regarded as natural and inevitable concomitants of human existence. They cannot be changed or improved, they are not subject to progress, nothing can be done about them except to submit and adjust to them; in short, they are not problems. The problematical situation is one where it appears that something can be done, something which is defined by the comparison of a better future and a worse present. Thus the concept of problems is closely linked historically and culturally with the idea of progress and the increase of man's power over nature. To the extent that the laboratories of General Electric raise hopes of regulating rainfall, the weather will become a problem. Thus, in the most advanced cultures almost any state of affairs can potentially be treated as a problem.

In considering matters like ill health, it may at first appear that for a state of affairs to be defined as problematic, it must inflict discomfort upon someone. Certainly it is true that many actions carried on by planning bodies are of this order; they are aimed at correcting some deficiency or restoring some status quo ante. It is also true, on the other hand, that many actions of planning bodies, if they can be said to originate in any form of distress at all, originate only in that "divine discontent" created by an awareness of a discrepancy between what is and what might be. For propaganda purposes, it may be an advantage to publish each problem as an evil to be disposed of, rather than a good to be attained. However, it must be noted how in the planning process it is often the unfolding of new possibilities that creates the problem, not the intensification of some threat of pain.

Failure to recognize the prospect of continuous, dynamic change leads not to planning but to fire-fighting, not to cumulative advance in power and technique but to stagnant routine. The definition of problems in terms of the progressive setting of new and positive goals is thus one of the major distinctions between the planning and the therapeutic approach to the conduct of family agencies. Also, the therapy, as well as the charity approach, is likely to assume the existence of a natural order. According to this view, problems arise when something goes wrong with the natural order. Some external disturbance is said to interfere with normal functioning, and the problem is assumed solved when the natural order is restored. The planning approach, in contrast, denies the assumption of some pre-existent natural order, and construes the social order as the product or construction of purposeful human activity. There is no valid question of whether to plan or not to plan, but only of which plans are good and which plans are bad. The structure of all human organizations—from the smallest to the largest—is taken as the embodiment of certain rules of the game which have been invented or accepted by their participants. Problems from this point of view require some reconstitution of the group to accomplish some change of purpose.[4] From the therapeutic point of view, it is common to speak of "society as the patient." But from the planning point of view, all parties affected by the problem are equally patients and therapists, who are engaged not in restoring their constitution but in modifying it continuously as new problems emerge. Instead of a sacred attitude toward the structure of the social order, the planning approach takes a very secular attitude.

Personality likewise becomes problematic when it is viewed as

4. Frank H. Knight, *Freedom and Reform: Essays in Economics and Social Philosophy* (New York: Harper, 1947), pp. 205–45.

a construction from the elements of experience. The basic assumption of all research on the development of personality is that ultimately something can be done about it, something distinguishable in terms of better and worse. How much can be done, of course, is not ascertainable a priori but only by exploration and experiment. As the reflection of the social order in which it occurs, personality can be no more a "natural order" than are the rules of the game which constitute the social order. The identity of Americans is a social problem in 1955.

2. *The formulation of proposals.*—Although the transition from the problem phase to the proposal phase of planning is usually gradual, the formulation of proposals is qualitatively distinct from the definition of public and problem. Proposals are creative responses; they call for imagination, invention, even genius. The making of proposals has to be properly timed, not coming too early in the planning process. For any given problem there may be a number of solutions, and thus new potentialities of divergence are introduced into the public's discussion. If those who make proposals are anxious that they be accepted or at least taken seriously and attended to, they should ideally wait until a public has become quite clear and coherent as to the nature of its problem and its desire to act. This is especially true when a proposal is likely to threaten this or that section of the public's interest; a premature proposal is more easily exiled from discussion by an alert minority, or even without opposition may lose force, when its relevance is not yet apparent.

Perhaps the proposal phase could be said to begin where "to act or not to act" ceases to be the question and consideration turns to serious alternatives. It ends when the proposal or proposals go before a policy-making body for decision. During the interim a considerable number of developments ideally must occur if the outcome is to be a full-fledged proposal of the planning type. During this phase, proposals may be legion, running from the most casual sort of suggestion to massive reports prepared by many experts and taking years of work. Despite such variation in their elaborateness, the proposal must contain the following basic elements if it is to deserve serious consideration:

1. A statement of an effective and feasible way of solving the

problem as it has been defined. 2. An estimate of the resources, human and material, required for carrying out the proposal. 3. A schedule of the rate at which these resources will be applied. 4. A statement of certain quantitative goals for achievement within the schedule set. Any proposal containing these elements is a planning proposal, and is often called a plan, sometimes with the name of its author prefixed, e.g., the Marshall Plan (although technically it does not become a plan until it has been subject to a policy commitment, and then of course it becomes a program).

The injection of proposals into the public's discussion of the problem is frequently, at first, on what might be called an amateur basis. While each serious proposal may contain the four essential elements, their development is neither elaborate nor exact. The multiplicity of proposals and their rudimentary nature, given a strong feeling of concern, then quite readily lead to a conscious demand for more careful study of the situation and comparative examination of the proposals. Then, and not before then in most cases, is the appropriate time for commencing the formal organization of the public.

At this point, another custom is often to constitute some expert committee, commission, or board and to charge it with making a study and some definite recommendations for action. The composition of the more successful committees tends to be drawn, with certain exceptions, from all the significant elements in the public to which the situation is a problem. To give them their charge may call for further definition of the appropriate scope of the planning area. This calls for judgment and may itself be a matter of disagreement. If action is truly desired, the planning area ought to be confined to those to whom the situation is definitely a problem in which they are actively involved, and it ought not to include everyone who might potentially experience some consequences from the action taken.

The method of appointment or invitation depends on the source of initiative. Persons representing dogmatic and intransigent minorities may have to be excluded, if they are incapable of discussion. On the other hand, difference of opinion is necessary for critical discussion and to avoid self-deception. Also, by including important interest groups at this early point, they are far more likely to make positive contributions, to become more deeply involved in a determination to solve the problem, and not to obstruct or refuse co-operation in later phases. Often voluntary community action is stultified because initiative in planning has been sequestered within a small, self-appointed elite.

These considerations emphasize the social context within which recommending bodies should be constituted. Such considerations are often neglected in favor of the personal qualities of potential members—interest, ability, free time, resources, prestige. These often matter, but they are also frequently sterile in terms of results. It takes much more than a coterie of enthusiasts or a list of prominent names adorning a letterhead to assure that a study committee will act and cause others to act.

As a sign of some degree of impartiality, the members of such a commission or board are customarily unpaid, though they may get their expenses or pay from the groups they represent. Thus they can rarely be expected to expend more than limited amounts of time in the business of the committee. Unless the whole operation is too small and rudimentary, this is the point at which a staff of full-time, paid professional experts may have to be engaged.

The professional staff usually consists of a number of specially qualified experts drawn from several fields or professions, their work being assigned and brought into a coherent pattern by a "generalist" with some facility in transcending special vocabularies and in promoting co-operation. He is often known as an executive secretary or staff director. On the other hand, the staff may consist of a single person who is at best an able amateur. *Ad hoc* commercial consultants are often useful in supplementing or providing an independent check on permanent staffs. Where expertness is required, the gains through specialization are obvious. Specialization may occur not only among various professions—as engineers, accountants, doctors, and attorneys—but with regard to various functions, such as researchers, idea-men, publicists, and patient drudges. The man of a creative turn may wilt before the task of tracing property titles, as the meticulous investigator may balk at championing a new idea. The creation of high standards of ethical and technical performance falls to a considerable degree to the professional societies to which the specialists belong; creation of co-operation and morale within the staff falls especially upon the generalist in charge. The specialists can normally be selected by various fairly objective measures of competence, while the role of the generalist has to be filled primarily through trial and error.

When proposal-making bodies are constituted *ad hoc*, they usually report their findings and recommendations, and then are disbanded. There is thus little opportunity for them or their professional staffs to accumulate experience as a group. Since proposal-making bodies almost universally try to settle upon a single proposal or integrated body of recommendations, with at most a single minority report rather than several alternatives, their work may be rejected or tabled by the policy-making body. Later, another study committee may therefore have to be set up; or a third or a fourth. In some instances of very complex problem situations, e.g., devising private expenditures of public funds, as in government-sponsored research, a succession of studies may have to be made before a workable scheme can be evolved. In this way, there is some accretion of experience even among *ad hoc* recommending bodies. On the other hand, except at the beginning of their existence, most planning agencies utilize permanently constituted advisory committees, which in turn often utilize permanently constituted professional staffs. Under such conditions, the accretion of experience is expedited, with many kinds of desirable consequences in the way of expert proficiency, e.g., the narrowing of estimates or the correct anticipation of opinion. Moreover, as needs to be stressed, the proposal-making or planning group can thus co-operate very closely with the group in charge of the actual execution of programs. The Tennessee Valley Authority, for example, takes pride in the fact that in its administrative structure planning and operation are merged. Such a setup is probably an extreme which is rarely feasible. On the other hand, severe and unnecessary complications develop when an advisory commission plus its staff get so far detached from operating agencies that neither feels responsible toward the other, and communication between them breaks down. There are certain guiding trends of expectation regarding such bodies which are becoming more explicitly defined as time goes on. These trends can be summarized under the general term of "professionalization." This term not only refers to formal membership of staff members in professional societies and their adherence to professional standards of ethics and competence, but to a subtle though substantial development of respect and support for professionals among the public at large. The development of professional standards has always depended to a large degree upon insistence by the community that the trust which it places in professionals be merited, and not solely dependent on the spontaneous enforcement of professional standards by the professional societies themselves.

Formerly, however, the professions were a quite distinct and even segregated group of occupations. In recent times the professional outlook has permeated extensively into many occupations and institutions where it once was absent, and their clientele has come to demand professional standards of conduct where much less used to be expected. This demand for professional conduct plainly applies to the status and role ascribed to the proposal-making bodies we have been discussing. They are expected to observe a steady not-self-interested, expert, responsible concern for the welfare of the public they serve. While their diagnoses and recommendations are not accepted as formally binding, they influence the course of the community's action to the extent that the community trusts them. Having such influence, there is no reason for the body of recommending experts to possess direct authority over the administrator of an action program or his agency, and certainly never over the clientele the agency serves. Having made their proposals, the members of the recommending body should have no more voice or vote in their adoption or rejection than any other citizens.

Often hearings are held in which the knowledge, views, and suggestions of all interested parties are sought. The scope of the problem must be defined and measured; all plausible ways of solving the problem must be canvassed or even invented; the resources available and required for each alternative solution must be estimated as closely as possible; reasonable rates of accomplishment for various quantitative goals must be proposed; the barriers set by the vital interests of affected groups must be assessed; and the proposal as a whole must be formulated in such a way as to conciliate, skirt, or dissolve all obstacles. It is not surprising that the intensive fact-finding and deliberation which goes into making a well-formulated proposal far exceeds anything of this sort that the public at large can do, so that the public comes to depend heavily on the integrity and competence of its expert recommending bodies. Also, it is perhaps not surprising that recommending bodies and reports often appear to the inexperienced public as luxuries which cannot be afforded, rather than as necessities for ultimate economy in planning.

In any planning proposal, the quantitative goals regularly receive major attention, and the success of the proposal often depends upon the response to such goals. It might thus appear that the goals recommended are primary and the rest of the report is derivative. The opposite, however, comes nearer the truth. It would be very hard to say which elements in the report are primary, since even the exact scope of the problem is likely to be much more indeterminate than the public is inclined to suppose. There are always alternative solutions which are discarded, sometimes reluctantly, and potential alternatives which are overlooked. Estimates of resources, and especially of costs, may be very loose. Above all, the human variables in the program are problematical. In considering these multiple uncertainties and fitting them into a semblance of an orderly plan, some factors can be determined exactly, but there are others which never can be. If this is so, why do agencies attempt to set quantitative goals and time limits for accomplishment? If predictions are so uncertain and contingent, why plan?

Quantitative goals are necessary if there are to be intelligent subdivision of responsibilities and co-ordination of the flow of work and resources. Secondly, the policy-making body and the public as well as the personnel of the program must know what is being asked of them. Finally, it is just this security of commitment which generates the motivation necessary to fulfil the goals. In order to stabilize motivation, there must be norms and a target for effort. The art of setting the level of aspiration for a group so that it will evoke optimum effort never ceases to be an expression of leadership. Goals which appear to have been imposed upon a group from above or from outside have a stifling effect even when they are set very low, whereas goals which emerge from a group's attempt to better its own record can stimulate prodigious effort. Thus goals are always most strategically calculated when they can be related to a recent cycle of similar experience, less perspicuously when they are proposed for the first time.

When the report has been finally assembled and approved, it is ready to be passed on to the executive or the policy-making body which commissioned its preparation. A question may remain whether and when it should be made available to the public concerned, and in what form. In general, of course, the best result is achieved by full and immediate publication. On the other hand, special circumstances may demand different timing, and publication in both popular and technical versions. The scale of distribution of the report depends on the degree to which it is to be part an educational campaign, or simply precipitated into public discussion on a take it or leave it basis. Generally speaking, the latter may appear preferable in most cases, leaving advocacy of its recommendations to such voluntary groups as have by this stage of the planning process come into existence. On the other hand, the authors of a report may have need to defend their thinking in public forums. Opportunity for the lay members of the public to see and question the experts in person is the most effective means to diminish any gulf of status or suspicion between them, and to encourage the public's participation in the solution of its problems.

3. *The decision on policies.*—From the first murmurings of awareness of the existence of a problem, there will normally have been a steady gain in definiteness of its conception among the public affected. If people always knew what they wanted, professional planners would then be in the happy position of being able to speak authoritatively about the best means. However, ends are not given, nor are ends and means so nicely distinguishable. Knowledge of limitations and possibilities affects the formulation of ends, and experts may be as influential as leaders in

helping to form public opinion. Nevertheless, while it is up to the experts to propose, it is up to the public to dispose, since no expert is qualified to know better than people themselves what they want. And they themselves do not know what they want until they have considered the matter.

Once an expertly formulated and timely proposal for action has been presented to the public, it might be supposed that the next phase of the planning process—the policy phase—would consist merely of a decision by the appropriate policy-making body empowered to represent the public. Much more is required, however, so much more that the act of decision comes only as the climax of a complex process of prior discussion, and may indeed never come at all, as can happen to the best-laid plans. Since discussion so little resembles certain popular notions of what planning is, and because of some of the semantic prejudices about its meaning, it is important to describe in some detail what takes place in this phase of democratic planning.

First of all, it has to be recognized from the outset that the type of discussion meant here is a very specific and limited kind of discussion, concerned with proposals for action, which, if adopted, become agreements binding upon the participants. Thus it could perhaps better be called bargaining or negotiation. Academic discussion of academic questions commits no one to action. Any sort of unilateral communication—preaching, persuading, selling, amusing—obviously does not constitute discussion, not even when two people or parties engage in it alternately. The phenomenon of two people talking past each other is widely known. As Professor Knight has discriminatingly pointed out, the mere assertion of interests ("I want . . .") by one party to another does not constitute discussion, even though it involves a question of action, since it does not tend to produce an agreement, or at least a decision, accepted as binding upon both parties.[5] What distinguishes discussion from propaganda, begging, or commanding is that it involves a moral commitment to act in a specified way. If a decision to act or co-operate is to be arrived at through genuine discussion, certain requirements must regularly be met. Otherwise any apparent decision might be called

5. Knight, *op. cit.*, pp. 205–45.

an agreement but is likely to prove unworkable as a basis for action. Planning can only proceed on the basis of binding commitments for specified periods; and under modern conditions, where apparent consent through custom is unreliable and the constant use of force repugnant, voluntary agreement is the only basis on which binding commitments can be obtained. It is necessary, therefore, to specify the requirements of genuine discussion. Most of the existing literature which claims to deal with discussion focuses on the form and content of what is said rather than on the conditioning context in which it occurs. It deals with the conduct of academic exchanges such as forums, debates, symposia, round tables, panels, and conferences—or else various forms of legal, commercial, and religious advocacy. The exceptions to this are the limited writings on parliamentary practice and actual collective bargaining, but even these tend to be preoccupied with form and content.

What follow seem to be the indispensable social conditions of genuine discussions:

a) Social equality among the participants: This is a social-psychological matter, depending upon how the parties to the discussion regard each other rather than upon external signs of status alone. Where there is a difference of status, superiors will have no success in asking inferiors to join in a discussion. Without rough equality, there can only be unilateral command, persuasion, or ostracism. Discussion may occur between, let us say, officers and enlisted men, but only on those subjects where they talk as equals. Similarly, among apparent equals, say among enlisted men, a genuine discussion is likewise disrupted and transformed into dual monologues as soon as any party lays claims to any special access to the truth or special authority to determine policy.

It is thus very important to distinguish experts and authorities from leaders in the process of opinion formation. The board member, for example, might be a leader among the citizens of his district, trusted as a representative rather than looked up to as an authority. In such an event, he is very likely to be an alert and attentive listener to what the people of the district have to say, entering into the discussion in such ways as to contribute to the clarification of the problem and the formulation of unified opinion. He would thus stand most definitely as a recognized inside leader rather than as an outside authority.

b) *A considerable area of values in common:* Usually there are not only a fund of values held in common, built up through common past experience, but various forms of functional interdependence and co-operation. It is the fact that the parties will "have to live with each other" in the future that makes it desirable and even urgent for them to work out agreement. Other values are as a rule at stake besides those immediately involved in discussion, and these add to the importance of the discussion. Should discussion break down and conflict ensue, much else might be lost besides the point at issue. Otherwise the discussion may either be academic or irresolvable, since the only constraint toward agreement would be some gain to each, as in a business transaction.

Not the least of the values usually held in common is the language of the group itself, which makes communication, understanding, and co-operation possible. This is acknowledged by the popular phrase, "He speaks my language," to express the fact that people are in agreement on fundamentals. A common vocabulary is encouraged by enlarging the flow of communication within the public concerned, through meetings, periodicals, correspondence, visits, parties, education, ceremonies, and celebrations. But the observation that a large measure of consensus on values and vocabulary improves the prospects of discussion, should not be taken to mean that discussion in any way presupposes unanimity.

c) *Dissent, based upon clashes of interest and alternative possibilities of action:* Knight points out that there is a dialectical sense in which the existence of opinion necessarily presupposes difference of opinion.[6] Without dissent, there would be nothing to discuss. There might be facts to ascertain, or indoctrination to perform upon recruits, but if all concerned are quite contented with current ways, and no one sees a better alternative, there is no problem of what is to be done. Dissent is possible only when the public has come to feel that there is a problem, and that

6. Knight, *op. cit.*, p. 210.

something should be done, and when one or more definite proposals are then put forward. Even discussion over whether there is a problem or something should be done is academic until some plan of action is suggested. Those who are against action must have something to be against, just as those who want action must have at least one notion which they favor.

Moreover, dissent over alternative lines of action (inaction being usually a synonym for traditional procedure) must be supported by clashes of interest lest it be merely academic and lead to no resolution.

It is only an apparent contradiction to insist that discussion is conditional both on values held in common and on clashes of interest. Because of the values held in common each party can advance his proposal not as a mere assertion of interest but as a right which ought to be binding upon the other. It is the justification of interests as rights which makes a discussion. Enemies of government by discussion exaggerate the ideological nature of a group's moral justification of its position, but the wisest friends of government by discussion do not altogether deny the basis of group interest for each partisan's view. To insist, however, that justifications set forth in advocacy or defense of an action program are derived in some direct way from the interest of a group is to reduce discussion to a mere war of words, which it is not. Moreover, it wilfully overlooks the variety of justifications which may be asserted for any one group interest, the often incoherent and contradictory diversity among the interests of a group, and, above all, the unformed, inchoate nature of any group's interests. Often it assumes that a group's interest is either an objective fact visible to all, or at least visible to some observers with special access to truth. This is never the case. A group, or even an individual, is often as divided within itself as to what it wants as the community of which it is a part. It may wish to justify its formulation of what it wants as much to itself as to the public. The integration of personality and the integration of the community are aspects of the same unceasing process.

Some professed friends of government by discussion, however, presume that there is an objective public interest, usually implicitly represented and defined by themselves. There is no pre-existing public interest, any more than there is a pre-existing group interest. It is the public interest which is to be determined by discussion; the definition of the public interest is the product of discussion; it is the determinant only in the sense of being the end sought. Those who insist that they represent the public good in any sense except in demanding that agreement be reached are like the prophets whom Knight describes as making discussion impossible through dogmatically proclaiming "God says. . . ."

d) *Willingness to compromise nonvital interests:* In a way, this is simply to say that there must be willingness to discuss. There must be some points on which each party must be willing to make concessions, accept half-measures, and consider alternatives. If one party takes an intransigent, all-or-nothing attitude, discussion is impossible, because there is nothing to discuss. The only alternatives for the others are capitulation or warfare.

Now this is not to say that each party must be prepared for possible concession on every point. This would be to say that there should be no fixed points of reference, no given identities or directions to guide discussion. All would be chaos and indecision unless some tentative hierarchy of values was established. The existence of some vital interests must be assumed; indeed, more than that, each party must mutually accept and respect the sacred previous commitments, the bias, the past history, and the unique outlook of the other parties, if its own are to be equally accepted and respected. If anyone professing an experimental philosophy were to carry it to the extreme of demanding that every value of every participant be at stake in every discussion, he would be doing a severe disservice to his own philosophy. The most general problem of a discussion is to compose the vital interests which clash, through negotiating modifications of the less vital.

Determined insistence on certain vital interests does not make discussion impossible, as long as their relationship to the vital interests of other parties may be freely talked about. The kind of dogmatism which forbids discussion is that which declares all interests of a party to be equally vital, that which declares there can be no even tentative distinction among ends, and no part without the whole. The highly comprehensive and closed systems of thought of various religious and political sects are of this character.

Policy commitments for limited periods of time, followed by reconsideration of policy, can win mutual compromises which indefinitely long commitments cannot. Another way of saying this is that an experimental attitude makes agreement on action possible, where agreement on principles would be impossible. Especially in a cosmopolitan society, it becomes necessary and desirable to base action upon proximate rather than ultimate arguments. An example of the experimental attitude carried to its ultimate form is furnished in simple play. Here no serious purpose at all must be alleged to justify engaging in the exploration of new possibilities and values. Play lies at the extreme pole from the grim seriousness which demands cosmic justification for the slightest deviation from traditional routine; the experimental attitude, lying somewhere in between, tends only to diminish the intransigence of ultimate commitments without attacking them.

e) Good faith: This means willingness to be bound by an agreement into which one has voluntarily entered. But this in turn is necessarily conditional on the good faith of the other parties to the agreement. It seems to be not only an explicit principle of law but a feature of the way in which conscience develops that a person does not feel morally bound—does not disapprove his own actions—if he violates an agreement exacted by another party through force or fraud. This does not apply to inherited loyalties, until they move into the area of deliberate and self-conscious choice. In the agreements made in actual life, threats are often used which come close to the use of force, bargaining occurs between parties of unequal power, and biased misrepresentations are made which approach wilful deception. The perfectly free and equal agreement is therefore an ideal, but one very useful as a standard for judging the quality of agreements, particularly for predicting their durability as a basis for planning.

Good faith must be manifest in the process of discussion itself, in the consistent maintenance of the conditions of genuine discussion. Filibustering, wilful postponement of decision by calling for more facts and study, frustration of parliamentary procedure, and persistent arguments *ad hominem* which impugn the good faith of others—these tactics soon dissipate the mutual trust without a minimum of which discussion cannot long continue. In industrial relations, where bargaining in good faith is required by law, the government defines good faith as the willingness to continue to talk. This seems to imply very little, but over time it has come to accomplish a lot. As trust in the good faith of others increases, discussion is facilitated by the greater ease with which clashes of interest can be confronted and dealt with in a matter-of-fact manner.

Although these five preconditions for genuine discussion may occur, they offer no guarantee that the discussion which follows will produce agreement and a binding commitment. Discussion may break down through the clash of vital interests which appear to be irreconcilable. Or a decision may be necessary due to the force of events, before there can be thorough discussion, so that some are forced into compliance by others. In some instances, through timidity or lack of interest, one party will submit to the proposal of another without discussion. Contrary to the naïve notion that deciding means only to take a vote, the many whose interests are only slightly affected may willingly defer to the few to whom the outcome is vital.

In those cases where discussion is not completed before decision and action must be taken, or where passive compliance takes the place of vigorous participation and agreement, it would be wrong to speak of a breakdown of the discussion. No doubt many discussions fall short in one way or another of the model described above, and this is only one of the imperfections to be expected. Rarely, for example, does a discussion end in unanimity, except in the proximate sense that minorities consent to majority rule as long as their vital interests are not too severely transgressed.

It is not defensible to insist that genuine discussion can only occur within the confines of some fixed rules of etiquette, any more than within fixed rules of grammar—although some etiquette and some grammar are indispensable. Attempts to manage discussion through the imposition of rules from without usually have the opposite effect from the improvement intended; any deliberative body almost by definition must be the custodian of its own rules of discussion. That discussion can and does improve is evident in many examples. It has done so, however, only where it has been pursued as a value by participants who have retained their sovereign equality and the other minimum conditions noted above. To set up an independent power to compel arbitration as a means of guaranteeing agreement in discussion is to destroy discussion and the whole principle of moral commitments to voluntary agreements.

One of the fascinating features of actual negotiation is the fact that a great deal of it is nonverbal, proceeding by gesture, posture, facial expression, grunts, sighs, smiles, cheers, snorts, and sneers. Many arguments advanced by literate and rational means are met not in kind but by ridicule, indifference, browbeating, threat, or suppression. Yet the outcome may be agreed to by all concerned. Some of the ideological justifications offered in defense of group interests are often discounted at far below face value without either party dropping its mask of seriousness in speaking or hearing them. On the other hand, profoundly sincere statements of devotion to community interest may be brutally condemned as window-dressing, without preventing later acceptance of highly formal and moral preambles to final agreements.

These necessary qualifications to practice, however, do not obviate the frequently pressing practical problem of when to terminate discussion. Where, between utter unanimity at one pole and outright conflict at the other, is the best point for decision? The principle of majority rule should not mean that as soon as 51 per cent of the participants in a decision-making body make up their minds, no more discussion is required. If attention is kept on the fact that, for planning operations, the essential function of the policy phase is to produce a binding commitment for a specified period of time, the attainment of a majority for a proposal may be quite an insufficient guide as to when to terminate discussion. Indeed, when affairs of this sort are well-handled in practice, they proceed quite the other way around; the termination of discussion is the moment to take the vote which officially and ceremonially signifies the reaching of the decision. When all relevant facts have been presented, when all possibilities have been explored, when all compromises and concessions have been bargained out, then it will be noticed that participants, if they have anything more to say at all, will begin to repeat themselves. Or, they cease to engage in discussion, and commence to talk only to delay action. Experienced discussants are quite able to discern this moment. To ask for a vote on the question prior to this point is to court later nonco-operation from dissident minorities; to postpone discussion after this point is to build up unnecessary impatience and hostile feelings. When the vote is taken, if the proposal wins, the bigger the majority for it, the better the chances of later getting the co-operation of the losing minorities. Also, the less chance of having to reopen the policy before its term of commitment runs out. When minorities have had their day in court, as it were, and have lost their case fairly after full debate, they become obligated to abide by the decision of the majority. Until there has been a full debate there is not likely to be mutual understanding, and a consensus on the nature of the specific differences between majority and minority ("agreement to disagree"), which, while not constituting unanimous agreement, yet preserves the integrity of the community.

As long as the conditions of discussion are maintained, minorities can become majorities in the future, especially when periodic opportunities for evaluation and reconsideration are given, along with the customary opportunities for re-election of officers. There is likely to be a series of issues, each of which divides the public in diverse ways. Opponents on one issue become allies on others, so that permanent alienation of any group is rare.

Up to this point, our model outline of the policy-making phase of the planning process may have seemed to imply some identity between the affected public and its policy-making body. In the smallest planning operations, such an identity is possible and a sort of direct democracy may exist. In most instances, however, even at the local level of operation, policy-making must be carried on by representative bodies. Moreover, the fact that the typical documents of the policy phase are minutes of meetings, hearings, and debates may serve to obscure that such formal encounters only condense a larger process of public involvement.

The vicarious participation by the affected public through its representative policy-making body needs to be stressed, because therein seems to be an important difference in content, if not in procedure, between the making of law and the setting of goals for action programs—between government in the classical sense and planning in the modern sense.

Once launched, a proposal can rarely be withdrawn to a more propitious time; it must meet its fate, whether it be rejection or acceptance. As the discussion by the public proceeds to a climax, it becomes fitting for the representative policy-making body to express a decision either by vote or by some other method. And such a decision, under the circumstances and in the atmosphere described, is ideally the formal culmination of a process by which in fact the public has already made up its mind as to what it wants.

One further important, but frequently neglected, item is necessary to complete the policy phase. This is the brief ceremony which, though performed in a multitude of formal and informal ways, is generally known as burying the hatchet. Discriminating and sincere dramatization of the values held in common among the erstwhile antagonists is a priceless asset in assuring the maximum degree of co-operation—or at least noninterference—by all parties in the execution of the program which has been finally adopted as policy.

4. *The execution of programs.*—After all the expedient modifications and political concessions, the plan of action which has been adopted as a policy may be much like the original proposal or it may resemble it only very slightly. In either case, what has been adopted is a broad and general set of goals plus an indication of ways and means such as budget, personnel, schedule, which are to be made available for achieving them. There has been a steady evolution from embryonic intention to definite commitment, but even by the end of the third phase of planning, only the broader outlines of the program can be discerned.

There is a considerable remaining margin for policy-formulation by the executives or administrators of the agency itself. Even their own status and powers are in part subject to their own definition. Utilizing this margin for initiative which has been left to them, many executives of agencies have distinguished themselves as leaders in conducting their programs. In order to lead successfully, they have to be responsive to their publics and to the policy-making bodies to which they are responsible, yet they prefer those programs which quite decisively state their responsibilities without spelling out in too great detail how they should be performed.

Experienced policy-making bodies have realized that just how a policy will work out in practice can be predicted only to a limited extent, due to changing conditions and adjustment of estimates, so that it is best not to weigh an administrator down with too many rigid rules, rather letting these develop from experience. It is better to outline the task and hold the administrator accountable for its performance than to bind his hands and hamper the initiative and morale of his agency through imposing rules, which may in the end seem more important than the success of the program.

Drawing the line between how far the policy-making body should go in spelling out details of the program and how much prerogative should be left to executive discretion is a matter of judgment and circumstance. Apart from the need to maintain the supremacy of the policy-making body, and the loyalty and morale of the personnel of the action agency, it is best to rely on ensuing experience rather than any general principles.

Perhaps the one general statement that can be made about the proper organizational structure for executing a program of planned action is this corollary of our consistent emphasis on the sharing of purpose as the compass for procedure: Administrative structure is best which, given the problem, resources, and policy determinations binding an agency, maximizes the participation of its personnel and its clientele in the execution of the program. Participation here is viewed in at least two senses, first, participation in the further development of policy, and second, personal involvement in the goals of the program, leading to maximum effort and ingenuity in contributing to its success.

Two of the typical documents of the program phase of the planning process are the organization charts, showing channels of authority and responsibility in hierarchical terms of staff and line, and the budget, showing allocations of funds for salaries, services, and supplies. While these are no doubt necessary, they are decidedly inferior in obtaining participation to the much less common flow chart, which shows the distribution of work among the components of the agency in terms of quotas and schedules. Such a chart gives each member of the personnel a graphic and comprehensive sense of his part in the total effort, and it also gives the public its most tangible notions of what to expect, when, where, and from whom. To the extent that the clientele itself actually participates in the execution of the program—through advisory boards, committees, teams, or voluntary associations—the distinction between personnel and clientele diminishes, and the roles of clients themselves must of course be entered on the flow chart.

The best test of participation in the program by the personnel of the agency is the degree to which each rank is consulted on the setting of quotas and schedules for its functional unit of the operation. It is precisely here that the two senses of participation, the matter of "voice" and the matter of motivation, will ideally merge.

It is probably not extreme to declare that any quota of work externally imposed upon a person is bound to seem coercive to some degree. While the ways in which coercion is exercised are often subtle and difficult to discern, even where no effort is made deliberately to conceal them, the effects of coercion are registered in the attitude of the person to his work. Instead of motivation to approach an ideal of performance, which removes all barriers to the release of energy, there is resistance to the coercion, a setting of limits to effort, and even discontent and sabotage. Instead of guilt over doing less than one's best, there is often the feeling that integrity and self-respect are best maintained by a refusal to surrender to the coercion. To be sure, it is obvious that employment utterly free of coercion is almost nonexistent; even play can become rapidly adulterated with compulsion as it gets organized by teams and clubs. Nevertheless, there are enormous differences in quality of performance as coercion fluctuates. Conversely, no organization can survive long if none of the personnel do more than their specified and required minimum; even in a prison, the prisoners must contribute more than is absolutely forced from them.

In practice the participation of personnel in setting the goals of their own effort can help to release the energy for attaining them. In determining their respective quotas and schedules, personnel are in effect spelling out of the interim or subgoals within the over-all goals of the agency. Yet, since initiative in evoking responsibility lies almost entirely with the administrator, the burden of achieving the personnel's genuine participation lies upon his shoulders, and failure to achieve it can only spuriously be blamed on the personnel. In other words, as generally recognized, the test of the administrator, although it may be expressed in terms of objective results in completing his program, is basically a test of his ability to minimize coercion and maximize participation. Where he has the least opportunity for coercion, his skill as an organizer and leader of group effort becomes most clearly manifest (such as in campaigns using unpaid volunteers). All other conditions being equal, it seems demonstrable that shared purpose will always release more energy and ingenuity, and produce better results, than coercion.

Too often the planning aspect of administration is discussed loosely in terms of controls. Not only has the term a popular connotation of some form or degree of coercion, but this is all too often so in practice. In other words, the various quotas and schedules are set up unilaterally and hierarchically by the administrator and his lieutenants, as tasks imposed externally upon subordinates. The best forms of planning break down the broad goals of a program to apply to the various functional units of the executive agency, but much is lost, and the success of the program is jeopardized, if this is done solely for the sake of co-ordination. If quotas and schedules are instead construed not as controls in this limited sense but as interim goals, their other functions in facilitating motivation of personnel and morale of the agency then become feasible.

Beyond stating these general characteristics of the program

phase of our model of the planning process, it is doubtful that much more could be said without getting down to particular cases. There are vast numbers of books about the familiar problems of administration, most of them conceived in terms of human relations. Undoubtedly great progress is being made, on a case by case basis, in solving these problems, but it is evident that no general principles of administration have become so firmly and reliably established that all agencies are beginning to follow them. The most hopeful sign is simply that a tremendous over-hauling of administrative concepts is going on, and that participation is guiding a great deal of such discussion. It would be inconsistent with the general principles of planning to make categorical prescriptions here.

It is well to note, however, that much of the academic discussion of the principles of administration, while admirably giving increasing emphasis to participation by personnel, tends to overlook the probably much more important matter of participation by clientele. Indeed, some of the academic discussions seem to take for granted that participation by the clientele is impossible, that at best the clientele may consume the services of the agency, and these services are related directly to their preconceived wants.

By some administrators and writers on administration, however, it is well understood that the benefits of participation by the clientele of an agency overweigh the hazards. The existence of an alert, informed, interested clientele may expose the inept administrator to observation and correction that he would escape if it were more apathetic; on the other hand, a favorable public goes far to assure the success of a program. The attempt to evoke such a favorable response from its clientele often leads agency administrators into unilateral forms of publicity, public relations, and propaganda. A free flow of valid information is rightly to be desired. A system of interim progress reporting, for the clientele as well as the personnel, is indispensable to optimum co-ordination and motivation in democratic planning agencies. Nevertheless, the practice of unilateral public relations is currently probably justly a little suspect. It produces far fewer results than might be supposed from its analogy to commercial advertising.

Though it will be granted by many that public relations will not take the place of participation by an agency's clientele, some continue to rely upon public relations as a means of obtaining participation. That is, they exhort and cajole their clients to participate, or to feel a sense of participation, as if such a feeling could be induced by will power. Participation to deepen must commence with the definition of the problem, and carry through the debate of proposals and the adoption of policy. It is too late in the process to commence trying to evoke participation after everything is cut and dried. Countless instances can be cited to demonstrate people's lack of enthusiasm for projects which have been fashioned and thrust on them by others. The best of intentions often go awry because of such methods.

Let us suppose, however, that the public has participated fully in the first three phases, in defining the problem, debating the alternative solutions, and, at least through representatives, making the policy decision which launches a program of action. And let us suppose that channels or mechanisms have been established for the clientele to participate in the conduct of the program. Is it then certain that their involvement will be high, with a resulting flow of effort and ingenuity, of initiative and responsibility? Unfortunately, this cannot be assumed.

If participation in the planning process were deemed to go only as far as participation in the conduct of programs and no farther, it would soon dwindle into routine. To the extent that participation of the clientele was voluntary, it would cease. The public would in a sense abdicate, becoming content to leave matters in the hands of the paid and delegated personnel of the agency, as long as they did not too greatly transgress routine expectations. This spectacle of a public which is satisfied after setting up a program to leave it to be run by a few is familiar in agencies of all kinds. In the beginning of its existence an agency may enjoy a high degree of interest from its clientele; there is hope, energy, idealism, enthusiasm; but once a permanent personnel is established, all this often wanes. A crisis may seem to waken it again, but only ephemerally. The most persistent obstacle to continuing participation is an intangible one. For the baffling opponent is complacency, especially the sort of complacency which seems permitted if not justified by the tolerable success of an agency in meeting some routine minimum of performance.

Some of the bitterest struggles of leadership can occur in the minds of leaders, as the same complacency infiltrates and begins to be felt as a dull poisoning of their energy. It is then that the question arises, "Why not relax? Why not let things find a level routine? As long as no one is complaining, why is it not sufficient just to let things amble along as they have been?" A swarm of rationalizations can be found to justify such doubts about the desirability of continued progress, and to support the policy of simply mending troubles as they arise. The decline and failure of participation may thus occur insidiously, from within, despite good will, as readily as from arbitrariness without.

When participation in the conduct of programs lags, these programs cease to represent planning, and become something else, for which epithets abound, if analytic concepts do not. Planning, by definition, stands for the guidance of present action by prospective and retrospective reference. It does not stand for mere maintenance of present routine, however well devised, or it does so only to the extent that this may be useful within the context of a more enveloping goal. The vital element, or condition, in maintaining participation by clientele and personnel in the programs of agencies is the constant emergence of new goals. Only thus can the sense of creation, of values in process of realization, be maintained.

In part, this is a task for leadership, by leaders who do not sink into mere office-holding, but continually find new and inspiring areas for effort. Viewed thus, leadership may spring from any member of a group; ideas are not the prerogative solely of constituted officers; if anything, the reverse may be true. It is the realization of such a relationship which provides the political solution to the problem of maintaining both citizen participation in government and clientele participation in social agencies.

One way of maintaining public interest is through competition for office, success in which occurs through appeals to the diverse interests and shifting ideas among the public. The dynamic effect of aspiring leaders setting forth rival promises regarding the future, as a means of securing office, is to generate new wants, new hopes and aspirations, new goals for concerted effort.

It happens, however, that even competition for office may be an insufficient source of renewal of group purpose. The insecurities of office-holding may be so intense that, by various schemes of co-optation, monopoly, quietism, or even more drastic devices, office-holders succeed in cementing themselves into place. Or it may be that imagination lags, and rivals come to be so little different that they make no difference. Or, on the other hand, the strife of competition for office may become so intense that its contribution to unified community action is nullified and reversed. Without depreciating the stimulus of competitive politics, or the part they play as a guarantee against worse events, as an incentive to progress they must be assessed as sporadic, inconsistent, and unpredictable. Happily, it is quite possible for new goals to form rationally, continually, and effectively without continual changes of personnel. This can come about through the vigorous and careful implementation of the fifth phase of the planning process, the making of periodic appraisals of progress.

5. *Periodic appraisals.*—The characteristic document of the fifth phase of the planning process is the annual report. It not only summarizes the events of the previous phases but, when fully developed, comes near to epitomizing planning. Its contents are intended to reveal the success of programs and the quality of an agency's practice, but the potential functions of annual reporting extend far beyond the matter-of-fact recording of activity. It is for this reason that periodic appraisal—though extremely neglected—is held to be a distinct and vital phase of the planning process.

If there has been good planning up to the last phase, goals will already have been stated in quantitative terms. The index of progress, therefore, is mainly a matter of comparing expected and achieved results. In many cases, however, especially among new agencies, goals may not have been given quantitative formulation in advance. Nevertheless, if there is to be an appraisal at all, there must be quantitative indices. In the course of constructing such measures, there is, or ought to be, a progressive evolution of objective bases of comparison between periods. That is, the process of evaluating results of a program leads to a clarification of the objectives of the program itself, which, as we shall discuss presently, is of great significance for the next cycle of planning. Even where there has been much previous experience and many careful estimates and predictions, there are always unexpected deviations and consequences in the actual working-out of the program. Thus the task of appraisal always to some degree involves the technical problem of modifying and applying indices of progress, and there is no end to the improvements that can be made in this process.

The task of index construction, however, is only part of the larger activity of evaluation. Are the indices applied actually valid measures of achievement and progress? Many so-called measures of progress which find their way into annual reports quite obviously are not valid. To illustrate, an adult education office may report that it has mailed out many thousands of pieces of literature, although these may be quite unreadable and unread. Or a health clinic may publicize how many free physical examinations or inoculations it has given, without disclosing whether it has demonstrated any effect upon morbidity in a community. Often the most accessible quantitative data have the least validity as indices of progress; massive effort is proffered as a substitute for results. Efficiency is the ratio of effect to effort, and indices of effect are the harder to come by.

The problem of developing valid indices is frequently a very difficult one. Professional statisticians, incidentally, have been of meager help, since they tend to concentrate on the manipulation of indices, once derived, rather than on their progressive validation. To be sure, they are in part excused by the uniqueness of the goals of each agency, yet it remains puzzling that theoretical contributions to such a basic feature of social statistics as index construction should remain almost primitive. Why should each family agency be left to struggle in an amateurish way with the technical problems of indexing?

The statistical expert cannot rule with propriety upon questions of policy. But where objectives are not clear or consistent, or where wishful or defeatist thinking prevails in the evaluation of results, the determined statistician makes a signal contribution to objectivity by insisting upon definitions of aims which he can convert into quantitative expressions. He calls loose talk to account. Also, by the same insistence upon converting goals and ideals into standards for measurement of change in desired directions, he promotes thinking about self-evaluation by comparisons of achievement in one planning period with that in another, rather than by reference to implied rivals. By such objective comparisons of self with self, over time, the identity and direction of development of a group (or a person) is confirmed, stimulated, and fortified against external counterinfluences.

In addition to descriptions and measures of achievement, annual reports usually include statements of the original objectives and goals of a program, names of leading personnel, jurisdiction, financial accounts, table of organization, and varying amounts of background information (history, maps, illustrations) and propaganda. The precise functions which the report is supposed to perform will regulate the inclusion or exclusion of such minor data. Where the annual report goes beyond the reporting of progress for the previous cycle, and becomes also the bearer of definitions of new problems and proposals for action in ensuing cycles, there is, of course, no ready way of determining in advance what further material will prove relevant.

Limiting ourselves to the annual report which is primarily a record of progress, it is still possible to extract a few general rules or criteria for the evaluation of annual reports themselves. Examination of even a limited sample of annual reports issued by planning agencies (and there are great differences in quality) reveals a pressing need for greater standardization in annual reporting.

For a start, annual reports ought to be issued annually, and certainly no more than a year after the period which they cover. Second, they ought to be reports, that is, they should record the degree of success or failure an agency has experienced in pursuing its goals. Not until an agency begins to appraise its achievement objectively can there be any possibility of cumulative improvement in the construction and validation of its indices of progress.

These are the fundamentals, yet they are not so obvious that their regular observance can be presupposed. For example, the parks and forests department of a certain great state—employing hundreds of personnel, caring for thousands of square miles, and controlling millions in budget and facilities—issued its only annual report in 1934, and that was a campaign pamphlet for the incumbent governor! In judging the planning practice of many an agency, one cannot begin with the niceties of index validation.

Perhaps it may seem superfluous to urge that annual reports should be veracious, but the exhortation is too often needed. One way of getting veracity might be to adopt the same means normally employed to assure honesty in financial accounting, i.e., the employment of outside, disinterested, presumably incorruptible auditors. For special purposes of increased assurance, resolution of intra-agency conflicts, fresh viewpoints and special expertness, outside audits of operations are to be recommended. But such audits ought to be viewed as supplementary only, and the main task of preparing annual reports be kept within the hands of the agency personnel itself. Otherwise much of the utility and regenerative function of annual reports in the planning process is necessarily lost. Sometimes actual preparation of the basic data is delegated to an internal policy-appraisal or progress-reporting unit. But an agency and its administrative chief ought to feel that the document by which their work is made known periodically is their report. And if the agency grasps the fact that its annual report can become a powerful instrument working for the success of its programs, the strong identification of the personnel with the showing it makes in print can support and augment the veracity of its annual reports.

For the declared purpose of the periodic appraisal is to assess the successes and failures of the program, and if the failures are concealed, little or no profit can be derived from them. Incentives to distort facts, to engage in judicious selection and emphasis, to offer tendentious interpretations and gratuitous justifications, will no doubt continue as long as rivalry for position persists, but they can be diluted and countered progressively by strengthening the experimental attitude inherent in planning as in science. Professional societies as independent bodies may also eventually assist in raising the standards of program audits.

If plans are construed as hypotheses, to be confirmed or refuted by experience, there is no reason to review results in the spirit of praise and blame. There will, no doubt, be gratification or disappointment over the outcome of each cycle of planning, but the important consideration is that each round of experience and its meaning for the next round will be evaluated objectively. Unless critical appraisal of success and failure occurs, the agency will go on repeating undiagnosed mistakes or ascribing efficacy to the wrong causes. Instead of progressive reduction of error and reliable achievement of intention, affairs will degenerate into a stabilized routine which evokes little enthusiasm from anyone concerned. The systematic scrutiny of experience can be a provocative stimulus to progress. Unless this is grasped, neither personnel nor clientele realize how much they have been robbed when their agency fails to publish regular, thorough, and veracious annual reports. Some of the less obvious functions of annual reports when properly utilized are their respective consequences for administrators, rank-and-file personnel, clientele, and similar agencies in other communities.

For the administrators of an agency, the appraisal of the planning process offers the opportunity for self-conscious accumulation of skill and know-how, of tried and tested techniques of action. If appropriately publicized, annual reports offer one of the most reliable means of communicating information to a clientele and quickening its involvement and support of the agency. Through unflinching reports, an agency can get the confidence of the public. The perspective derived from its annual appraisals gives balance and wisdom to day-by-day decisions on policy and personnel. Periodicity itself is a security-giving organization of work, and reports contribute to periodicity.

Like interim reporting, and supplementing it, annual reporting helps a worker in an organization to visualize his place in the whole, to aid in co-ordinating his work with that of others with less requirement of supervision. It strengthens discipline of members of a group by each other, instead of by supervision, and thereby can accentuate the morale of personnel. By facilitating adoption by working groups of quotas and schedules as personal commitments, annual reporting like interim reporting adds appreciably to the motivation and sense of responsibility among personnel. By causing reflection upon the methods employed by an agency in achieving its results, the systematic backward look at how far they have come encourages personnel to ingenuity in devising new methods to economize effort and resources. Since the annual report, unlike interim types of reporting, goes out to the public of the agency, the mere existence of annual reports tends to increase the consciousness by personnel of their responsibilities toward clientele, and invites a sense of identification with clientele.

Lest these claims for the virtues of annual reporting seem too unrealistic, let note be made of the nuisance and imposition that report-writing becomes to administrators when conceived as mere record-keeping. Interim reporting especially can easily register as a *pro forma* duty, whose principal function is to interrupt and distract ongoing activity. Interim reporting, however, should principally apply intramurally to agency personnel, and be for them not only a report to others but a means of exhibiting to themselves, in a graphic and economical way, just how they are doing in the execution of their interlocking quotas and schedules. Annual reporting, on the other hand, suffers more from under- than from overdoing—not so much in the sense of quantity as in the sense of profundity of retrospection. Unless it achieves the degree of detachment, of withdrawal from action, which permits basic and imaginative reconsideration of what the activity is all about, its result is undoubtedly stultification instead of stimulation. But reporting itself, like agency programs, benefits from inclusion within the scope of regular review; if it is working poorly, it deserves improvement, not rejection.

With regard to clientele, annual reports, when properly exploited, also function to bring about identification. Thorough reporting provides the factions among the clientele at once with non-hearsay material for criticism and appreciation of an agency's operation, and for defending it against its opponents. The public is going to evaluate an agency anyway, but when the clientele feels itself a party to the formulation and revision of agency programs, their judgments are more likely to be responsible, sound, and fair; their own overt participation in execution, more vigorous and effective. The reporting of success enhances the appetite for more success, especially when the reaching of goals is not only matter-of-factly reported but given ceremonial recognition in meetings of personnel and clientele, e.g., awards made to leaders and outstanding performers by the voluntary associations among the clientele.

Finally, there is a fourth group for whom annual reports perform an extremely valuable function. That is the planners in similar agencies elsewhere, the professionals and technical specialists who, in fashioning proposals, must draw upon as much relevant prior experience as possible. Each instance of planning is in a sense a pilot project for similar ventures by others confronted with matching problems. And if the experience of planning is to be made available to others, the ideal form for its communication is adequate annual reports. Like the journals of scientific societies, the annual reports of planning agencies, as they come to be prepared by professional standards, develop as the media for the more rapid evolution of planning technology through its sharing. Very much like the duty of the scientist to publish his findings, it has become the obligation of planners to make known the assessments of their own experience in return for sharing the findings of others.

Planning of the piecemeal, democratic character which we have outlined above is not a dream of the future. It is a *fait accompli* on the American scene, and our model is already descriptive of the operation of hundreds if not thousands of family agencies. Yet though many agencies perform these phases without explicit formulation of what they are doing, they may find it helpful to unify and clarify their activities as they examine themselves from this point of view. That is, the model of the planning process which we have sketched offers itself as a standard for the evaluation of the practice of any action agency, whether it already conceives of itself as practicing planning or not. And to evaluate is already to commence to plan, for one cannot assign a value to anything, including past experience itself, save by reference to its potential role in future action.[7] It is, however, the task and prerogative of each family agency itself to judge its own

7. David G. French, *An Approach to Measuring Results in Social Work* (New York: Columbia University Press, 1952).

proper degree and quality of planning. To attempt to usurp such functions would be futile as well as inconsistent with what has already been said about outside experts.

The notion of planning is comparable to embarking upon an endless journey. Any existing ways can be improved upon. Development is cumulative, one cycle of change leads to another. Planning therefore implies a sociology, a psychology, a philosophy. It is at once a theory of social organization and of social change, of motivation and personality formation, of valuation and metaphysics.[8]

Some of these implications, though not explorable further here, become visible in part as we note how the fifth phase of one cycle of planning merges into the first phase of the next. By considering in a matter-of-fact way each previous cycle, as well as its current situation, a group can voluntarily and advisedly alter its existing procedures. Culture and social organization then become cumulatively the self-conscious product of rational intent. The group is freed from those bonds of necessity which were only necessary because they were thought to be so. This does not mean that the lessons of the past are discarded or ignored. It means that according to circumstance, what is worthy is conserved, and what is not is changed.

CONCLUSION

The proper unit of analysis of the activities of family agencies is the planning year, but the cumulative feature of planning—the way new values and knowledge accrue from one cycle of experience to another—is an unending process. As put at the outset of this chapter, the history of a planning agency is similar to the career of an autonomous person who transforms his identity as he increases his competence to utilize available conditions for purposeful development. Neither a family nor any of its members is likely to conform as closely in behavior to an annual cycle as an agency which must schedule the collaboration of many people. In an agricultural society, the calendar of events may more fully exhibit regular seasonality than in a city where the requirements of social rhythm are more artificial.

8. Charner M. Perry, "Knowledge as a Basis for Social Reform," *The International Journal of Ethics*, XLV, No. 3 (April, 1935), 253–81.

On the other hand, episodes of behavior, whether vast or small, have a structure not set by the clock or the calendar. And they contribute cumulatively to the emerging life-history of which they compose the elementary units. The scheme of phases in our planning model must be conceived within a context of multiple cycles, more or less consistently elaborating certain themes of intent, which distinguish the person, his family, his group, or an agency. The longer, more rigidly structured cycle of agency action, as mentioned earlier, may furnish suggestions for the analysis of the less regular episodes of interaction in the family or other small group.

The anti-historical bias of the functionalist thinkers who dominated the interwar period discouraged attention to the effects on forward development of retrospective evaluation of experience. As the planning process gets incorporated in the lives of clients, the phases of the cycle will seem less like a scheme of eternal recurrence, but rather as steps in a sequence leading to interpersonal competence at a professional level.

The notion that the development of the group and the development of the person are not only parallel but instrumental to each other is a concept important to agencies seeking to cultivate the growth of interpersonal competence. The growth of competence is not separable from the elaboration of identity.[9] Although frequently taken as models by clients, professional personnel are no more likely to be paragons than anyone else; it is important however, if by their example they are not to undo the effect of their declared intentions, that they are moving in the same direction as their clients. If the professional personnel of an agency see themselves as simply endowing their clients with competence, but not changing themselves, there is only a small chance that they will achieve a continuing improvement in their clients' competence. If, on the other hand, the client identifies with the agency, as fully as its personnel do, which is only possible if built on participation—then the agency and the clients will foster each other's growth in competence.

9. This point is elaborated in Nelson N. Foote, "Concept and Method in the Study of Human Development," in Muzafer Sherif and M. O. Wilson (eds.), *Emerging Problems in Social Psychology* (Harper and Brothers, in press).

VI *Conclusion: Participant Experimentation with Quasi-Families*

IN AMERICA, THE RAPID EVOLUTION of agencies for concerted action has coincided with remarkable progress in social science. Each development has long roots into the past and strong claims to legitimacy in American public opinion. Current planning agencies trace back to the many types of voluntary mutual aid associations which have always distinguished this society, and social science in turn professes to be the offspring of natural science, the most potent canon of truth in modern times. Administrators of action agencies seek professional status for themselves and scientific guidance for their policies; social scientists seek public recognition by administrators and expanded use of their research findings; and the future bodes their co-operation.

Not only have social science and social planning acted on each other, but each development has had its opponents, who have also interacted. The most severe critics of the administrators of action agencies have charged that, far from implementing the principle of voluntary association and increasing the power of the citizen over his destiny, they are destroying it through bureaucratic centralization of power. The most severe critics of social science have denied that social science is or ever can be a science at all. Other critics have condemned social science as a sinister technique for the manipulation of the majority by a self-interested elite of experts and administrators. We call attention to these contemporary clashes of opinion not for the purpose of intensifying them, but only to record in general terms the existence of a controversy which could be documented by numberless references.[1] The current context of discussion into which any proposals for scientific action upon any problems of personality or social organization must plunge is thus highly polarized.

1. A recent treatment is William H. Whyte, *Is Anybody Listening?* (New York: Simon and Schuster, 1952), pp. 206 ff.

This context is not static, however; the controversy does not simply revolve in fixed channels. Out of the dialectical interplay of thought and action, of creation and criticism, some synthesis is emerging. This synthesis can appropriately be named participant experimentation. This concept brings research and planning into an integral relation, closer than they are generally thought to be at present. By deriving future proposals for research and planning from this synthesis, the force of current opposition may be gradually dissolved, and the terms of previous controversies be made obsolete. Furthermore, if the synthesis is real, it will release motivation for carrying forward a movement of research and action suitable for the next few decades.

Research of one kind or another has been applied already in every phase of the planning process—in defining the scope of the problem, in calculating the goals and resources for each alternative proposal, in canvassing the views and values of each interest group concerned in a policy decision, in translating the broad program adopted into specific tasks, and in reporting progress periodically through the application of valid indices.

The reflexive consequences of proper reporting of progress by agencies need to be restated for special stress: (1) the clarification of an agency's identity by the mirror of its recent history, (2) the motivating effects of comparing its present achievement with that of past and projected periods, and (3) the involvement effected by avoiding absolute commitments and encouraging the exploration or creation of new values. It is in the appraisal phase of the planning process—the measurement of change and the evaluation of progress—that the nexus between research and planning becomes most clear.

In the spread of group work among social workers—a sort of transitional step along the way from the therapeutic to the planning approach in community action—one of the most effective techniques for stimulating action by a community has been the community self-survey.[2] The social worker employing this technique begins dealing with a problem, interracial tension,

2. See M. H. Wormser and Claire Selltiz, "Community Self-surveys: Principles and Procedures," chapter xix in Marie Jahoda *et al.*, *Research Methods in Social Relations*, Part II (New York: Dryden Press, 1951).

for example, by organizing a study committee of interested and affected citizens. This group itself carries on the work of obtaining facts and figures about the problem. In the course of meeting together, this committee usually irons out personal and group differences, educates its members and gets them working together in such a way that they are far more ready to take action on their own recommendations than they would have been had the same recommendations been made by the social worker at the outset. Extension workers in agriculture and home economics are now moving beyond their older demonstration methods toward the same group-decision technique. Of course, the community self-survey, promising as it is when properly employed, does not always lead to sufficient action nor can it guarantee the success of a program. Nevertheless, as a transitional development, it has already pointed the way to adoption of the full-scale model of planning. It provides empirical evidence of the motivating effects to be derived from the self-analysis of a group.

FROM THE RECOGNITION TO THE EXPLOI-
TATION OF REFLEXIVITY

Through periodic reports and appraisals, the reflexive thrust of self-analysis can potentially be intensified to a far higher degree than is usual in the community self-survey. Also, periodic self-appraisal can be varied and adjusted for maximum effect, as well as being handled in a less amateurish and more scientific manner, with each cycle of experience. As annual reports become more and more like the records of statistical and historical surveys and comparisons, research by a group upon itself becomes more and more an instrument of self-conscious self-change.

Just as the conduct of social action has evolved in the direction of scientific procedure, so research in some of the social sciences —notably social psychology—has as the result of a series of important discoveries been approaching a model of social action. One of the most striking of these discoveries was what has been called by Dewey and others the Heisenberg effect in social science research.[3] In physics, the Heisenberg principle of inde-

3. John Dewey, *The Quest for Certainty: A Study of the Relation of Knowledge and Action* (New York: Minton, Balch and Company, 1929), pp. 201–4.

terminacy is the finding that in making minute measurements, the effect of the measuring instrument upon the phenomenon measured under certain conditions distorts the phenomenon so substantially that measurement is impossible. In some cases this effect can be prevented by use of more delicate measuring instruments, but in other cases the dilemma is theoretically insoluble. In social science there are countless expressions of an analogous dilemma. If a person is interviewed about his occupational aspirations, for example, these are quite frequently changed, or new ones are created, in the course of the interview. Voters when canvassed on their political opinions often find those opinions altered by having attention directed to them—the alterations sometimes being differentially affected by the status of interviewers, even when the latter make every effort not to influence respondents. One of the writers early in the war had to interview dairy farmers regarding their plans for increasing milk production, and despite a carefully followed sampling procedure decided that the answers were unrepresentative, because they were the only farmers in their counties who had been interviewed. The mere asking of questions, as Socrates found long ago, can have reorganizing and occasionally distressing consequences. Indeed, mere listening may have profound effects upon the person listened to, as psychotherapists have learned recently.

A second kind of repercussion to social research is the oft noted episode in which people of some group or category react to predictions of their behavior in such a way as to falsify the prediction or to knowledge of trends in their behavior in such ways as to diminish or intensify the trends. A companion phenomenon —the way in which some attribution or prediction made known to a group by its author will cause them to behave in a way to validate it—has been called by Robert K. Merton "the self-fulfilling prophecy" and also was designated earlier by Gunnar Myrdal as "the principle of cumulation."[4] The success of the technique of psychoanalysis may be taken as still another instance of the reflexive influence of inquiry upon the characteristic be-

4. Robert K. Merton, *Social Theory and Social Structure* (Glencoe: The Free Press, 1949), pp. 175–95. Gunnar Myrdal, *An American Dilemma* (New York: Harper, 1944), Appendix 3.

havior of the persons studied, since it accomplishes desirable changes in personal integration by causing the subjects to raise to conscious recollection the meaning of past acts and relations. The effects of books of history on the further course of history illustrates almost the identical phenomenon; rewriting history books is always a necessary instrument of any revolution. Though there is as yet no systematic review of this phenomenon, various other illustrations of it could be given, but these should suffice to demonstrate that the findings of social science have as definite impact upon the subjects of the research as do the methods employed.

Are the concepts of social science to be included among its findings or its methods? If neither, their popular adoption may be added as a third channel through which social science alters the character of the phenomena it studies. For as long ago as 1927 Morris R. Cohen noted that "the invention of a technical term often creates facts for social science. Certain individuals become *introverts* when the term is invented, just as many persons begin to suffer from a disease the moment they read about it. . . ."[5] The burden of certain criticisms of the Warner scheme for analysis of social classes is that by becoming generally known his six-level concept tends to intensify or to create the phenomenon which it purports to describe.[6] That is, the mere sociological concept of class—if widely employed—may have a normative effect upon popular behavior, just as the Marxian concept of class struggle is said to encourage class struggle. And so there may be some genuine rather than sentimental justification for those professing equalitarians who do not want the existence of social classes to be discussed. Similarly, the popular dissemination of the concept of intelligence as a quantitative variable has encouraged—and has often intended to encourage—effort by individuals to achieve higher rankings; also, and this is a notorious example, the concept of the normal curve has been employed in reverse to make people fit it. In view of the fact that all human beings organize their experience and actions through the medium of verbal categories,

5. W. F. Ogburn and A. Goldenweiser, *The Social Sciences and Their Interrelations* (Boston: Houghton Mifflin, 1927), p. 459.
6. Walter Goldschmidt, "America's Social Classes—Is Equality a Myth?" *Commentary*, X (1950), 175–81.

and that social science concepts are usually as accessible to the ordinary citizen as to the social scientist, it probably should be expected that descriptive and analytical concepts would lead to revisions of self-conception and social distinction among the human beings to whom applied.

Finally, account must be taken of the common implication of citizens and scientists alike, not only in the methods, findings, and concepts of social science, but also in the interests which motivate social studies. It is not as if a special class of beings called scientists withdrew from the rest of humanity, and became mere spectators of life, knowledge of which they gathered and stored for its own sake. Moreover, the extent of resources made available for social science in general tends to vary with the importance accorded to social science in a community, as against the alternative uses to which the same resources might be put. The economics of research and teaching quite clearly reveal the relative values placed upon particular problems. The sociologists of knowledge have for some time been exploring the interests which have animated the work of certain scholars in various periods, places, and settings. Thus far, however, they have only begun to explore the implications which general adoption by their own community of a scientific interest toward itself would have for their own specialty.

To recognize that social facts are the creation of the persons observed, that neither persons nor institutions are permanently given but are in constant process of reconstruction, and that the verbal categories by which self and others are construed are the materials of which social organization is constructed, leads to a conception of human nature and the social order which is less a substantive description than a methodology. This is the ultimate outcome of the interactional approach of social psychology, which was first developed in studies of personality in the family. The evolution of social science is not in the direction of permanently definitive statements about human nature and society, but toward the specification of the methods whereby human nature and society come to be what they are. Social theory thus becomes only suspended social action. The famous *mot* of Poincaré, that natural scientists talk about their results while social scientists talk about their methods, is rendered pointless when it becomes evident that the methods of social science are, in this sense, its most valuable findings.

The social scientists who have given most attention to the reflexive consequences of social research upon its subjects are probably Kurt Lewin and his followers.[7] Some might name Elton Mayo and his followers, but this is debatable, since the famous observation in the Western Electric study, that the productivity of certain workers rose as a consequence of being studied, was converted only into a counseling program and not generalized to the point of making the workers fuller participants in the research. The Lewin group, on the other hand, has systematically consulted with its subjects in the planning of research on themselves, involved them in carrying it out, and shown them its findings, often with the deliberate intent of engaging them in further cycles of what Lewin termed "action research." Up to the present, however, there has unfortunately been no systematic study by any social scientist of the precise nature of the reflexive effects of social research and of the conditions under which they occur. That they do occur seems firmly established, and so there no longer remains justification for ignoring the methodological problems or the practical opportunity they present.

Scientific attitudes toward this methodological problem vary. Some incline to regard reflexive effects as no more than minor complications or hindrances to valid observation, to be reduced to a minimum or eliminated entirely if possible. It is probably from such a point of view that most researchers would attempt to refute Frank Knight's statement[8] that it is this reflexive feature of social science data which prevents social science from really becoming a science. The defenders of the obsolete image of social science hold that as with other sources of bias or distortion in observation, if discipline is exerted sufficiently, this type of error can be controlled. In particular, research findings may be kept secret from the subjects of the research, so as to avoid influencing their behavior, as for example the arguments against

7. Kurt Lewin, *Resolving Social Conflicts* (New York: Harper and Brothers, 1948).

8. Frank H. Knight, *Freedom and Reform: Essays in Economic and Social Philosophy* (New York: Harper and Brothers, 1947), pp. 205–45.

the publication of polls lest they cause a "bandwagon effect" or, as perhaps in the 1948 election, a "boomerang effect." For some, the perfect subject is the most naïve.

Instead of denying or seeking to minimize the effects of social investigation on the behavior of the people investigated, it is probable that social science has much to gain by making them the focus of greater attention. For if the reflexive consequences of social inquiry can be isolated and studied, it is possible that the precise conditions under which they occur can be predicted, and ultimately utilized. This outcome is far from certain; it may be that with every cycle of self-examination new conditions are generated, so that prediction is always one move behind self-knowledge, and the concrete outcomes will always remain indeterminate, as Knight insists. Abstractly, on the other hand, each increment of self-knowledge is likely to produce at least an enhanced sense of self-determination. If in all social research, furthermore, the subjects were systematically made party to the research, as well as to the findings—as the subjects' curiosity and co-operation have always seemed in fairness to warrant—the result promises new techniques of self-expression and social planning.

Perhaps the argument can be summed up as follows:

Thesis: The way to develop the most reliable generalizations about human behavior is through applying the methods of natural science.

Antithesis: But the regularities in behavior which are studied by the social scientist are matters of convention, and are continually transformed by the process of investigation, since subjects can and do respond normatively to generalizations about themselves. Thus the generalizations of social science are doomed to a limited and temporary kind of reliability not found in the natural sciences.

Synthesis: Let us grant the criticism, and conclude that, as in any other science, the methods must be appropriate and adequate to the phenomena studied. Let us grant that human behavior cannot legitimately be reduced to less than what it is, and that the investigator is always implicated in a system of social relations with his subjects, and that these reciprocal relations largely determine what will be included or excluded from his observations. The standard procedures of scientific investigation may nevertheless be applied, but the type of generalizations derived will differ. As the subjects respond to these generalizations, they may make them invalid, but only in the sense that a new regularity appears. In this manner, the reflexive effects of social science —including motives, methods, concepts, and findings—instead of being rejected as impediments, may be pursued and utilized as a major *raison d'être:* a method of controlled self-change.

At this point, a hypothetical example may be helpful. Suppose that a survey of all parents in a certain community reveals that 75 per cent of these parents beat their children for defying commands and 25 per cent do not. The mere interviewing of parents to find this out may have caused large numbers of them to reflect upon beating as a debatable practice, and to discuss it with others. Suppose that the figures found are then published for the information of the whole community. Some parents who beat their children may be encouraged by realizing how many others do likewise; others may be influenced by the fact that many parents get along without beating. Some parents who do not go in for beating may be encouraged to learn that there are many others who do not; others may be discouraged to realize they are in a minority. But since many parents do not fall neatly into one category or the other, and may resort to beating only under extreme circumstances, it is likely that the interviewing process will force them to clarify their conceptions of themselves as beaters or nonbeaters. Also, when the results are published, knowledge of how many endorse or condemn each practice is likely to send further waverers in one direction or the other. Suppose then that a second survey is made, to check upon the effects of the first survey. Instead of obtaining a mere net percentage change in the total population, suppose the response of each parent is matched with his previous response, so as to take account of any cancellation of opposite changes. And suppose that the results of the second survey are also published. By then much more thought and discussion will have been provoked, and possibly not a smaller but an even greater change will occur as a result of the second survey. Moreover, a third or a fourth survey might occur before diminishing returns in the form of induced change would set in. Of course, resistance to further interviewing might before then have mounted to the point of being prohibitive, because human beings quickly lose patience with being studied—unless they are studying themselves. Suppose that the community itself adopted a scientific attitude toward itself and took over responsibility for such a third and fourth survey, conducting a survey each year, the results being regularly reported back to the community. It becomes evident that the direction of change will probably become a matter of dismay or gratification to all who are made aware of it; discussion will occur and opinion form. Instead of the findings remaining mere factual records objectively gathered by disinterested observers, they become indices of progress and achievement; the community commences to measure itself against itself, to accentuate a direction of change guided by a preferred self-characterization; goals of the "Let's do better next year!" type are informally or formally set up for each period. The adoption of these goals releases the energy for their achievements; new values and motives are created.

This sequence which flows from community self-study is a hypothetical one, but this kind of development—though not anywhere systematically exploited—has actually happened in recognizable form many times more than is required to prove its practical possibility. And yet the example given involves social research only at its most elementary level. If, beyond mere interviewing and reporting, a single further step in analysis of results were taken, such as the making of comparisons among various strata of the population, the publication of these results might stimulate action of an even more diverse and still less predictable kind. Suppose, for example, it were shown that Protestants beat their children twice as often as Catholics; what would be the reaction of the Protestants to this, in that community? It is likely that a year later the next report would show some consequent change. Let the community add the scientific study of family relations to its school curricula, let it finance and carry out further research, introduce more and more scientific findings into all media of communication and discussion; while the nature of the results will not be foreseeable, it is foreseeable that there will be substantial results. Let each citizen adopt a scientific attitude, participate in research as a consciously co-operating subject, and follow the latest findings of research as an interest, and he will progressively become a different person.

Frank Knight's contention that human beings change their behavior as a consequence of studying it does not make social science generalizations impossible; it means that the generalizations evolved are likely to be of a quite different sort from generalizations about the behavior of atoms, stars, violets, or rabbits, which cannot react to what is said about them. The broadest generalizations of social science are more likely to be procedural than substantive (in the sense of invariable universal predictions about behavior).

Consider a family agency with a personnel of experts and a clientele of people affected by some common problem of family relations. If it follows the model of democratic planning, it can readily be noted how much its procedure resembles the conventional sequence of scientific method:

PHASES OF PLANNING	PHASES OF RESEARCH METHOD
1. Definition of problem	Observation, description, classification
2. Formation of proposals and their discussion	Theoretical speculation and formulation of hypotheses
3. Policy decision	Choice of hypothesis for testing
4. Execution of program	Experimental verification of hypothesis
5. Periodic appraisal and revision of goals	Publication for replication or criticism and revision

In other words, the proposal for action in planning has the same status as the hypothesis for testing in research. Family agencies can readily conceive their programs in experimental terms, as some do already. Then, if the outcomes of their programs are carefully and periodically examined in a scientific manner, it becomes progressively difficult to detect where science ends and action begins. The general form of theoretical propositions ("if these conditions, then that outcome") is not altered by whether the specified dependent variables are of practical interest or not. The successful procedure—if understood—is the valid generalization. This is the ideal form of applied science, of scientifically guided action. The futile philosophical arguments over whether value judgments can be made scientifically are not so much solved as rendered obsolete and irrelevant when practical and theoretical experiment merge. To the extent that every man becomes an informed and participating citizen in the publics to which he belongs, the only manipulation possible is that of selves, by themselves, and for themselves. The citizen is not subordinated to the expert, nor is the expert prostituted by an administrator; they form a professionalized society of equals. Planning becomes not a procedure for reducing freedom but for increasing the scope of self-determination. Social science becomes not a technique for manipulation but a means for everyone to explore new possibilities of self-development. Family life becomes a lifelong series of experiments in personality reorganization conducted by the persons involved, and family agencies become their sources of leadership.

If the goal of family research and family agencies is to be the development of competent personalities then this implies a good deal more than the acquisition and application of matter-of-fact knowledge. It requires above all the will to carry out these theoretical and practical programs. Not the least of the threats confronting western communities is a dangerous paralysis of the general will. How is the motivation to commit resources and effort to the propagation of more competent personalities to be aroused, sustained, and enhanced? There is compelling evidence in the volume of sales of self-help books for the existence of an almost universal desire for greater competence. Everyone prefers his favorite brand of such literature, and scorns the others, but the person who utilizes none is rare. The appetite for wealth, which has characterized the western world throughout modern times, is a close and pregnant analogy to the craving for competence. As men achieve a competence with respect to the social world comparable to their mastery over the material world, some old values may make way for new, but others are realized in higher degree. As some means become ends in themselves, so some former ends are reduced to the function of means. Perhaps the substitution of the pursuit of competence for the pursuit of wealth will be such an instance. In the contemporary world, a parent is far better advised to endow his child with competence in the new sense than to leave him with "a competence" in the old sense.

Karl Mannheim has declared[9] that democracies do not know

9. Karl Mannheim, *Freedom, Power and Democratic Planning* (New York: Oxford University Press, 1950), chap. ix.

what kind of citizen they want to create. It is likely, however, that a later generation will look back and observe that we were not trying to create a fixed type of man, as other ages and places have done. Instead, we were groping toward the creation of a person who, not conforming to a predetermined image, is unprecedentedly capable of determining himself. Such a person would no longer answer to Sullivan's description of most of us as "poor caricatures of what we might have been."

The problem for the researcher or the agency administrator is not primarily how to intensify the public's appetite for interpersonal competence, but how to ascertain the reproducible conditions for its development. Such knowledge as there is at present is mainly in the form of hypotheses, and it is of such hypotheses that this book has largely been fashioned. Some trends of research in the past decade, however, promise to lead to participant experimentation on a larger scale than previously attempted. Moreover, soon the agencies may be so ready to venture into research that the family researchers, who are supposed to supply the ideas and hypotheses, will be in danger of lagging behind.

QUASI-FAMILIES AS GENERIC

The strategy of participant experimentation extends potentially far beyond the borders of family research. Wherever a group attempts to change itself through study, and thinks of the program it follows as a hypothesis to be tested in action, it is employing the strategy of participant experimentation. And any agency no matter how vast and complex can adopt such a program. The way social research has recently been used to assist the economic development in preindustrial countries illustrates the scope of social experiment which can be explored. The universalization of social science as the basis of a way of life is a prospect far more realistic now than a century or more ago when its founders proclaimed their faith that it would spread as far as the natural science which had inspired it.

On the other hand, the study of families is uniquely appropriate for perfecting the immediate tactics of participant experimentation. The members of a family change and develop, and it is other family members who are the principal determinants of such development. If this is assumed to be true, then the reflexivity quotient of any participant experiment is maximized, the more the behavior of the subjects resembles that of the members of a family. The more each means to the others, and they to him, the greater the consequences of their interaction. Conversely, the influence of others upon the self sharply declines as they move outside one's constellation of significant others.

The family is the model for the quasi-family, but the resemblance between quasi- and real families varies greatly. It is this variability, however, that creates the occasion for experimentation with quasi-families. Family patterns are normally transferred to interpersonal relations in other institutions, as noted at the outset of this work. It may be that investigation of this finding will help solve some of the problems of these other institutions. But our interest here is more in what might result from application in the other direction. It is the possibility of progressively reconstituting the family through experimentally establishing its preferred relations in quasi-families which offers hope of raising the quality of family life and of making accessible to experimental research a subject previously almost inviolate to observation.

The reader has been spared the kind of account which stresses the gap between what exists in practice and the ideals of family life that members or students might hold. It is clear that incompetence in marriage and parenthood are very common, and its consequences are difficult for millions to bear. The usual reference to rates of divorce only crudely suggests how far families fall short of the hopes they inspire when formed, since even families that last often fail to achieve the optimal development of their members, so much so that many writers incline to assume that marital and parental misfeasance are the normal human condition.

Although the program of research suggested in this book will take many hands and years, a very slight beginning has been made at the Family Study Center. Other publications will have to carry the account and analysis of results. In brief, however, the basic finding is simply that changes in certain components of competence can be produced through series of meetings of quasi-family groups of young adults, who role-play and discuss problematic family life situations. The procedures employed are being made available, not only in print, but through the medium of summer workshops for practitioners drawn from several types of family agencies. The workshop experience in itself is an intensive kind of quasi-family experience, which widens the way for collaboration between academic researchers and mature practitioners.

In the research to date, a major stratagem has been the formulation through imagination, criticism, and sharing through demonstration of models of improved performance in family relations, on a hypothetical or "as-if" basis. By overt performance a member learns to exhibit greater competence within the sheltered forum of a small group of comparable others, before whom he is willing to expose himself in challenging tasks of learning. The carry-over to actual life—in his real family and interpersonal relations—is a problem not only of competence but of identity-change. It can be accomplished by a process of identification and progressive involvement in his practice group from week to week. How stable such gains are is yet to be determined, but as other investigators have frequently found, the only permanent change is structural change. Thus it is assumed that only as increments in competence are stabilized through changed conceptions of identity, and fortified through the actual growth of friendship, commitment, and obligation to other members of the practice group, is there reasonable chance of achieving the substantial results envisaged. This is not the place to expand on the managed transition from quasi- to real situations, from role-playing to role-taking, in these limited ventures in participant experimentation. It is more important by way of conclusion to reiterate that the instance cited is only a single application of the general strategy we have proposed in the course of this document.

On the other hand, while granting that interpersonal relations within small groups only constitute one among six classes of conditions affecting development of interpersonal competence, it may very well be that this class of conditions is the most strategic at the present time. Two strong trends in postwar research, closely related to the study of families, are the small-group movement and the elaboration of ego-psychology.[10] There is conspicuously great interest in small group behavior among younger social scientists, even though the study of small groups is unhappily divided between two approaches. There are those who emphasize the revitalizing functions of small groups in advanced urban communities, and those who attempt to emulate natural science by studying them under laboratory conditions. In the field of ego-psychology, neo-Freudian emphasis on coping behavior in life situations has moved far from the confines of the pathological. If through the medium of an experimental approach to family life, paralleled in practice as in research, these two broad streams of thought and action can be thoroughly joined, the hopes based on social science may not prove unjustified. And if the family as the cellular component of society can be reconstituted through participant experimentation—if the gap from quasi-family to real life situations can be steadily bridged through wider development of interpersonal competence in the next generation—then the family itself will gain in value and public honor.

10. J. L. Moreno, "Old and New Trends in Sociometry: Turning Points in Small Group Research," *Sociometry*, XVII, No. 2 (May, 1954), 179–93.

Bibliographical Appendix: American Family Research, 1945–54

THE conclusion of the Battle of the Bulge at the close of 1944 made clear that World War II was nearing its end. Thus 1945 rather than 1946 is taken here as the first postwar year of the decade which we wish to characterize through its reflection in family research. That events in the world intimately affect the choice of problems for academic investigation will be clearly evident.

The Bibliography which follows was intended to include every article and monograph reporting American family research which appeared from January 1, 1945, through December 31, 1954. Only items published in the United States by American investigators about American subjects are listed, although excluded thereby are documents as important as Georg Karlsson's *Adaptability and Communication in Marriage* (Swedish) and Paul K. Hatt's *Backgrounds of Human Fertility in Puerto Rico*. A journal like the *American Anthropologist* is not covered at all on the same account. Notwithstanding these temporal and spatial limits, the remaining literature is vast, and its boundaries are hard to define.

To speak of family research implies definitions of both "family" and "research." As mentioned in chapter i, we are concerned with investigations directed at the family as a unit or at a level of human behavior midway between the individual and the community or larger society embracing other institutions. There is little written that explicitly addresses the complete family unit, while much is written that is tangential in emphasizing the individual family member or the effects of the family on other phenomena. Within the range of truly family behavior are taken to be such component phenomena as husband-wife, parent-child, and sibling relationships, as well as their precursors and successors, such as courtship and widowhood. Friendship, however, although an intimate relationship, is included only where it clearly is studied within a context of family behavior. In other words, it would be too rigorous a definition to select only those items which deal simultaneously with the family as a complete unit: husband-wife, parent-child, and sibling interrelationships. But it does not require reduction to the level of individual behavior to accept as within the scope of family research any work which deals with at least one of these relationships of persons allied by descent or marriage (or adoption). This definition of what is covered by "the family" in terms of family relationships seems consistent with both common usage and our special emphasis upon identity and interpersonal competence. At many points, however, it was hard to distinguish whether the main focus of an item was upon the family or upon delinquency, psychopathology, genetics, sex, population, or gerontology; judgment finally had to be employed where our definition of "family" proved insufficient.

Our definition of "research" is not intended to represent our stand upon the many controversies about the application of scientific method to the study of human behavior, but it is not inconsistent with the position already taken in chapter vi. As simply a means of deciding which articles and monographs to include in the Bibliography, we have taken the general view that any item ought to report the results of investigation in which data were gathered and an effort was made to generalize from it. Neither mere data alone nor mere speculation alone is thus meant to be included. Nonetheless, there are undoubtedly exceptions, marginal cases, and mistakes of both omission and commission.

We have deliberately ignored all textbooks, collections of previously published articles, manuals, tracts, popular essays, conference proceedings, and unpublished theses. Even Burgess and Locke's influential *The Family: From Institution to Companionship* (1945; 2d ed., 1953), which advances a thesis with assembled evidence, is thus left out as a textbook. Professor William L. Ludlow, of Muskingum College, compiled an exhaustive bibliography of all types of literature about the family in 1951, which ran to thousands of items. Many items of a philosophical sort may carry much weight in discussion of policy, but here they would interfere with a scrutiny of trends in actual research.

In the research process a function of leadership is often played by certain books which synthesize previous thought and investigations and, in response to such secondary findings, proffer new lines of investigation. In the past decade notable examples have been provided by such writers as Erich Fromm, Harry Stack Sullivan, and Erik H. Erikson; so, with discretion, a few of their works have been included. Another exception to including only monographs and articles which report firsthand the results of original investigations consists of several well-edited symposiums. Written by major theorists who confront therein the frontier problems of their field, these symposiums also often affect the formulation of research problems and thus deserve recognition, as in the case of the volume edited by Ruth N. Anshen in 1949. On the other hand, apart from the nine volumes of *The Psychoanalytic Study of the Child* (an annual) and despite the great influence of this vein of thought in studies of the family, most of the printed material in psychoanalytic publications is so far removed from being definable as research that it is omitted.

At the other pole from simple case studies and undisciplined speculation are certain major sources of statistical data which the professional family researcher would not be without. Because they usually appear in raw form without interpretation or generalization, they are not separately listed in the Bibliography but deserve emphatic mention:

Metropolitan Life Insurance Company, *Statistical Bulletin* (monthly)
U.S. Bureau of the Census, *Current Population Reports*, Ser. P-20
U.S. Bureau of the Census, *Population—Special Reports*
U.S. Bureau of the Census, *Statistical Abstract of the United States*
U.S. National Office of Vital Statistics, *Monthly Vital Statistics Bulletin*
U.S. National Office of Vital Statistics, *Special Reports*
U.S. Women's Bureau, Department of Labor, *Bulletins*

With regard to the periodical journals in which virtually all research articles appear, it was found that family research as defined here appears in a variety of journals too numerous relative to our limited resources to be examined exhaustively. Fortunately, however, the principal mediums could be limited to twenty, in each of which at least ten items had appeared in the last ten years. Five of these were sociological journals, five psychological, and five miscellaneous. Five monograph series were also included; the monograph series which have carried substantial contributions to family research are these:

> "Child Development Monographs"
> "Genetic Psychology Monographs"
> "Psychodrama Monographs"
> "Psychological Monographs"
> "Smith College Studies in Social Work"

The fifteen journals are ranked here in each group in order of frequency of family research items published during the decade covered:

American Sociological Review
American Journal of Sociology
Rural Sociology
Sociology and Social Research
Social Forces

———

Journal of Genetic Psychology
Journal of Abnormal and Social Psychology
Journal of Educational Psychology

Journal of Social Psychology
Journal of Psychology

———

Marriage and Family Living
Journal of Home Economics
American Journal of Orthopsychiatry
Child Development
Sociometry

This ranking is not representative of the relative current status of these journals as mediums for family research. *Marriage and Family Living* now leads all the rest in frequency of items, having published more in the last three years than in the previous thirteen. *Sociology and Social Research* has likewise recently climbed in quantity and quality. *Child Development* would hold higher rank, were it not for the peculiar bias derived from individualistic psychology whereby many of its contributors treat the child as if he were isolated from his family.

Certain other journals carry family research reports often enough to indicate that during the next decade some are likely to cross our minimum line of one article per year; they are:

Quarterly Journal of Child Behavior
Journal of Clinical Psychology
Journal of Consulting Psychology
Review of Educational Research
Journal of Experimental Education
Eugenics Quarterly
Journal of Gerontology

Human Relations
Mental Hygiene
Milbank Memorial Fund Quarterly
Psychiatry
School and Society
International Journal of Sexology
Social Problems

While certain items in these journals have attracted attention and are included in the bibliography below, they have been examined only closely enough to ascertain that they fell below the minimum standard achieved by the leading fifteen which were systematically scrutinized. In distributing the collected items in ten alphabetical series according to year, some authors' names stood out as highly recurrent. To produce a ranking of individual productivity might make interesting reading. The purpose of this particular arrangement, however, would have been better served if titles rather than authors could have been alphabetized. We want to discern the principal themes that have been employed since the war in the definition and choice of problems, in order to apply the criterion of relevance which has been advanced throughout this work.

1945

1. AMES, VIOLA CAPREZ. "Socio-psychological Vectors in the Behavior and Attitudes of Children. II. Awareness of Acceptance Status," *Journal of Educational Psychology*, XXXVI, No. 4 (April, 1945), 271–88.
2. BACH, G. R. *Young Children's Play Fantasies.* ("Psychological Monographs, General and Applied," Vol. LIX, No. 2 [1945].)
3. BAIN, READ. "Needed Research in Parent-Child Fixation," *American Sociological Review*, X, No. 2 (April, 1945), 208–16.
4. BALDWIN, A. L., KALHORN, J., and BREESE, F. H. *Patterns of Parent Behavior*, pp. 1–75. ("Psychological Monographs, General and Applied," Vol. LVIII, No. 3 [1945].)
5. BALDWIN, ALFRED L. "An Analysis of Some Aspects of Feeding Behavior," *Journal of Genetic Psychology*, LXVI (1945), 221–32.
6. BAUM, PEARL. "When Is It Worth While To Reopen a Case for Child Guidance," *Smith College Studies in Social Work*, XV, No. 3 (March, 1945), 216–26.
7. BEAGLEHOLE, ERNEST. "A Critique of 'The Measurement of Family Interaction,'" *American Journal of Sociology*, LI (September, 1945), 145–47.
8. BLOOM, LEONARD, RIEMER, RUTH, and CREEDON, CAROL. *Marriages of Japanese-Americans in Los Angeles County: A Statistical Study.* Berkeley and Los Angeles: University of California Press, 1945.
9. BOSSARD, JAMES H. S. "Family Modes of Expression," *American Sociological Review*, X, No. 2 (April, 1945), 226–37.
10. ——. "Family Problems of the Immediate Future," *Journal of Home Economics*, XXXVII, No. 7 (September, 1945), 383–87.
11. ——. "The Law of Family Interaction," *American Journal of Sociology*, L, No. 4 (January, 1945), 292–94.

12. BRADWAY, KATHERINE P. "An Experimental Study of Factors Associated with Stanford-Binet IQ Changes from the Preschool to the Junior High School," _Journal of Genetic Psychology_, LXVI (1945), 107–28.

13. BURGESS, ERNEST W. "Unemployment and the Family," _Marriage and Family Living_, VII, No. 4 (autumn, 1945), 87.

14. BURMA, JOHN H. "Attitudes of College Youth on War Marriage," _Social Forces_, XXIV, No. 1 (October, 1945), 96–100.

15. DEUTSCH, HELENE. _The Psychology of Women: A Psychoanalytic Interpretation._ Vol. II: _Motherhood._ New York: Grune & Stratton, 1945.

16. DICKENS, DOROTHY. "Home Management and Family Level of Living," _Journal of Home Economics_, XXXVII, No. 1 (January, 1945), 13–18.

17. DUVALL, EVELYN MILLIS, and MOTZ, ANNABELLE BENDER. "Age and Education as Factors in Social Experience and Personal Family Adjustments," _School Review_, LIII (September, 1945), 413–21.

18. ———. "Are Country Girls So Different?" _Rural Sociology_, X, No. 3 (September, 1945), 263–74.

19. ———. "Attitudes of Second Generation Daughters to Family Living," _Journal of Consulting Psychology_, November-December, 1945, pp. 281–86.

20. DYER, DOROTHY TUNELL. "Are Only Children Different?" _Journal of Educational Psychology_, XXXVI, No. 5 (May, 1945), 297–302.

21. FLEEGE, URBAN H. _Self-revelation of the Adolescent Boy: A Key to Understanding the Modern Adolescent._ Milwaukee: Bruce Publishing Co., 1945.

22. FORD, CLELLAN STEARNS. _A Comparative Study of Human Reproduction._ New Haven: Yale University Press, 1945.

23. FREUD, ANNA, HARTMANN, HEINZ, and KRISS, ERNST. _The Psychoanalytic Study of the Child_, Vol. I. New York: International Universities Press, 1945.

24. GARDNER, G. E., and GOLDMAN, N. "Childhood and Adolescent Adjustment of Naval Successes and Failures," _American Journal of Orthopsychiatry_, XV (1945), 584–96.

25. GRINKER, ROY R., and SPIEGEL, JOHN P. _Men under Stress._ Philadelphia: Blakiston Co., 1945.

26. HILL, REUBEN. "Campus Values in Mate Selection," _Journal of Home Economics_, XXXVII, No. 9 (November, 1945), 554–58.

27. ———. "The Returning Father and His Family," _Marriage and Family Living_, VII, No. 1 (winter, 1945), 31 ff.

28. HOFFER, CHARLES R. "The Impact of War on the Farm Family," _Rural Sociology_, X, No. 2 (June, 1945), 151–56.

29. HOLDEN, MARCIA. "Treatability of Children of Alcoholic Parents," _Smith College Studies in Social Work_, XVI (1945), 44–61.

30. KARDINER, ABRAM, with the collaboration of RALPH LINTON, CORA DuBOIS, and JAMES WEST. _The Psychological Frontiers of Society._ New York: Columbia University Press, 1945.

31. KING, CHARLES E. "The Negro Maternal Family: A Product of an Economic and a Cultural System," *Social Forces,* XXIV, No. 1 (October, 1945), 100–104.

32. KIRKPATRICK, CLIFFORD, and CAPLOW, THEODORE. "Courtship in a Group of Minnesota Students," *American Journal of Sociology,* LI, No. 2 (September, 1945), 114–25.

33. ———. "Emotional Trends in the Courtship Experience of College Students as Expressed by Graphs, with Some Observations on Methodological Implications," *American Sociological Review,* X, No. 5 (October, 1945), 619–26.

34. KVARACEUS, W. C. "Prenatal and Early Developmental History of 136 Delinquents," *Journal of Genetic Psychology,* LXVI (1945), 267–71.

35. LAFORE, G. G. *Practices of Parents in Dealing with Preschool Children* ("Child Development Monographs," No. 31 [1945].)

36. LANDIS, PAUL H., and DAY, KATHERINE H. "Education as a Factor in Mate Selection," *American Sociological Review,* X, No. 4 (August, 1945), 558–60.

37. LATIMER, R. H. "The Parent-Child Relationships in Children Afflicted with Tics," *Nervous Child,* IV (1945), 353–58.

38. LEWIS, WILLIAM DRAYTON. "Influence of Parental Attitudes on Children's Personal Inventory Scores," *Journal of Genetic Psychology,* LXVII (December, 1945), 195–201.

39. LOCKE, HARVEY J. "Contemporary American Farm Families," *Rural Sociology,* X, No. 2 (June, 1945), 142–51.

40. McCORMICK, JANE L. "Why Some Foster Home Applications Are Withdrawn," *Smith College Studies in Social Work,* XVI, No. 2 (December, 1945), 83–103.

41. McDONAGH, EDWARD, and McDONAGH, LOUISE. "War Anxieties of Soldiers and Their Wives," *Social Forces,* XXIV, No. 3 (December, 1945), 195–200.

42. McPHERSON, E. GLEN, and McPHERSON, MARIAN WHITE. "An Exploratory Investigation of Tenant Reactions to a Federal Housing Project," *Journal of Psychology,* XX (1945), 199–215.

43. MORENO, JACOB L. *Psychodrama and the Psychopathology of Interpersonal Relations.* ("Psychodrama Monographs," No. 16.) Boston: Beacon House, Inc., 1945.

44. MUELLER, DOROTHY DANIELS. "Paternal Domination: Its Influence on Child Guidance Results," *Smith College Studies in Social Work,* XV (1945), 184–215.

45. ORBISON, M. "Some Effects of Parental Maladjustment on First-born Children," *Smith College Studies in Social Work,* XVI (1945), 138–39.

46. PATRICK, C. "Relation of Childhood and Adult Leisure Activities," *Journal of Social Psychology,* XXI (1945), 65–79.

47. PREVY, ESTHER ELIZABETH. "A Quantitative Study of Family Practices in Training Children in the Use of Money," *Journal of Educational Psychology,* XXXVI, No. 7 (October, 1945), 411–28.

48. READ, K. H. "Parents' Expressed Attitudes and Children's Behavior," *Journal of Consulting Psychology*, IX (1945), 95–100.

49. REEVES, GRACE. "The New Family in the Postwar World," *Marriage and Family Living*, VII, No. 4 (autumn, 1945), 73–76, 89.

50. REIK, THEODOR. *Psychology of Sex Relations*. New York: Rinehart & Co., Inc., 1945.

51. REINEMANN, J. O. "Extra-marital Relations with Fellow Employees in War Industry as a Factor in Disruption of Family Life," *American Sociological Review*, X, No. 3 (June, 1945), 399–404.

52. RHINEHART, JESSE BATTEY. "A Comparative Evaluation of Two Nursery School–Parent Education Programs," *Journal of Educational Psychology*, XXXVI, No. 5 (May, 1945), 309–17.

53. RICHARDSON, HENRY B. *Patients Have Families*. New York: Commonwealth Fund, 1945.

54. RIEMER, SVEND. "Farm Housing Behavior: An Analysis of Housing Census Data," *Rural Sociology*, X, No. 2 (June, 1945), 157–68.

55. ———. "Maladjustment to the Family Home," *American Sociological Review*, X, No. 5 (October, 1945), 643–48.

56. ROBERTS, HARRY W. "Effects of Farm Ownership on Rural Family Life," *Social Forces*, XXIV, No. 2 (December, 1945), 185–94.

57. ROCKWOOD, LEMO D., and FORD, MARY E. N. *Youth, Marriage, and Parenthood: The Attitudes of 364 University Juniors and Seniors toward Courtship, Marriage, and Parenthood*. New York: John Wiley & Sons, Inc., 1945.

58. ROE, ANNE, and BURKS, BARBARA. *Adult Adjustment of Foster-Children of Alcoholic and Psychotic Parentage and the Influence of the Foster-Home*. New Haven: Quarterly Journal of Studies on Alcohol, 1945.

59. RUSTAD, RUTH M., and REULEIN, PAULINE B. "Child Study in High School," *Journal of Home Economics*, XXXVII, No. 6 (June, 1945), 321–23.

60. SANTULLI, MARY L. "Criteria for Selection of Families for Housekeeper Service," *Smith College Studies in Social Work*, XV, No. 4 (June, 1945), 327–46.

61. SEWARD, GEORGENE H. "Cultural Conflict and the Feminine Role: An Experimental Study," *Journal of Social Psychology*, XXII (November, 1945), 177–94.

62. SKODAK, MARIE, and SKEELS, HAROLD M. "A Follow-up Study of Children in Adoptive Homes," *Journal of Genetic Psychology*, LXVI (1945), 21–58.

63. SMITH, JANE HARRIS. "The Relation of Masculinity-Femininity Scores of Sorority Girls on a Free Association Test to Those of Their Parents," *Journal of Social Psychology*, XXII (August, 1945), 79–85.

64. SMITH, WILLIAM C. "The Stepchild," *American Sociological Review*, X, No. 2 (April, 1945), 237–42.

65. STEINER, LEE R. *Where Do People Take Their Troubles?* Boston: Houghton Mifflin Co., 1945.

66. STOTT, LELAND H. "Family Prosperity in Relation to the Psychological Adjustment of Farm Folk," *Rural Sociology*, X, No. 3 (September, 1945), 256–63.

67. ——. "Research in Family Life in Nebraska," *Journal of Home Economics*, XXXVII, No. 2 (February, 1945), 80–83.

68. TAYLOR, LOUIS. "The Social Adjustment of the Only Child," *American Journal of Sociology*, LI, No. 3 (November, 1945), 227–32.

69. TORRANCE, P. "The Influence of the Broken Home on Adolescent Adjustment," *Journal of Educational Sociology*, XVIII (1945), 359–64.

70. WARNER, W. LLOYD, and SROLE, LEO. *The Social Systems of American Ethnic Groups*. New Haven: Yale University Press, 1945.

71. WEST, JAMES (pseud.). *Plainville, U.S.A.* New York: Columbia University Press, 1945.

72. WHITE, THELMA E., and BANKS, ETHEL LEWIS. "Adventures in Housing," *Journal of Home Economics*, XXXVII, No. 2 (February, 1945), 72–73.

73. WITTMAN, MARY PHYLLIS, and HUFFMAN, ARTHUR V. "A Comparative Study of Developmental, Adjustment, and Personality Characteristics of Psychotic, Psychoneurotic, Delinquent, and Normally Adjusted Teen Aged Youths," *Journal of Genetic Psychology*, LXVI (1945), 167–82.

74. WOOFTER, T. J. "Southern Children and Family Security," *Social Forces*, XXIII, No. 3 (March, 1945), 366–75.

1946

1. ADAMS, CLIFFORD R. "The Prediction of Adjustment in Marriage," *Educational and Psychological Measurement*, VI (1946), 185–93.

2. ANDERSON, JOHN E. "Parents' Attitudes on Child Behavior: A Report of Three Studies," *Child Development*, XVII, Nos. 1–2 (March-June, 1946), 91–97.

3. ANDERSON, W. A. "The Challenge of Tomorrow's Rural Life," *Rural Sociology*, XI, No. 2 (June, 1946), 120–27.

4. ——. "Family Social Participation and Social Status Self-ratings," *American Sociological Review*, XI, No. 3 (June, 1946), 253–58.

5. ——. "Types of Participating Families," *Rural Sociology*, XI, No. 4 (December, 1946), 355–61.

6. BACH, GEORGE R. "Father-Fantasies and Father-typing in Father-separated Children," *Child Development*, XVII, Nos. 1–2 (March-June, 1946), 63–80.

7. BALDWIN, ALFRED L. "Differences in Parent Behavior toward Three- and Nine-Year-old Children," *Journal of Personality*, XV (December, 1946), 143–65.

8. BANDER, VIOLET. "Services of a Family Case Worker to Day Nursery Applicants," *Smith College Studies in Social Work*, XVI, No. 3 (March, 1946), 179–97.

9. BARRON, MILTON L. "The Incidence of Jewish Intermarriage in

Europe and America," *American Sociological Review*, XI, No. 1 (February, 1946), 6–13.

10. BARRON, MILTON L. *People Who Intermarry: Intermarriage in a New England Industrial Community*. Syracuse: Syracuse University Press, 1946.

11. BEARD, MARY RITTER. *Woman as Force in History: A Study in Traditions and Realities*. New York: Macmillan Co., 1946.

12. BEEGLE, J. ALLEN, and SMITH, T. LYNN. *Differential Fertility in Louisiana*. (Louisiana Bull. 103.) Baton Rouge: Louisiana State University and A. & M. College, 1946.

13. BENEDEK, THERESE. *Insight and Personality Adjustment—a Study of the Psychological Effects of War*. New York: Ronald Press Co., 1946.

14. BERGLER, EDMUND. "Six Types of Neurotic Reaction to a Husband's Request for a Divorce," *Marriage and Family Living*, VIII, No. 4 (autumn, 1946), 81 ff.

15. BORDEN, B. "The Role of Grandparents in Children's Behavior Problems," *Smith College Studies in Social Work*, XVII (1946), 115–16.

16. BOSSARD, JAMES H. S., and BOLL, ELEANOR S. "The Immediate Family and the Kinship Group: A Research Report," *Social Forces*, XXIV, No. 4 (May, 1946), 379–84.

17. BOWMAN, CLAUDE C. "Hidden Valuations in the Interpretation of Sexual and Family Relationships," *American Sociological Review*, XI, No. 5 (October, 1946), 536–44.

18. BRODBECK, ARTHUR J., and IRWIN, ORVIS C. "The Speech Behavior of Infants without Families," *Child Development*, XVII, No. 3 (September, 1946), 145–56.

19. COLE, STEWART G. "The Intercultural Workshop," *Sociology and Social Research*, XXX, No. 6 (July–August, 1946), 476–83.

20. DAVIS, ALLISON, and HAVIGHURST, ROBERT J. "Social Class and Color Differences in Child-rearing," *American Sociological Review*, XI, No. 6 (December, 1946), 698–710.

21. DREIKURS, RUDOLPH. *The Challenge of Marriage*. New York: Duell, Sloan & Pearce, 1946.

22. DURAND, JOHN D. "Married Women in the Labor Force," *American Journal of Sociology*, LII, No. 3 (November, 1946), 217–23.

23. DUVALL, EVELYN MILLIS. "Conceptions of Parenthood," *American Journal of Sociology*, LII, No. 3 (November, 1946), 193–203.

24. ELDRIDGE, HOPE T., and SIEGEL, J. S. "The Changing Sex Ratio in the United States," *American Journal of Sociology*, LII, No. 3 (November, 1946), 224–34.

25. ELIOT, THOMAS D. "War Bereavements and Their Recovery," *Marriage and Family Living*, VIII, No. 1 (winter, 1946), 1–6.

26. ELKIN, HENRY. "Aggressive and Erotic Tendencies in Army Life," *American Journal of Sociology*, LI, No. 5 (March, 1946), 408–13.

27. ERICSON, MARTHA. "Child-rearing and Social Status," *American Journal of Sociology*, LII, No. 3 (November, 1946), 190–92.

28. ESSIG, MARY, and MORGAN, D. H. "Adjustment of Adolescent

Daughters of Employed Women to Family Life," *Journal of Educational Psychology*, XXXVII, No. 4 (1946), 219–33.
29. EVJE, MARGARET. "Outlook for Treatment of Children Who Have Had Neonatal Difficulties," *Smith College Studies in Social Work*, XVI, No. 4 (June, 1946), 223–64.
30. FITZSIMMONS, CLEO. "Family Economics Research Evaluated," *Journal of Home Economics*, XXXVIII, No. 9 (November, 1946), 586–90.
31. "Fortune Survey, The: Women in America," *Fortune*, XXXIV, No. 2 (August, 1946), 5–6.
32. FOSTER, ROBERT G. "The Family," *Rural Sociology*, XI, No. 1 (March, 1946), 35–42.
33. FRAZIER, E. FRANKLIN, and BERNERT, ELEANOR H. "Children and Income in Negro Families," *Social Forces*, XXV, No. 2 (December, 1946), 178–82.
34. FREUD, ANNA, et al. *The Psychoanalytic Study of the Child*, Vol. II. New York: International Universities Press, 1946.
35. GATES, MARY FRANCES. "A Comparative Study of Some Problems of Social and Emotional Adjustments of Crippled and Non-crippled Girls and Boys," *Journal of Genetic Psychology*, LXVIII (June, 1946), 219–44.
36. GESELL, ARNOLD L., and ILG, FRANCES L., in collaboration with LOUISE B. AMES and GLENNA E. BULLIS. *The Child from Five to Ten.* New York: Harper & Bros., 1946.
37. GILLETTE, J. M. "Farm Enlargement in North Dakota: Reasons and Causes," *Rural Sociology*, XI, No. 3 (September, 1946), 253–69.
38. GLICK, PAUL C. "Estimates of the Future Number of Families," *American Journal of Sociology*, LII, No. 3 (November, 1946), 235–42.
39. GOULDNER, ALVIN W. "Basic Personality Structure and the Subgroup," *Journal of Abnormal and Social Psychology*, XLI (1946), 356–58.
40. GREEN, ARNOLD W. "The Middle-Class Male Child and Neurosis," *American Sociological Review*, XI, No. 1 (February, 1946), 31–41.
41. HARRIS, RAYMOND P. " 'Grass Root' Project—Consumer Buying," *Journal of Home Economics*, XXXVIII, No. 10 (December, 1946), 639–40.
42. HEATH, C. W., and GREGORY, L. W. "Problems of Normal College Students and Their Families," *School and Society*, Vol. LXIII (1946).
43. HELLERSBERG, E. F. "Food Habits of Adolescents in Relation to Family, Training, and Present Adjustment," *American Journal of Orthopsychiatry*, XVI (1946), 34–51.
44. VON HENTIG, HANS. "The Sociological Function of the Grandmother," *Social Forces*, Vol. XXIV (May, 1946).
45. HORROCKS, JOHN E., and THOMPSON, GEORGE G. "A Study of the Friendship Fluctuations of Rural Boys and Girls," *Journal of Genetic Psychology*, LXIX (December, 1946), 189–98.
46. JENKINS, R. L., and GLICKMAN, S. "Common Syndromes in Child

Psychiatry. I. Deviant Behavior Traits. II. The Schizoid Child," *American Journal of Orthopsychiatry*, XVI (April, 1946), 244–54, 255–61.

47. JOHNSON, HILDEGARD BINDER. "Intermarriages between German Pioneers and Other Nationalities in Minnesota in 1860 and 1870," *American Journal of Sociology*, LI, No. 4 (January, 1946), 299–304.

48. KASANIN, J., RHODE, C., and WERTHEIMER, E. "Observations from a Veteran's Clinic on Childhood Factors in Military Adjustment," *American Journal of Orthopsychiatry*, XVI (1946), 640–59.

49. KERR, MARION JEAN. "The Importance of Preparing Children for Psychiatric Treatment," *Smith College Studies in Social Work*, XVII, No. 2 (December, 1946), 69–104.

50. KOMOROVSKY, MIRRA. "Cultural Contradictions and Sex Roles," *American Journal of Sociology*, LII, No. 3 (November, 1946), 184–89.

51. KOOS, EARL LOMON. *Families in Trouble*. New York: King's Crown Press, 1946.

52. LAMSON, HERBERT D. "Marriage of Co-eds to Fellow Students," *Marriage and Family Living*, VIII, No. 2 (May, 1946), 27 ff.

53. LANDIS, JUDSON T. "Length of Time Required To Achieve Adjustment in Marriage," *American Sociological Review*, XI, No. 6 (December, 1946), 666–77.

54. LANDIS, PAUL H. "Rural-urban Migration and the Marriage Rate—an Hypothesis," *American Sociological Review*, XI, No. 2 (April, 1946), 155–58.

55. LARSEN, CECIL E. "Control Patterns in an Intracultural School," *Sociology and Social Research*, XXX, No. 5 (May-June, 1946), 383–90.

56. LEEVY, J. ROY. "Social Education for Housing," *Sociology and Social Research*, XXX, No. 5 (May-June, 1946), 379–82.

57. LEWIS, CLAUDIA. *Children of the Cumberland*. New York: Columbia University Press, 1946.

58. LOCKE, HARVEY J. "Disposition of Divorce Applications," *Sociology and Social Research*, XXX, No. 6 (July-August, 1946), 439–51.

59. McDONAGH, EDWARD C. "The Discharged Serviceman and His Family," *American Journal of Sociology*, LI, No. 5 (March, 1946), 451–54.

60. MacDONALD, JOYCE, and GILBERT, CHARLOTTE. "Social Adjustment of Hypothyroid Children," *Smith College Studies in Social Work*, XVII, No. 1 (September, 1946), 1–31.

61. McMILLAN, ROBERT T. "School Acceleration and Retardation among Open Country Children in Southern Oklahoma," *Rural Sociology*, XI, No. 4 (December, 1946), 339–45.

62. MASLOW, A. H., and SZILAGYI-KESSLER, I. "Security and Breastfeeding," *Journal of Abnormal and Social Psychology*, XLI (1946), 83–85.

63. MATTHEWS, M. TAYLOR. "The Wheeler County, Texas, Rural Health Services Association," *Rural Sociology*, XI, No. 2 (June, 1946), 128–37.

64. MEAD, MARGARET. "What Women Want," *Fortune*, XXXIV, No. 6 (December, 1946), 172 ff.

65. MERRILL, BARBARA. "A Measurement of Mother-Child Interaction," *Journal of Abnormal and Social Psychology*, XLI (1946), 37–49.

66. PASAMANICK, BENJAMIN. "A Comparative Study of the Behavioral Development of Negro Infants," *Journal of Genetic Psychology*, LXIX (September, 1946), 3–44.

67. PATTERSON, CECIL H. "The Relationship of Bernreuter Scores to Parent Behavior, Child Behavior, Urban-rural Residence, and Other Background Factors in 100 Normal Adult Parents," *Journal of Social Psychology*, XXIV (August, 1946), 3–49.

68. PORTERFIELD, AUSTIN L., and SALLEY, H. ELLISON. "Current Folkways of Sexual Behavior," *American Journal of Sociology*, LII, No. 3 (November, 1946), 209–16.

69. PREVEY, ESTHER E. "Developing Good Habits in the Use of Money," *Journal of Home Economics*, XXXVIII, No. 2 (February, 1946), 79–81.

70. RADKE, MARIAN J. *The Relation of Parental Authority to Children's Behavior and Attitudes.* ("University of Minnesota Child Welfare Monographs," No. 22.) Minneapolis: University of Minnesota Press, 1946.

71. REDFIELD, MARGARET PARK. "The American Family: Consensus and Freedom," *American Journal of Sociology*, LII, No. 3 (November, 1946), 175–83.

72. RINER, ELIZABETH. "Stork Club: Adventure in Adult Education," *Journal of Home Economics*, XXXVIII, No. 3 (March, 1946), 133–36.

73. ROBINSON, ELIZABETH F. "Doll Plan as a Function of the Doll Family Constellation," *Child Development*, XVII, No. 3 (September, 1946), 99–119.

74. ROGERS, PAULINE AUNGST. "Case Work with Spouses of Psychiatric Patients," *Smith College Studies in Social Work*, XVI, No. 4 (June, 1946), 265–81.

75. SEARS, ROBERT R., PINTLER, MARGARET H., and SEARS, PAULINE S. "Effect of Father Separation on Preschool Children's Doll Play Aggression," *Child Development*, XVII, No. 4 (December, 1946), 219–43.

76. SEWARD, GEORGENE H. *Sex and the Social Order.* New York: McGraw-Hill Book Co., Inc., 1946.

77. SHERMAN, ARTHUR WESLEY. "Emancipation Status of College Students," *Journal of Genetic Psychology*, LXVIII (June, 1946), 171–80.

78. SNYDER, BARBARA JUNE, and SNYDER, WILLIAM U. "Some Relationships between Children's Symptoms of Maladjustment and Background Factors," *Journal of Clinical Psychology*, Vol. XIII (April, 1946).

79. SPITZ, R. A. *The Smiling Response: A Contribution to the Onto-*

genesis of Social Relations. ("Genetic Psychology Monographs," Vol. XXXIV, No. 1 [1946].)

80. STRAUSS, ANSELM. "The Ideal and the Chosen Mate," *American Journal of Sociology,* LII, No. 3 (November, 1946), 204–8.

81. ———. "The Influence of Parent-Images upon Marital Choice," *American Sociological Review,* XI, No. 5 (October, 1946), 554–59.

82. STRECKER, EDWARD A. *Their Mothers' Sons: The Psychiatrist Examines an American Problem.* Philadelphia: J. B. Lippincott Co., 1946.

83. SULLENGER, T. EARL, and LINDEVALL, GWEN. "The Urban Church in a Changing Social Scene," *Sociology and Social Research,* XXX, No. 3 (January-February, 1946), 196–200.

84. VAUGHAN, THEO L., and PRYOR, HERBERT. "Prepayment Medical Care in Nevada County, Arkansas," *Rural Sociology,* XI, No. 2 (June, 1946), 137–47.

85. VERVILLE, ELINOR. "The Effect of Emotional and Motivational Sets on the Perception of Incomplete Pictures," *Journal of Genetic Psychology,* LXIX (December, 1946), 133–45.

86. WINCH, ROBERT F. "Interrelations between Certain Social Background and Parent-Son Factors in a Study of Courtship among College Men," *American Sociological Review,* XI, No. 3 (June, 1946), 333–41.

87. WOLFENSTEIN, MARTHA. *The Impact of a Children's Story on Mothers and Children.* ("Monographs of the Society for Research in Child Development," Vol. XI, No. 1 [1946].)

88. ZIMMERMAN, CARLE C. "The Social Conscience and the Family," *American Journal of Sociology,* LII, No. 3 (November, 1946), 263–68.

1947

1. ANDERSON, W. A. "The Spacing of Births in the Families of University Graduates," *American Journal of Sociology,* LIII, No. 1 (July, 1947), 23–33.

2. BACH, GEORGE R., and BREMER, GLORIA. "Projective Father Fantasies of Pre-adolescent, Delinquent Children," *Journal of Psychology,* XXIV (1947), 3–17.

3. BALDWIN, ALFRED L. "Changes in Parent Behavior during Pregnancy: An Experiment in Longitudinal Analysis," *Child Development,* XVIII, Nos. 1–2 (March-June, 1947), 29–39.

4. BICKSLER, PAUL H. "Tangibles in Marriage Counseling," *Marriage and Family Living,* IX, No. 3 (September, 1947), 61–62, 65.

5. BLOOM, LEONARD. "Transitional Adjustments of Japanese-American Families to Relocation," *American Sociological Review,* XII, No. 2 (April, 1947), 201–9.

6. BOSSARD, JAMES H. S. "The Guest and the Family," *Marriage and Family Living,* IX, No. 2 (May, 1947), 40.

7. BOSSARD, JAMES H. S., and BOLL, ELEANOR S. "The Role of the Guest: A Study in Child Development," *American Sociological Review,* XII, No. 2 (April, 1947), 192–201.

8. ———. "School Situations in Behavior Studies: An Autobiographical

Analysis," *Sociology and Social Research*, XXXI, No. 6 (July-August, 1947), 423–28.

9. BRAV, STANLEY R. "Note on Honeymoons," *Marriage and Family Living*, IX, No. 1 (February, 1947), 60 ff.

10. BROWN, ANDREW W., MORRISON, JOAN, and COUCH, GERTRUDE B. "Influence of Affectional Family Relationships on Character Development," *Journal of Abnormal and Social Psychology*, XLII, No. 4 (October, 1947), 422–28.

11. BROWN, MARJORIE M. "Factors Influencing the Outcome of Treatment of Adolescents in a Family Agency," *Smith College Studies in Social Work*, Vol. XVIII, No. 1 (September, 1947).

12. BURGESS, ERNEST W. "The Family and Sociological Research," *Social Forces*, XXVI, No. 5 (October, 1947), 1–6.

13. CANNON, KENNETH L. "Marriage and Divorce in Iowa, 1940–47," *Marriage and Family Living*, IX, No. 1 (February, 1947), 81–83, 98.

14. CHRISTENSEN, HAROLD T. "Student Views on Mate Selection," *Marriage and Family Living*, IX, No. 4 (autumn, 1947), 85–88.

15. COOPER, MARCIA MANN. *Evaluation of the Mother's Advisory Service* ("Monographs of the Society for Research in Child Development," Vol. XII, No. 1 [1947].)

16. CUPPS, RAYANNE D., and HAYNER, NORMAN S. "Dating at the University of Washington," *Marriage and Family Living*, IX, No. 2 (May, 1947), 30–31.

17. CUTLER, VIRGINIA F. "A Technique for Improving Family Housing," *Journal of Home Economics*, XXXIX, No. 3 (March, 1947), 141–47.

18. DAVIS, W. ALLISON, and HAVIGHURST, ROBERT J. *Father of the Man: How Your Child Gets His Personality*. Boston: Houghton Mifflin Co., 1947.

19. ELLIS, ALBERT. "Questionnaire versus Interview Methods in the Study of Human Love Relationships," *American Sociological Review*, XII, No. 5 (October, 1947), 541–53.

20. ENGLAND, A. O. "Cultural Milieu and Parental Identification," *Nervous Child*, XI (1947), 301–5.

21. FARIS, ROBERT E. L. "Interaction of Generations and Family Stability," *American Sociological Review*, XII, No. 2 (April, 1947), 159–64.

22. FITZSIMMONS, CLEO, and PERKINS, NELLIE L. "Some Illinois Clothing Consumption Patterns," *Journal of Home Economics*, XXXIX, No. 8 (October, 1947), 495–97.

23. ———. "Some Illinois Food Consumption Patterns," *ibid.*, No. 9 (November, 1947), pp. 572–74.

24. ———. "Some Illinois Housing Consumption Patterns," *ibid.*, No. 10 (December, 1947), pp. 633–36.

25. FROMM, ERICH. *Man for Himself: An Inquiry into the Psychology of Ethics*. New York: Rinehart & Co., Inc., 1947.

26. GAMBLE, CLARENCE J. "The College Birthrate," *Journal of Heredity*, XXXVIII (1947), 358.

27. GARDNER, L. PEARL. "An Analysis of Children's Attitudes toward Fathers," *Journal of Genetic Psychology*, LXX (March, 1947), 3–28.

28. GLICK, PAUL C. "The Family Cycle," *American Sociological Review*, XII, No. 2 (April, 1947), 164–74.

29. ———. "The Family Cycle," *Marriage and Family Living*, IX, No. 3 (September, 1947), 58.

30. GOLDFARB, WILLIAM. "Variations in Adolescent Adjustment of Institutionally Reared Children," *American Journal of Orthopsychiatry*, XVII (July, 1947), 449–57.

31. GRAVES, WINIFRED SIBLEY. "Factors Associated with Children's Taking Music Lessons, Including Some Parent-Child Relationships. I. History and Procedures," *Journal of Genetic Psychology*, LXX (March, 1947), 65–89.

32. ———. "Factors Associated with Children's Taking Music Lessons, Including Some Parent-Child Relationships. II. Results and Conclusions," *ibid.*, pp. 91–125.

33. GREENACRE, PHYLLIS. "Child Wife as Ideal: Sociological Consideration," *American Journal of Orthopsychiatry*, XVII (January, 1947), 167–71.

34. HAGOOD, MARGARET JARMAN. "Construction of County Indexes for Measuring Change in Level of Living of Farm Operator Families, 1940–45," *Rural Sociology*, XII, No. 2 (June, 1947), 139–50.

35. HILL, REUBEN. "The American Family: Problem or Solution?" *American Journal of Sociology*, LIII, No. 2 (September, 1947), 125–30.

36. HOHMAN, LESLIE B., and SCHAFFNER, BERTRAM. "The Sex Lives of Unmarried Men," *American Journal of Sociology*, LII, No. 6 (May, 1947), 501–7.

37. KIRKPATRICK, CLIFFORD. *What Science Says about Happiness in Marriage*. Minneapolis: Burgess Publishing Co., 1947.

38. KISER, CLYDE V., and WHELPTON, P. K. "Progress Report on the Study of Social and Psychological Factors Affecting Fertility," *American Sociological Review*, XII, No. 2 (April, 1947), 175–86.

39. KNAPP, PATRICIA, and CAMBRIA, SOPHIE T. "The Attitudes of Negro Unmarried Mothers toward Illegitimacy," *Smith College Studies in Social Work*, XVII, No. 3 (March, 1947), 185–203.

40. KOSHUK, RUTH PEARSON. "Developmental Records of 500 Nursery School Children," *Journal of Experimental Education*, Vol. XVI (December, 1947).

41. KUHN, ANNE L. *The Mother's Role in Childhood Education: New England Concepts, 1830–1860*. New Haven: Yale University Press, 1947.

42. LANDIS, JUDSON T. "Adjustments after Marriage," *Marriage and Family Living*, IX, No. 2 (spring, 1947), 32.

43. LEVISON, FRANCES. "American Woman's Dilemma," *Life*, XXII (June 16, 1947), 101–16.

44. LEVY, R. J. "Effects of Institutional vs. Boarding Home Care on a Group of Infants," *Journal of Personality*, XV (1947), 233–41.

45. LIPPITT, ROSEMARY. *Psychodrama in the Home*. ("Psychodrama Monographs," No. 22.) Beacon: Beacon House, Inc.

46. LOCKE, HARVEY J. "Predicting Marital Adjustment by Comparing a Divorced and a Happily Married Group," *American Sociological Review*, XII, No. 2 (April, 1947), 187–91.

47. LOOMIS, C. P., BEEGLE, J. A., and LONGMORE, T. W. "Critique of Class as Related to Social Stratification," *Sociometry*, X, No. 4 (November, 1947), 319–37.

48. LOOMIS, STUART D., and GREEN, ARNOLD W. "The Pattern of Mental Conflict in a Typical State University," *Journal of Abnormal and Social Psychology*, XLII, No. 3 (July, 1947), 342–55.

49. LUNDBERG, FERDINAND, and FARNHAM, MARYNIA F. *Modern Woman: The Lost Sex*. New York: Harper & Bros., 1947.

50. MADOW, LEO, and HARDY, SHERMAN E. "Incidence and Analysis of the Broken Family in the Background of Neurosis," *American Journal of Orthopsychiatry*, XVII (July, 1947), 521–28.

51. MEAD, MARGARET. "Age Patterning in Personality Development," *American Journal of Orthopsychiatry*, XVII, No. 2 (April, 1947), 231–40.

52. ———. "What Is Happening to the American Family?" *Journal of Social Casework*, XXVIII (November, 1947), 323–30.

53. MEYER, CHARLENE TRUMBO. "The Assertive Behavior of Children as Related to Parent Behavior," *Journal of Home Economics*, XXXIX, No. 2 (February, 1947), 77–80.

54. MEYER, R. "The Deposed Child," *Archives of Disease in Childhood*, XXII (1947), 86–90.

55. MITCHEL, SUZANNE BERGEL. "Outcome of Family Agency Work with Feebleminded Clients," *Smith College Studies in Social Work*, Vol. XVIII, No. 1 (September, 1947).

56. MOORE, JEAN K. "Speech Content of Selected Groups of Orphanage and Non-orphanage Children," *Journal of Educational Research*, Vol. XVI (December, 1947).

57. ———. *Psychodramatic Treatment of Marriage Problems*. ("Psychodrama Monographs," No. 7.) Beacon: Beacon House, Inc., n.d.

58. MORENO, JACOB L. *Life-Situation Test*. ("Psychodrama Monographs," No 20.) Beacon: Beacon House, Inc., 1947.

59. MOWRER, ERNEST, and MOWRER, HARRIET. "The Marital Adjustment of Twins," *Marriage and Family Living*, IX, No. 2 (May, 1947), 39.

60. MURDOCK, GEORGE P. "Family Universals," *Marriage and Family Living*, IX (November, 1947), 9 ff.

61. NOTTINGHAM, ELIZABETH K. "Effects of Two World Wars on Middle Class Women," *American Sociological Review*, XII, No. 6 (December, 1947), 666–75.

62. PFLEGER, JANET. " 'The Wicked Stepmother' in a Child Guidance Clinic," *Smith College Studies in Social Work*, XVII, No. 3 (March, 1947), 159–84.

63. POPENOE, PAUL. "Recent Trends in American Marriages," *Eugenical News*, XXXII, No. 1 (March, 1947), 9–11.

64. PORTERFIELD, AUSTIN L. "New and Old Themes in the Folkways of the Family," *Marriage and Family Living*, IX (May, 1947), 25–27.

65. PRICE, LOVEL. "Casework with Parents of Feebleminded Children," *Smith College Studies in Social Work*, Vol. XVIII, No. 1 (September, 1947).

66. REMMERS, H. H., and WILTMAN, N. "Attitude Interrelationships of Youth, Their Parents, and Their Teachers," *Journal of Social Psychology*, XXVI (1947), 61–68.

67. RIEMER, SVEND. "Married Veterans Are Good Students," *Marriage and Family Living*, IX (February, 1947), 11–12.

68. RODEHAVER, MYLES. "Fringe Settlement as a Two Directional Movement," *Rural Sociology*, XII, No. 1 (March, 1947), 49–57.

69. ROTENBERG, GERTRUDE. "Can Problem Adolescents Be Aided Apart from their Parents?" *Smith College Studies in Social Work*, XVII, No. 3 (March, 1947), 204–22.

70. SCHULMAN, MARY JEAN, and HAVIGHURST, ROBERT J. "Relations between Ability and Social Status in a Midwestern Community. IV. Size of Vocabulary," *Journal of Educational Psychology*, XXXVIII, No. 7 (November, 1947), 437–42.

71. STRAUSS, ANSELM. "Personality Needs and Marital Choice," *Social Forces*, XXV, No. 3 (March, 1947), 332–35.

72. SULLIVAN, HARRY STACK. *Conceptions of Modern Psychiatry: The First William Alanson White Memorial Lecture.* Washington: William Alanson White Psychiatric Foundation, 1947.

73. TAYLOR, DONALD W. "An Analysis of Predictions of Delinquency Based on Case Studies," *Journal of Abnormal and Social Psychology*, XLII, No. 1 (January, 1947), 45–56.

74. TERMAN, LEWIS M., and ODEN, M. H. *The Gifted Child Grows Up: Twenty-five Years Follow-up of a Superior Group.* Stanford, Calif.: Stanford University Press, 1947.

75. THOMPSON, GEORGE G., and HORROCKS, JOHN E. "A Study of the Friendship Fluctuations of Urban Boys and Girls," *Journal of Genetic Psychology*, LXX (March, 1947), 53–63.

76. TIETZE, CHRISTOPHER. "Human Fertility in Puerto Rico," *American Journal of Sociology*, LIII, No. 1 (July, 1947), 34–40.

77. WAKELEY, RAY E. "Selecting Leaders for Agricultural Programs," *Sociometry*, X, No. 4 (November, 1947), 384–95.

78. WATSON, GOODWIN. *Youth after Conflict.* New York: Association Press, 1947.

79. WINCH, ROBERT F. "Primary Factors in a Study of Courtship," *American Sociological Review*, XII, No. 6 (December, 1947), 658–66.

80. YOUNG, FLORENE M. "Psychological Effects of War on Young Children," *American Journal of Orthopsychiatry*, XVII (July, 1947), 500–510.

81. YOUNG, LOUISE M. (ed.). "Women's Opportunities and Responsibilities," *Annals of the American Academy of Political and Social Science*, CCLI (May, 1947), 1–186.

82. ZIMMERMAN, CARLE C. *Family and Civilization*. New York: Harper & Bros., 1947.

1948

1. ANDERSON, W. A. "The Control of Child-spacing in University Graduate Families," *Rural Sociology*, XIII, No. 3 (September, 1948), 307–14.
2. AUSTIN, MARY C., and THOMPSON, GEORGE G. "Children's Friendships: A Study of the Bases on Which Children Select and Reject Their Best Friends," *Journal of Educational Psychology*, XXXIX, No. 2 (February, 1948), 101–16.
3. AVERY, C. B. "The Social Competence of Pre-school Acoustically Handicapped Children,"*Volta Review*, L (1948), 256–57, 286, 288.
4. BALDWIN, ALFRED L. "Socialization and the Parent-Child Relationship," *Child Development*, XIX, No. 3 (September, 1948), 127–36.
5. BARNETT, JAMES H., and GRUEN, RHODA. "Recent American Divorce Novels, 1938–1945: A Study in the Sociology of Literature," *Social Forces*, Vol. XXVI (March, 1948).
6. BECKER, HOWARD, and HILL, REUBEN (eds.). *Family, Marriage, and Parenthood*. Boston: D. C. Heath & Co., 1948.
7. BECKER, M. "The Effects of Activity Group Therapy on Sibling Rivalry," *Journal of Social Casework*, XXIX (1948), 217–21.
8. BEELEY, ARTHUR L. *Impact of the War on the Family and Children in Metropolitan Salt Lake (Report of the Utah Preparatory Commission)*. ("Publications of the Institute of World Affairs.") Salt Lake City: University of Utah Press, 1948.
9. BROWN, L. GUY. "The Family as a Universal Culture Pattern," *American Journal of Sociology*, LIII, No. 6 (May, 1948), 460–63.
10. BURGESS, ERNEST W. "The Family in a Changing Society," *American Journal of Sociology*, LIII, No. 6 (May, 1948), 417–22.
11. CAMPISI, PAUL J. "Ethnic Family Patterns: The Italian Family in the United States," *American Journal of Sociology*, LIII, No. 6 (May, 1948), 443–49.
12. CAVAN, RUTH SHONLE. "Regional Family Patterns: The Middle Western Family," *American Journal of Sociology*, LIII, No. 6 (May, 1948), 430–31.
13. CEDARQUIST, H. T. "The 'Good Mother' and Her Children," *Smith College Studies in Social Work*, XIX (1948), 1–26.
14. CHRISTENSEN, HAROLD T. "Courtship Conduct as Viewed by Youth," *Journal of Home Economics*, XL, No. 4 (April, 1948), 187–88.
15. ———. "Mormon Fertility: A Survey of Student Opinion," *American Journal of Sociology*, LIII, No. 4 (January, 1948), 270–75.
16. COHEN, BARBARA, and KAPNEK, JOANNE. "When the Family Meets for Meals," *Journal of Home Economics*, XL (1948), 577–78.
17. CONRAD, S. J. "A Study of Preschool Children," *American Journal of Orthopsychiatry*, XVIII (1948), 340–44.
18. COTTRELL, LEONARD S., JR. "The Present Status and Future Orientation of Research on the Family," *American Sociological Review*, XIII, No. 2 (April, 1948), 123–36.

19. Cushing, Hazel M., Phillips, Velma, and Stevenson, Ailcie. "Economic Status of Married College Students," *Journal of Home Economics*, XL, No. 1 (January, 1948), 25–26.

20. Das, Sonya Ruth. *The American Woman in Modern Marriage.* New York: Philosophical Library, 1948.

21. Davis, W. Allison. *Social-Class Influences upon Learning.* Cambrige: Harvard University Press, 1948.

22. Deutsch, Leopold, and Wiener, Louise L. "Children with Epilepsy: Emotional Problems and Treatment," *American Journal of Orthopsychiatry*, XVIII (1948), 65–72.

23. Dickins, Dorothy. "Consumption Patterns of Cotton-Farm Families and an Agricultural Program for the South," *Rural Sociology*, XIII, No. 1 (March, 1948), 22–31.

24. Ellis, Albert. "Questionnaire versus Interview Methods in the Study of Human Love Relationships. II. Uncategorized Responses," *American Sociological Review*, XIII, No. 1 (February, 1948), 61–65.

25. ———. "The Value of Marriage Prediction Tests," *ibid.*, No. 6 (December, 1948), pp. 710–18.

26. Ellsworth, John S., Jr. "The Relationship of Population Density to Residential Propinquity as a Factor in Marriage Selection," *American Sociological Review*, XIII, No. 4 (August, 1948), 444–48.

27. Fernberger, Samuel W. "Persistence of Stereotypes concerning Sex Differences," *Journal of Abnormal and Social Psychology*, XLIII, No. 1 (January, 1948), 97–101.

28. Fisher, Jacob. *Workers and Dependents in Urban Families.* ("Bureau Memos," No. 64.) Washington: Federal Security Agency, Social Security Administration, Bureau of Research and Statistics, 1948.

29. Fisher, Sarah Carolyn. "Relationships in Attitudes, Opinions, and Values among Family Members," *University of California Publications in Culture and Society*, II, No. 2, 29–100. Berkeley and Los Angeles: University of California Press, 1948.

30. Folsom, Joseph K. "Regional Family Patterns: The New England Family," *American Journal of Sociology*, LIII, No. 6 (May, 1948), 423–25.

31. Frank, Lawrence K. "What Families Do for the Nation," *American Journal of Sociology*, LIII, No. 6 (May, 1948), 471–73.

32. Frazier, E. Franklin. "Ethnic Family Patterns: The Negro Family in the United States," *American Journal of Sociology*, LIII, No. 6 (May, 1948), 435–38.

33. Freid, Edrita G., and Stern, Karl. "The Situation of the Aged within the Family," *American Journal of Orthopsychiatry*, XVIII (1948), 31–53.

34. Fuller, Elizabeth Mechem. "Injury-prone Children," *American Journal of Orthopsychiatry*, XVIII (1948), 708–23.

35. Gorer, Geoffrey. *The American People: A Study in National Character.* New York: W. W. Norton & Co., Inc., 1948.

36. Gross, Neal. "Sociological Variation in Contemporary Rural Life," *Rural Sociology*, XIII, No. 3 (September, 1948), 256–69.

37. HAGOOD, MARGARET JARMAN. "Changing Fertility Differentials among Farm-Operator Families in Relation to Economic Size of Farm," *Rural Sociology*, XIII, No. 4 (December, 1948), 363–73.

38. HARE, ALEXANDER P., and HARE, RACHEL T. "Family Friendship within the Community," *Sociometry*, XI, No. 4 (November, 1948), 329–34.

39. HARRIS, D. B. "Social Change in the Beliefs of Adults concerning Parent-Child Relationships," *American Psychologist*, III (1948), 264.

40. HARTLEY, EUGENE L., and KRUGMAN, DOROTHY C. "Note on Children's Social Role Perception," *Journal of Psychology*, XXVI (1948), 399–405.

41. HAY, DONALD G. "A Scale for the Measurement of Social Participation of Rural Households," *Rural Sociology*, XIII, No. 3 (September, 1948), 285–94.

42. HAYNER, NORMAN S. "The Sociologist Views Marriage Problems," *Sociology and Social Research*, XXXIII, No. 1 (September-October, 1948), 20–24.

43. ———. "Regional Family Patterns: The Western Family," *American Journal of Sociology*, LIII, No. 6 (May, 1948), 432–34.

44. HOFFER, CHARLES R. "The Family Doctor Sociometric Relationships," *Sociometry*, XI, No. 3 (August, 1948), 244–45.

45. INGERSOLL, HAZEL L. "A Study of the Transmission of Authority Patterns in the Family," *Genetic Psychology Monographs*, XXXVIII, No. 2 (October, 1948), 225–302.

46. ———. "Transmission of Authority Patterns in the Family," *Marriage and Family Living*, X, No. 2 (spring, 1948), 36.

47. JONES, ROBERT C. "Ethnic Family Patterns: The Mexican Family in the United States," *American Journal of Sociology*, LIII, No. 6 (May, 1948), 450–52.

48. JUDKINS, BARBARA. "Adoptive Parents in a Child Guidance Clinic," *American Journal of Orthopsychiatry*, XVIII (1948), 257–64.

49. JUROVSKY, ANTON. "The Relations of Older Children to Their Parents," *Journal of Genetic Psychology*, LXXII (March, 1948), 85–100.

50. KERSTETTER, LEONA M. "Variability of Audience Responses in the Measurement of Marriage Partner Roles," *Sociatry*, II (1948), 375–84.

51. KINSEY, ALFRED C., POMEROY, W. B., and MARTIN, C. E. *Sexual Behavior in the Human Male*. Philadelphia: W. B. Saunders Co., 1948.

52. KOLB, WILLIAM L. "Sociologically Established Family Norms and Democratic Values," *Social Forces*, XXVI, No. 4 (May, 1948), 451–56.

53. KOLLER, MARVIN R. "Residential and Occupational Propinquity," *American Sociological Review*, XIII (1948), 613–16.

54. KOOS, EARL L. *The Middle Class Family and Its Problems*. New York: Columbia University Press, 1948.

55. ———. "Middle Class Family Crises," *Marriage and Family Living*, X (February, 1948), 25 ff.

56. LANDIS, JUDSON T. "Evaluation of Marriage Education," *Marriage and Family Living*, X, No. 4 (fall, 1948), 81 ff.

57. LOCKE, HARVEY J., and KLAUSNER, WILLIAM J. "Marital Adjustment of Divorced Persons in Subsequent Marriages," *Sociology and Social Research*, XXXIII, No. 2 (November-December, 1948), 97–101.

58. LOOMIS, CHARLES P. "The Most Frequently Chosen Sociogram or the Seduction of Rural Sociologists by the Neighborhood Theory," *Sociometry*, XI, No. 3 (August, 1948), 230–34.

59. LOWRIE, SAMUEL H. "Dating, a Neglected Field of Study," *Marriage and Family Living*, X, No. 4 (fall, 1948), 90.

60. MacNAUGHTON, MARGARET A. "Re the Economic Status of Faculty Families," *Journal of Home Economics*, XL, No. 3 (March, 1948), 133–34.

61. MANGUS, A. R. "Personality Adjustment of Rural and Urban Children," *American Sociological Review*, XIII (October, 1948), 566–75.

62. MEAD, MARGARET. "The Contemporary American Family as an Anthropologist Sees It," *American Journal of Sociology*, LIII, No. 6 (May, 1948), 453–59.

63. NIMKOFF, MEYER, and WOOD, ARTHUR L. "Courtship and Personality," *American Journal of Sociology*, LIII, No. 4 (January, 1948), 263–69.

64. OGBURN, WILLIAM F. "Education, Income, and Family Unity," *American Journal of Sociology*, LIII, No. 6 (May, 1948), 474–82.

65. PHILLIPS, VELMA, CUSHING, HAZEL, and STEVENSON, AILCIE. "Rural Family Life Pattern Affected by Land," *Journal of Home Economics*, XL, No. 6 (June, 1948), 313–14.

66. REIDER, NORMAN. "The Unmarried Father," *American Journal of Orthopsychiatry*, XVIII (1948), 230–37.

67. SAENGER, GERHART, and SHULMAN, HARRY MANUEL. "Some Factors Determining Intercultural Behavior and Attitudes of Members of Different Ethnic Groups in Mixed Neighborhoods," *Journal of Psychology*, XXV (1948), 365–80.

68. SIMSARIAN, FRANCES P. "Self-Demand Feeding of Infants and Young Children in Family Settings," *Mental Hygiene*, XXXII (April, 1948), 217–25.

69. SIRJAMAKI, JOHN. "Culture Configurations in the American Family," *American Journal of Sociology*, LIII, No. 6 (May, 1948), 464–70.

70. SKEELS, HAROLD M., and HARMS, IRENE. "Children with Inferior Social Histories; Their Mental Development in Adoptive Homes," *Journal of Genetic Psychology*, LXXII (June, 1948), 283–94.

71. SLOMAN, SOPHIE SCHROEDER. "Emotional Problems in 'Planned for' Children," *American Journal of Orthopsychiatry*, XVIII (1948), 523–28.

72. SOLOMON, JOSEPH C. "Play Technique," *American Journal of Orthopsychiatry*, XVIII (1948), 402–13.

73. SOWER, CHRISTOPHER. "Social Stratification in Suburban Communities," *Sociometry*, XI, No. 3 (August, 1948), 235–43.

74. STONE, L. GORDON. "Student Problems in a Teachers' College,"

Journal of Educational Psychology, XXXIX, No. 7 (November. 1948), 404–16.

75. TAVES, MARVIN J. "A Direct versus an Indirect Approach in Measuring Marital Adjustment," *American Sociological Review*, XIII, No. 5 (October, 1948), 538–41.

76. THOMPSON, WARREN S. "Differentials in Fertility and Levels of Living in the Rural Population of the United States," *American Sociological Review*, XIII, No. 5 (October, 1948), 516–34.

77. VAN HOUTEN, JANNY. "Mother-Child Relationships in Twelve Cases of School Phobia," *Smith College Studies in Social Work*, XVIII, No. 3 (1948), 161–80.

78. VANCE, RUPERT B. "Regional Family Patterns: The Southern Family," *American Journal of Sociology*, LIII, No. 6 (May, 1948), 426–29.

79. WESSEL, BESSIE BLOOM. "Ethnic Family Patterns: The American Jewish Family," *American Journal of Sociology*, LIII, No. 6 (May, 1948), 439–42.

80. WOLFORD, O. P. "How Early Background Affects Dating Behavior," *Journal of Home Economics*, XL (1948), 505–8.

81. WOOFTER, T. J., JR. "Trends in Rural and Urban Fertility Rates," *Rural Sociology*, XIII, No. 1 (March, 1948), 3–9.

1949

1. AMMONS, R. B., and AMMONS, H. S. "Parent Preferences in Young Children's Doll-Play Interviews," *Journal of Abnormal and Social Psychology*, XLIV, No. 4 (October, 1949), 490–505.

2. ANSHEN, RUTH NANDA (ed.). *The Family: Its Function and Destiny.* New York: Harper & Bros., 1949.

3. BALDWIN, ALFRED L. "The Effect of Home Environment on Nursery School Behavior," *Child Development*, XX (June, 1949), 49–62.

4. BALDWIN, ALFRED L., KALHORN, JOAN, and BREESE, FAY HUFFMAN. *The Appraisal of Parent Behavior.* ("Psychological Monographs," Vol. LXIII, No. 4 [1949].)

5. BIBER, B., and LEWIS, C. "An Experimental Study of What Young School Children Expect from Their Teachers," *Genetic Psychology Monographs*, XL (1949), 3–97.

6. BLAKE, ROBERT R. "The Relation between Childhood Environment and the Scholastic Aptitude and Intelligence of Adults," *Journal of Social Psychology*, XXIX (1949), 37–41.

7. BOSSARD, JAMES H. S., and BOLL, ELEANOR S. "Ritual in Family Living," *American Sociological Review*, XIV, No. 4 (August, 1949), 463–69.

8. BOWMAN, CLAUDE C. "Cultural Ideology and Heterosexual Reality: A Preface to Sociological Research," *American Sociological Review*, XIV, No. 5 (October, 1949), 624–33.

9. BOWMAN, HENRY A. "Marriage Education in the Colleges," *Journal of Social Hygiene*, XXXV (December, 1949), 407–17.

10. BURKS, B. S. *Studies of Twins Reared Apart.* ("Psychological Monographs," Vol. LXIII, No. 5 [1949].)
11. BURMEISTER, EVA. *Forty-five in the Family: A Story of a Home for Children.* New York: Columbia University Press, 1949.
12. BURNS, EVELINE M. *The American Social Security System.* Boston: Houghton Mifflin Co., 1949.
13. CAVAN, RUTH S., BURGESS, ERNEST W., HAVIGHURST, ROBERT J., and GOLDHAMER, HERBERT. *Personal Adjustment in Old Age.* Chicago: Science Research Associates, Inc., 1949.
14. CAVAN, RUTH SHONLE. "Family Life and Family Substitutes in Old Age," *American Sociological Review*, XIV, No. 1 (February, 1949), 71–83.
15. CENTERS, RICHARD. "Marital Selection and Occupational Strata," *American Journal of Sociology*, LIV, No. 6 (May, 1949), 530–35.
16. CHITTENDEN, GERTRUDE E. "Breaking Ground in Family Life Research," *Journal of Home Economics*, XLI, No. 7 (September, 1949), 364–66.
17. COLES, JESSIE, and SHENK, NORMA. "A Study of Family Clothing Expenditures," *Journal of Home Economics*, XLI, No. 4 (April, 1949), 193–94.
18. COMMUNITY SERVICES SOCIETY. *The Family in a Democratic Society: Anniversary Papers of the Community Service Society of New York.* New York: Columbia University Press, 1949.
19. CRUICKSHANK, WILLIAM M., and DOLPHIN, JANE E. "A Study of the Emotional Needs of Crippled Children," *Journal of Educational Psychology*, XL, No. 5 (May, 1949), 295–305.
20. DAMRIN, E. E. "Family Size and Sibling Age, Sex, and Position as Related to Certain Aspects of Adjustment," *Journal of Social Psychology*, XXIX (February, 1949), 93–102.
21. DANIEL, GERTRUDE. "A Community Plans for Better Family Living," *Journal of Home Economics*, XLI, No. 6 (June, 1949), 305–7.
22. DAWE, HELEN C., EKERN, DOROTHY, and BERGER, HARRIET. "Differences in Adult Contacts with Children," *Journal of Home Economics*, XLI, No. 2 (February, 1949), 87–88.
23. EDMISTON, R. W., and BAIRD, FRANCES. "The Adjustment of Orphanage Children," *Journal of Educational Psychology*, XL, No. 8 (December, 1949), 482–88.
24. ELDER, RACHEL ANN. "Traditional and Developmental Conceptions of Fatherhood," *Marriage and Family Living*, XI (summer, 1949), 98–101.
25. ELLIS, ALBERT. "Some Significant Correlates of Love and Family Attitudes and Behavior," *Journal of Social Psychology*, XXX (August, 1949), 3–16.
26. ———. "A Study of Human Love Relationships," *Journal of Genetic Psychology*, LXXV (September, 1949), 61–71.
27. ELLIS, ALBERT, and BEECHLEY, ROBERT M. "Assortative Mating in the Parents of Child Guidance Clinic Patients," *American Sociological Review*, XIV, No. 5 (October, 1949), 678–79.

28. ELLZEY, CLARK W. "Marriage Questionnaire Report," *Marriage and Family Living*, XI, No. 4 (fall, 1949), 133–35.

29. FEINBERG, HENRY. "Achievement of a Group of Children in Foster Homes as Revealed by the Stanford Achievement Test," *Journal of Genetic Psychology*, LXXV (December, 1949), 293–303.

30. FREUD, ANNA, *et al. The Psychoanalytic Study of the Child*, Vols. III–IV. New York: International Universities Press, 1949.

31. GLASS, NETTA. "Eating, Sleeping, and Elimination Habits in Children Attending Day Nurseries and Children Cared for at Home by Mothers," *American Journal of Orthopsychiatry*, XIX (1949), 697–711.

32. GLICK, PAUL C. "Family Life and Full Employment," *American Journal of Sociology*, LIV, No. 6 (May, 1949), 520–29.

33. ———. "First Marriages and Remarriages," *American Sociological Review*, XIV, No. 6 (December, 1949), 726–34.

34. GOODE, WILLIAM J. "Problems in Postdivorce Adjustment," *American Sociological Review*, XIV, No. 3 (June, 1949), 394–401.

35. GRAY, HORACE. "Psychological Types in Married People," *Journal of Social Psychology*, XXIX (May, 1949), 189–200.

36. GREENBERG, JOSEPH H. "Sex Distribution and Marital Status," *Sociology and Social Research*, XXXIII, No. 5 (May-June, 1949), 368–72.

37. GROSS, IRMA H., and EVERETT, ESTHER. "Home Management Is a Family Affair," *Journal of Home Economics*, XLI, No. 3 (March, 1949), 127–29.

38. HAVIGHURST, ROBERT J., and TABA, HILDA, in collaboration with ANDREW W. BROWN, *et al. Adolescent Character and Personality*. New York: John Wiley & Sons, Inc., 1949.

39. HENRY, WILLIAM E. "The Business Executive: The Psychodynamics of a Social Role," *American Journal of Sociology*, LIV, No. 4 (January, 1949), 286–91.

40. HILL, REUBEN, in collaboration with ELISE BOULDING and assisted by LOWELL DUNIGAN and RACHEL ELDER. *Families under Stress: Adjustment to the Crises of War Separation and Reunion*. New York: Harper & Bros., 1949.

41. HIMES, JOSEPH SANDY, JR. "Mate Selection among Negro College Students," *Sociology and Social Research*, XXXIII, No. 3 (January-February, 1949), 204–11.

42. HOLLINGSHEAD, AUGUST B. "Class and Kinship in a Middle Western Community," *American Sociological Review*, XIV, No. 4 (August, 1949), 469–75.

43. ———. *Elmtown's Youth: The Impact of Social Classes on Adolescents*. New York: John Wiley & Sons, Inc., 1949.

44. HOLLIS, FLORENCE. *Women in Marital Conflict*. New York: Family Service Association of America, 1949.

45. HOLWAY, AMY R. "Early Self-regulation of Infants and Later Behavior in Play Interviews," *American Journal of Orthopsychiatry*, XIX, No. 4 (October, 1949), 612–23.

46. JERSILD, ARTHUR T., WOODYARD, ELLA S., and DEL SOLAR, CHARLOTTE, in collaboration with ERNEST G. OSBORNE and ROBERT C. CHALLMAN. *Joys and Problems of Child Rearing.* New York: Bureau of Publications, Teachers College, Columbia University, 1949.

47. JONES, MARY COVER. "Attitudes toward Family Living," *Journal of Home Economics,* XLI, No. 9 (November, 1949), 494–96.

48. KALLMAN, F. J., DEPORTE, E., and FEINGOLD, L. "Suicide in Twins and Only Children," *American Journal of Human Genetics,* I (1949), 113–26.

49. KANNER, LEO. "Problems of Nosology and Psychodynamics of Early Infantile Autism," *American Journal of Orthopsychiatry,* XIX (July, 1949), 416–26.

50. KENT, EDITH. "A Study of Maladjusted Twins," *Smith College Studies in Social Work,* Vol. XIX, No. 2 (February, 1949).

51. KINGSLEY, A., and REYNOLDS, E. L. "The Relations of Illness Patterns in Children to Ordinal Position in the Family," *Journal of Pediatrics,* XXXV (1949), 17–24.

52. KORNER, ANNELIESE F. *Some Aspects of Hostility in Young Children.* New York: Grune & Stratton, 1949.

53. LANDIS, JUDSON T. "Marriages of Mixed and Non-mixed Religious Faith," *American Sociological Review,* XIV, No. 3 (June, 1949), 401–7.

54. LANDIS, PAUL H. "Personality Differences of Girls from Farm, Town, and City," *Rural Sociology,* XIV, No. 1 (March, 1949), 10–20.

55. LENROOT, KATHARINE F. "Children and Youth at Midcentury," *Journal of Home Economics,* XLI, No. 9 (November, 1949), 710–13.

56. LIDZ, R. W., and LIDZ, T. "The Family Environment of Schizophrenic Patients," *American Journal of Psychiatry,* CVI (1949), 332–45.

57. LOCKE, HARVEY J., and MACKEPRANG, MURIEL. "Marital Adjustment and the Employed Wife," *American Journal of Sociology,* LIV, No. 6 (May, 1949), 536–38.

58. LONG, ALMA. "Social Development among Adolescents," *Journal of Home Economics,* XLI, No. 4 (1949), 201–2.

59. LONGMORE, WILSON. "Planning Health Services for Rural Families," *Journal of Home Economics,* XLI, No. 3 (March, 1949), 135–37.

60. LOOMIS, C. P., BAKER, W. B., and PROCTOR, C. "The Size of the Family as Related to the Social Success of Children," *Sociometry,* XII (February-August, 1949), 313–20.

61. MACDONALD, MARGHERITA, MCGUIRE, CARSON, and HAVIGHURST, ROBERT J. "Leisure Activities and the Socioeconomic Status of Children," *American Journal of Sociology,* LIV, No. 6 (May, 1949), 505–19.

62. MANGUS, A. R. "Marriage and Divorce in Ohio," *Rural Sociology,* XIV, No. 2 (June, 1949), 128–37.

63. MARSHALL, DOUGLAS G. "The Decline in Farm Family Fertility and

Its Relationship to Nationality and Religious Background," *Rural Sociology*, XV, No. 1 (March, 1949), 42–49.

64. MEAD, MARGARET. *Male and Female: A Study of the Sexes in a Changing World*. New York: William Morrow & Co., Inc., 1949.
65. MOHR, JENNIE. "Home-making Problems of Working Women," *Smith College Studies in Social Work*, Vol. XIX, No. 1 (February, 1949).
66. MONTGOMERY, JAMES E. "Three Southern Appalachian Communities: An Analysis of Cultural Variables," *Rural Sociology*, XIV, No. 2 (June, 1949), 138–48.
67. MURDOCK, GEORGE PETER. *Social Structure*. New York: Macmillan Co., 1949.
68. NATIONAL CONFERENCE ON FAMILY LIFE, INTERAGENCY COMMITTEE ON BACKGROUND MATERIALS. *The American Family: A Factual Background*. Washington: Government Printing Office, 1949.
69. ORLANSKY, HAROLD. "Infant Care and Personality," *Psychological Bulletin*, XLVI (January, 1949), 1–48.
70. PAN, JU-SHU. "Social Adjustment of Aged People," *Sociology and Social Research*, XXXIII, No. 6 (July-August, 1949), 424–30.
71. PARSONS, TALCOTT. *Essays in Sociological Theory Pure and Applied*. Glencoe, Ill.: Free Press, 1949.
72. PHEARMAN, LEO T. "Comparisons of High-School Graduates Who Go to College with Those Who Do Not," *Journal of Educational Psychology*, XL, No. 7 (November, 1949), 405–14.
73. PICKFORD, R. W. "The Genetics of Intelligence," *Journal of Psychology*, XXVIII (1949), 129–45.
74. POWELL, MIRIAM. "Illegitimate Pregnancy in Emotionally Disturbed Girls," *Smith College Studies in Social Work*, Vol. XIX, No. 3 (June, 1949).
75. QUISENBERRY, RUTH. "Significance of the City Worker's Family Budget," *Journal of Home Economics*, XLI, No. 1 (January, 1949), 11–13.
76. RICHARDS, MARY. "When To Include the Father in Child Guidance," *Smith College Studies in Social Work*, Vol. XIX, No. 2 (February, 1949).
77. ROFF, MERRILL. "A Factorial Study of the Fels Parent Behavior Scales," *Child Development*, XX, No. 1 (March, 1949), 29–45.
78. ROHWER, ROBERT A. "Social Relations in Beginning as a Farm Operator in an Area of Prosperous Commercial Farming," *Rural Sociology*, XIV, No. 4 (December, 1949), 325–35.
79. ROSENCRANZ, MARY LOU LERCH. "A Study of Women's Interest in Clothing," *Journal of Home Economics*, XLI, No. 8 (October, 1949), 460–62.
80. SHEELEY, ARLENE, LANDIS, PAUL H., and DAVIES, VERNON. *Marital and Family Adjustment in Rural and Urban Families of Two Generations*. (Bull. 506 [May, 1949].) Pullman: State College of Washington, Institute of Agricultural Sciences, Agricultural Experiment Stations, 1949.

81. SHOBEN, EDWARD JOSEPH, JR. "The Assessment of Parental Attitudes in Relation to Child Adjustment," *Genetic Psychology Monographs,* XXXIX (1949), 103–48.

82. SKIDMORE, REX A., SMITH, THERESE L., and NYE, DELBERT L. "Characteristics of Married Veterans," *Marriage and Family Living,* XI, No. 3 (summer, 1949), 102.

83. SKODAK, MARIE, and SKEELS, HAROLD M. "A Final Follow-up Study of One Hundred Adopted Children," *Journal of Genetic Psychology,* LXXV (September, 1949), 85–125.

84. SMITH, WILLIAM C. "The Stepmother," *Sociology and Social Research,* XXXIII, No. 5 (May-June, 1949), 342–47.

85. SMITH, WILLIAM M., JR. "So Old Nobody Wants You," *Journal of Home Economics,* XLI, No. 6 (June, 1949), 308–10.

86. SOLAR, C. DEL. *Parents and Teachers View the Child: A Comparative Study of Parents' and Teachers' Appraisals of Children.* New York: Teachers College, Columbia University, 1949.

87. SPERRY, IRWIN, and BAGGS, BETTY COX. "New Techniques for Studying Children," *Journal of Home Economics,* XLI, No. 9 (November, 1949), 723–26.

88. SPITZ, RENÉ A. "The Role of Ecological Factors in Emotional Development in Infancy," *Child Development,* XX, No. 3 (September, 1949), 145–55.

89. STENDLER, CELIA BURNS. *Children of Brasstown.* (Bulletin of the Bureau of Research and Service of the College of Education, Vol. XLVI, No. 59.) Urbana: University of Illinois Press, 1949.

90. TERMAN, LEWIS M., and WALLIN, PAUL. "The Validity of Marriage Prediction and Marital Adjustment Tests," *American Sociological Review,* XIV, No. 4 (August, 1949), 497–504.

91. THOMAS, JOHN L. "The Urban Impact on the American Catholic Family," *American Catholic Review,* X, No. 4 (December, 1949), 258–68.

92. TIETZE, TRUDE. "A Study of Mothers of Schizophrenic Patients," *Psychiatry,* XII, No. 1 (February, 1949), 55–65.

93. TURBEVILLE, GUS, and SCHULER, EDGAR A. "Reading and Reading Interests of Housewives in a Rural County: A Comparison of Library Users and Non-library Users in Families of Leaders and a Cross-section Sample in Lenawee County, Michigan, 1946–1947," *Rural Sociology,* XIV, No. 3 (September, 1949), 220–32.

94. UNDERWOOD, VIRGINIA VAN METER. "Student Fathers with Their Children," *Marriage and Family Living,* XI, No. 3 (summer, 1949), 101 ff.

95. VALIEN, PRESTON, and FITZGERALD, ALBERTA PRICE. "Attitudes of the Negro Mother toward Birth Control," *American Journal of Sociology,* LV, No. 3 (November, 1949), 279–83.

96. WALLIN, PAUL. "An Appraisal of Some Methodological Aspects of the Kinsey Report," *American Sociological Review,* XIV, No. 2 (April, 1949), 197–210.

97. WARNER, W. LLOYD, and ASSOCIATES. *Democracy in Jonesville: A Study in Quality and Inequality.* New York: Harper & Bros., 1949.

98. WATTENBERG, WILLIAM W. "Delinquency and Only Children: Study of a 'Category,'" *Journal of Abnormal and Social Psychology,* XLIV, No. 3 (July, 1949), 356–57.
99. WHELPTON, P. K. "Cohort Analysis of Fertility," *American Sociological Review,* XIV, No. 6 (December, 1949), 735–49.
100. WHITELOCK, FRANCES. "Married Women in Today's Labor Force," *Journal of Home Economics,* XLI, No. 10 (December, 1949), 549–51.
101. WILLIAMS, MELVIN J. "Personal and Familial Problems of High School Youths and Their Bearing upon Family Education Needs," *Social Forces,* XXVII, No. 3 (March, 1949), 279–85.
102. WINCH, ROBERT F. "Courtship in College Women," *American Journal of Sociology,* LV, No. 3 (November, 1949), 269–78.
103. ———. "The Relation between Loss of a Parent and Progress in Courtship," *Journal of Social Psychology,* XXIX (February, 1949), 51–56.
104. WOODSIDE, MOYA. "Psychological and Sexual Aspects of Sterilization in Women," *Marriage and Family Living,* XI, No. 2 (spring, 1949), 72–73.
105. WOOFTER, T. J. "Factors Sustaining the Birth Rate," *American Sociological Review,* XIV, No. 3 (June, 1949), 357–66.
106. YOUNG, GRACE C., and RATHBUN, CONSTANCE. "Security as a Motivation for Early Growth in a Group of Adoptive Children," *Quarterly Journal of Child Behavior,* Vol. I (October, 1949).
107. ZIMMERMAN, CARLE C. *The Family of Tomorrow.* New York: Harper & Bros., 1949.

1950

1. ADAMS, CLIFFORD R. "Evaluating Marriage Prediction Tests," *Marriage and Family Living,* XII, No. 2 (spring, 1950), 55–58.
2. ADAMS, E. M. "The Philosophical Approach to Marriage and Family Research," *Social Forces,* XXIX, No. 1 (October, 1950), 62–64.
3. ADORNO, T. W., FRENKEL-BRUNSWIK, ELSE, LEVINSON, DANIEL J., and SANFORD, R. NEVITT, in collaboration with BETTY ARON, MARCIA HERTZ LEVINSON, and WILLIAM MORROW. *The Authoritarian Personality.* New York: Harper & Bros., 1950.
4. ANDERSON, W. A. *Marriages and Families of University Graduates.* Ithaca: Cornell University Press, 1950.
5. BANHAM, KATHARINE M. "The Development of Affectionate Behavior in Infancy," *Journal of Genetic Psychology,* LXXVI (June, 1950), 283–89.
6. BEALE, CALVIN L. "Increased Divorce Rates among Separated Persons as a Factor in Divorce since 1940," *Social Forces,* XXIX, No. 1 (October, 1950), 72–74.
7. BETTELHEIM, BRUNO, and SYLVESTER, EMMY. "Notes on the Impact of Parental Occupations: Some Cultural Determinants of Symptom Choice in Emotionally Disturbed Children," *American Journal of Orthopsychiatry,* XX (1950), 785–95.
8. BIESANZ, JOHN. "Inter-American Marriages on the Isthmus of Panama," *Social Forces,* XXIX, No. 2 (December, 1950), 159–63.

9. BLUM, LUCILLE HOLLANDER. "Some Psychological and Educational Aspects of Pediatric Practice: A Study of Well Baby Clinics," *Genetic Psychology Monographs*, Vol. XLI (February, 1950).

10. BOSSARD, JAMES H. S. (ed.). "Toward Family Stability," *Annals of the American Academy of Political and Social Science*, Vol. CCLXXII (November, 1950). Philadelphia, 1950.

11. BOSSARD, JAMES H. S., and BOLL, ELEANOR S. *Ritual in Family Living: A Contemporary Study*. Philadelphia: University of Pennsylvania Press, 1950.

12. BRUNNER, EDMUND DE S. *Case Studies of Family Farms*. New York: Columbia University Seminar on Rural Life, 1950.

13. BURGESS, ERNEST W. "The Value and Limitations of Marriage Prediction Tests," *Marriage and Family Living*, XII, No. 2 (spring, 1950), 54–55.

14. COHEN, LILLIAN. "Family Characteristics of Home Owners," *American Journal of Sociology*, LV, No. 6 (May, 1950), 565–71.

15. CRAMER, M. WARD. "Leisure-Time Activities of Economically Privileged Children," *Sociology and Social Research*, XXXIV, No. 6 (July-August, 1950), 444–50.

16. DICKINS, DOROTHY. "The Southern Farm Family in an Era of Change," *Rural Sociology*, XV, No. 3 (September, 1950), 232–41.

17. EDELSTON, H. "Educational Failure with High Intelligence Quotient," *Journal of Genetic Psychology*, Vol. LXXVII (1950).

18. EISSLER, RUTH S., FREUD, ANNA, HARTMAN, H., and KRIS, E. (eds.). *The Psychoanalytic Study of the Child*, Vol. V. New York: International Universities Press, 1950.

19. ELLIS, ALBERT. "Love and Family Relationships of American College Girls," *American Journal of Sociology*, LV, No. 6 (May, 1950), 550–56.

20. ELLIS, ALBERT, and FULLER, EARL W. "The Sex, Love, and Marriage Questions of Senior Nursing Students," *Journal of Social Psychology*, XXI (May, 1950), 209–16.

21. ERIKSON, ERIK H. *Childhood and Society*. New York: W. W. Norton & Co., Inc., 1950.

22. FESTINGER, LEON, SCHACHTER, STANLEY, and BACK, KURT. *Social Pressures in Informal Groups*. New York: Harper & Bros., 1950.

23. FITZSIMMONS, CLEO, and PERKINS, NELLIE L. "The Homemaking Plans of 50 Farm Homemakers," *Rural Sociology*, X, No. 2 (December, 1950), 403–13.

24. GINZBERG, ELI, GINSBURG, SOL W., AXELRAD, SIDNEY, and HERMA, JOHN L. "The Problem of Occupational Choice," *American Journal of Orthopsychiatry*, XX (1950), 166–201.

25. GLICK, PAUL C., and LANDAU, EMANUEL. "Age as a Factor in Marriage," *American Sociological Review*, XV, No. 4 (August, 1950), 517–29.

26. GROSS, LLEWELLYN. "A Hypothesis of Feminine Types in Relation to Family Adjustment," *American Journal of Orthopsychiatry*, XX (April, 1950), 373–81.

27. HARRIS, DALE B., GOUGH, HARRISON G., and MARTIN, WILLIAM E. "Children's Ethnic Attitudes: Relationship to Parental Beliefs concerning Child Training," *Child Development*, XXI (September, 1950), 169–81.
28. HARRIS, IRVING, RAPOPORT, LYDIA, RYNERSON, MARY ANN, and SAMTER, MAX. "Observations on Asthmatic Children," *American Journal of Orthopsychiatry*, XX (1950), 490–505.
29. HAVIGHURST, ROBERT J., and SHANAS, ETHEL. "Adjustment to Retirement: The Fossils—a Case Study," *Sociology and Social Research*, XXXIV, No. 3 (January-February, 1950), 169–76.
30. HOLLINGSHEAD, AUGUST B. "Cultural Factors in the Selection of Marriage Mates," *American Sociological Review*, XV, No. 5 (October, 1950), 619–27.
31. HOMANS, GEORGE C. *The Human Group.* New York: Harcourt, Brace & Co., 1950.
32. HORNEY, KAREN. *Neurosis and Human Growth: The Struggle toward Self-realization.* New York: W. W. Norton & Co., 1950.
33. HOULT, THOMAS FORD, and BOLIN, RUTH SMITH. "Some Factors Involved in High School Friendship Choices," *Sociology and Social Research*, XXXIV, No. 4 (March-April, 1950), 273–79.
34. JACOBSON, PAUL H. "Differentials in Divorce by Duration of Marriage and Size of Family," *American Sociological Review*, XV, No. 2 (April, 1950), 235–44.
35. KARPMAN, BEN (chairman). "The Psychopathic Delinquent Child Round Table, 1949," *American Journal of Orthopsychiatry*, XX (1950), 223–65.
36. KAUFMAN, IRVING, PECK, ALICE L., and TAGIURI, CONSUELO K. "The Family Constellation and Overt Incestuous Relations between Father and Daughter," *American Journal of Orthopsychiatry*, XX (1950), 266–79.
37. KEPHART, WILLIAM M. "Status after Death," *American Sociological Review*, XV, No. 5 (October, 1950), 619–27.
38. KINNEMAN, JOHN A., and McWILLIAMS, RAJEAN. "Family Size of Students at a Teacher's College," *American Sociological Review*, XV (May, 1950), 293–94.
39. KOLB, WILLIAM L. "Family Sociology, Marriage Education, and the Romantic Complex: A Critique," *Social Forces*, XXIX, No. 1 (October, 1950), 65–72.
40. KOMAROVSKY, MIRRA. "Functional Analysis of Sex Roles," *American Sociological Review*, XV, No. 4 (August, 1950), 508–16.
41. KOOS, EARL L. "Class Differences in Family Reactions to Crisis," *Marriage and Family Living*, XII, No. 3 (summer, 1950), 77–85.
42. LANDIS, JUDSON T., POFFENBERGER, THOMAS, and POFFENBERGER, SHIRLEY. "The Effects of First Pregnancy upon the Sexual Adjustment of 212 Couples," *American Sociological Review*, XV, No. 6 (December, 1950), 766–72.
43. LANDIS, PAUL H. "Sequential Marriage," *Journal of Home Economics*, XLII, No. 8 (October, 1950), 625–28.

44. LANDIS, PAUL H. "Sex Education: The Facts about Two Generations," *Clearing House: A Journal for Modern Junior and Senior High Schools,* XXIV (April, 1950), 451–55.

45. LEEVY, J. ROY. "Leisure Time of the American Housewife," *Sociology and Social Research,* XXXV, No. 2 (November-December, 1950), 97–105.

46. LEWIS, GORDON F. "Attitudes toward Contraceptives among Residents of a University Housing Project," *American Sociological Review,* XV (1950), 663–67.

47. LEWIS, OSCAR. "An Anthropological Approach to Family Studies," *American Journal of Sociology,* LV, No. 5 (March, 1950), 468–75.

48. LOOMIS, CHARLES P. "The Nature of Rural Social Systems—a Typological Analysis," *Rural Sociology,* XV, No. 2 (June, 1950), 156–74.

49. McDONAGH, EDWARD C. "Television and the Family," *Sociology and Social Research,* XXXV, No. 2 (November-December, 1950), 113–22.

50. McKEOWN, JAMES E. "The Behavior of Parents of Schizophrenic, Neurotic, and Normal Children," *American Journal of Sociology,* LVI, No. 2 (September, 1950), 175–79.

51. MARCSON, SIMON. "A Theory of Intermarriage and Assimilation," *Social Forces,* XXIX, No. 1 (October, 1950), 75–78.

52. MARKEY, OSCAR B. "A Study of Aggressive Sex Misbehavior in Adolescents Brought to Juvenile Court," *American Journal of Orthopsychiatry,* XX (1950), 719–31.

53. MILLER, HYMAN, and BARUCH, DOROTHY W. "A Study of Hostility in Allergic Children," *American Journal of Orthopsychiatry,* XX (1950), 506–19.

54. MONAHAN, THOMAS P. "The United States Census and Calculations of Age at Marriage," and comment by A. Ross ECKLER, *American Journal of Sociology,* LVI, No. 2 (September, 1950), 180–87.

55. MORRIS, W. W., and NICHOLAS, A. L. "Intrafamilial Personality Configurations among Children with Primary Behavior Disorders and Their Parents: A Rorschach Investigation," *Journal of Clinical Psychology,* XI (1950), 309–19.

56. MOTZ, ANNABELLE BENDER. "Conceptions of Marital Roles by Status Groups," *Marriage and Family Living,* XII (1950), 136 ff.

57. MULLEN, FRANCES A. "Truancy and Classroom Disorder as Symptoms of Personality Problems," *Journal of Educational Psychology,* XLI, No. 2 (February, 1950), 97–109.

58. NEWMAN, SAMUEL C. "The Development and Status of Vital Statistics on Marriage and Divorce," *American Sociological Review,* XV, No. 3 (June, 1950), 426–29.

59. ———. "Trends in Vital Statistics of Marriages and Divorces in the United States," *Marriage and Family Living,* XII, No. 3 (summer, 1950), 89–90.

60. NYE, IVAN. "Adolescent-Parent Adjustment—Rurality as a Variable," *Rural Sociology,* XV, No. 4 (December, 1950), 334–39.

61. ORT, ROBERT S. "A Study of Role-Conflicts as Related to Happiness

in Marriage," *Journal of Abnormal and Social Psychology*, XLV, No. 4 (October, 1950), 691–99.

62. PAN, JU-SHU. "Personal Adjustments of Old People: A Study of Old People in Protestant Church Homes for the Aged," *Sociology and Social Research*, XXXV, No. 1 (September-October, 1950), 3–11.

63. PLANT, JAMES. *The Envelope: A Study of the Impact of the World upon the Child*. New York: Commonwealth Fund, 1950.

64. PRESTON, MALCOLM G., MUDD, EMILY HARTSHORNE, FROSCHER, HAZEL BAZETT, and PELTZ, WILLIAM L. "Some Results from Research at the Marriage Council of Philadelphia," *Marriage and Family Living*, XII, No. 3 (summer, 1950), 104–5.

65. RABBAN, M. "Sex-Role Identification in Young Children in Two Diverse Social Groups," *Genetic Psychology Monographs*, XLII (1950), 81–158.

66. REICHARD, SUZANNE, and TILLMAN, CARL. "Patterns of Parent-Child Relationships in Schizophrenia," *Psychiatry*, Vol. XIII (May, 1950).

67. RIESMAN, DAVID, in collaboration with REUEL DENNEY and NATHAN GLAZER. *The Lonely Crowd: A Study of the Changing American Character*. New Haven: Yale University Press, 1950.

68. ROFF, MERRILL. "Intra-family Resemblances in Personality Characteristics," *Journal of Psychology*, XXX (1950), 199–227.

69. ROSE, ARNOLD M. "The Role of Self-direction in Child Development," *Sociology and Social Research*, XXXIV, No. 6 (July-August, 1950), 424–30.

70. ROY, KATHARINE. "Parents' Attitudes toward Their Children," *Journal of Home Economics*, XLII, No. 8 (October, 1950), 652–53.

71. SCHLEGEL, MARTHA M. "Family Living Vitalizes the Language Arts," *Clearing House: A Journal for Modern Junior and Senior High Schools*, XXIV (January, 1950), pp. 264–70.

72. SEARS, ROBERT R. "Ordinal Position in the Family as a Psychological Variable," *American Sociological Review*, XV, No. 3 (June, 1950), 397–401.

73. ——. "Relation of Fantasy Aggression to Interpersonal Aggression," *Child Development*, Vol. XXI (March, 1950).

74. SEARS, ROBERT R., and WISE, GEORGE W. "Approaches to a Dynamic Theory of Development Round Table, 1949. I. Relation of Cup Feeding in Infancy to Thumbsucking and the Oral Drive," *American Journal of Orthopsychiatry*, XX (1950), 123–38.

75. SIMON, ABRAHAM. "Social and Psychological Factors in Child Placement," *American Journal of Orthopsychiatry*, XX (1950), 293–304.

76. SKODAK, MARIE. "Mental Growth of Adopted Children in the Same Family," *Journal of Genetic Psychology*, LXXVII (September, 1950), 3–9.

77. SKRABANEK, R. L., and PARENTON, VERNON J. "Social Life in a Czech-American Rural Community," *Rural Sociology*, XV, No. 3 (September, 1950), 221–31.

78. STENDLER, CELIA. "Sixty Years of Child Training Practices," *Journal of Pediatrics*, XXXVI (1950), 122–34.
79. STENDLER, CELIA BURNS, and YOUNG, NORMAN. "The Impact of Beginning First Grade upon Socialization as Reported by Mothers," *Child Development*, Vol. XXI (December, 1950).
80. STEWART, ROBERT S. "Personality Maladjustment and Reading Achievement," *American Journal of Orthopsychiatry*, XX (1950), 410–17.
81. STOTT, LELAND H. "Some Environmental Factors in Relation to the Personality Adjustments of Rural Children," *Rural Sociology*, X, No. 4 (December, 1950), 394–403.
82. STOUT, IRVING W., and LANGDON, GRACE. "A Study of the Home Life of Well-adjusted Children," *Journal of Educational Sociology*, XXIII (1950), 442–60.
83. STRAUS, ROBERT. "Excessive Drinking and Its Relationship to Marriage," *Marriage and Family Living*, XII, No. 4 (November, 1950), 79 ff.
84. SUSSMAN, MARVIN B., and YEAGER, HAROLD C., JR. "Mate Selection among Negro and White College Students," *Sociology and Social Research*, XXXV, No. 1 (September-October, 1950), 46–49.
85. SWANSON, G. E. "The Development of an Instrument for Rating Child-Parent Relationships," *Social Forces*, XXIX, No. 1 (October, 1950), 84–90.
86. TERMAN, LEWIS M. "Predicting Marriage Failure from Test Scores," *Marriage and Family Living*, XII (February, 1950), 51–54.
87. THOMAS, JOHN L. "Marriage Prediction in *The Polish Peasant*," *American Journal of Sociology*, LV, No. 6 (May, 1950), 572–77.
88. TIMMONS, BENJAMIN F. "Background Factors in Preparation of Teachers and Leaders in Family Life Education," *Marriage and Family Living*, XII, No. 1 (winter, 1950), 9–10.
89. VAIL, JAMES P., and STAUDT, VIRGINIA M. "Attitudes of College Students toward Marriage and Related Problems. I. Dating and Mate Selection," *Journal of Psychology*, XXX (1950), 171–82.
90. WADE, ANDREW L., and BERREMAN, JOEL V. "Are Ministers Qualified for Marriage Counseling?" *Sociology and Social Research*, XXXV, No. 2 (November-December, 1950), 106–12.
91. WALLIN, PAUL. "Cultural Contradictions and Sex Roles: A Repeat Study," *American Sociological Review*, XV (April, 1950), 288–93.
92. WALLIN, PAUL, and RILEY R. "Reactions of Mothers to Pregnancy and Adjustment of Offspring in Infancy," *American Journal of Orthopsychiatry*, XX (July, 1950), 616–22.
93. WEISSKOPF, EDITH A. "A Transcendence Index as a Proposed Measure in the TAT," *Journal of Psychology*, XXIX (1950), 379–90.
94. WHELPTON, P. K., and KISER, CLYDE V. (eds.). *Social and Psychological Factors Affecting Fertility*, Vol. I. New York: Milbank Memorial Fund, 1950.
95. WHITE, LYNN TOWNSEND, JR. *Educating Our Daughters: A Challenge to the Colleges*. New York: Harper & Bros., 1950.

96. WILLIAMS, CORNELIA D. "College Students' Family Problems," *Journal of Home Economics*, XLII, No. 3 (March, 1950), 179–81.
97. WILSON, PAULINE PARK. *College Women Who Express Futility.* New York: Teachers College, Columbia University, 1950.
98. WINCH, ROBERT F. "Some Data Bearing on the Oedipus Hypothesis," *Journal of Abnormal and Social Psyhcology*, XLV, No. 3 (July, 1950), 481–89.
99. ———. "The Study of Personality in the Family Setting," *Social Forces*, XXVIII, No. 3 (March, 1950), 310–16.
100. WORCESTER, DEAN A., JR., and LAMPINAN, ROBERT J. "Income, Ability, and Size of Family in the United States," *Journal of Political Economy*, LVIII (1950), 436–42.
101. YANKAUER, ALFRED, JR. "The Relationship of Fetal and Infant Mortality to Residential Segregation," *American Sociological Review*, XV, No. 5 (October, 1950), 644–48.
102. ZIMMERMAN, CARLE C. "The Family Farm," *Rural Sociology*, XV, No. 3 (September, 1950), 211–21.
103. ZUKERMAN, JACOB T. "A Socio-legal Approach to Family Desertion," *Marriage and Family Living*, XII (November, 1950), 83.

1951

1. ALBRECHT, RUTH. "The Social Roles of Old People," *Journal of Gerontology*, Vol. VI (April, 1951).
2. ———. "Social Roles in the Prevention of Senility," *ibid.*, Vol. VII (1951).
3. ALEXANDER, THERON. "Certain Characteristics of the Self as Related to Affection," *Child Development*, XXII (December, 1951), 285–90.
4. ANDREWS, ROBERT O., and CHRISTENSEN, HAROLD T. "Relationship of Absence of a Parent to Courtship Status: A Repeat Study," *American Sociological Review*, XVI, No. 4 (August, 1951), 541–44.
5. AUBLE, JACQUELINE FULLER. "Independent Boarding Home Parents," *Journal of Home Economics*, XLIII, No. 10 (December, 1951), 785–87.
6. AUSUBEL, D. P. "Prestige Motivation of Gifted Children," *Genetic Psychology Monographs*, XLIII (1951), 53–117.
7. BARKER, ROGER G., *et al. One Boy's Day: A Specimen Record of Behavior.* New York: Harper & Bros., 1951.
8. BARRON, MILTON L. "Research on Intermarriage: A Survey of Accomplishments and Prospects," *American Journal of Sociology*, LVII, No. 3 (November, 1951), 249–55.
9. BARSCHAK, ERNA. "A Study of Happiness and Unhappiness in the Childhood and Adolescence of Girls in Different Cultures," *Journal of Psychology*, XXXII (1951), 173–215.
10. BEIGEL, HUGO G. "Romantic Love," *American Sociological Review*, XVI, No. 3 (June, 1951), 326–34.
11. BELCHER, JOHN C. "Evaluation and Restandardization of Sewell's Socio-economic Scale," *Rural Sociology*, XVI, No. 3 (September, 1951), 246–55.

12. BEYER, GLENN H. *Housing and Journey to Work.* (Cornell University Agricultural Experiment Station Bull. 877.) Ithaca: Cornell University Agricultural Experiment Station, 1951.

13. BIESANZ, JOHN, and SMITH, LUKE M. "Adjustment of Interethnic Marriages on the Isthmus of Panama," *American Sociological Review,* XVI, No. 6 (December, 1951), 819–22.

14. BISHOP, BARBARA MERRILL. *Mother-Child Interaction and the Social Behavior of Children.* ("Psychological Monographs," Vol. LXV, No. 11 [1951].)

15. BOSSARD, JAMES H. S. "Marrying Late in Life," *Social Forces,* XXIX, No. 4 (May, 1951), 405–8.

16. ———. "Process in Social Weaning: A Study of Childhood Visiting," *Child Development,* XXII, No. 3 (1951), 211–20.

17. ———. "A Spatial Index for Family Interaction," *American Sociological Review,* XVI, No. 2 (April, 1951), 243–45.

18. BOWLBY, JOHN. *Maternal Care and Mental Health.* Geneva: World Health Organization, 1951.

19. BRENNER, R. F. *A Follow-up Study of Adoptive Families.* New York: Child Adoption Research Committee, Inc., 1951.

20. BROWN, JAMES STEPHEN. "Social Class, Intermarriage, and Church Membership in a Kentucky Community," *American Journal of Sociology,* LVII, No. 3 (November, 1951), 232–42.

21. BUKOWSKI, A. F. "Stability of Marriage of Catholic College Graduates," *American Catholic Sociological Review,* XII (1951), 11–16.

22. BURGESS, ERNEST W., and LOCKE, HARVEY J. "Comment on Lowrie's 'Dating Theories and Student Responses,'" *American Sociological Review,* XVI, No. 6 (December, 1951), 843–44.

23. CALIGER, L. "The Determination of the Individual's Unconscious Concept of His Own Masculinity-Femininity Identification," *Journal of Projective Techniques,* XV (1951), 494–510.

24. CUNNINGHAM, RUTH, and ASSOCIATES. *Understanding Group Behavior of Boys and Girls.* New York: Teachers College, Columbia University, 1951.

25. DEEGAN, DOROTHY YOST. *The Stereotype of the Single Woman in American Novels: A Social Study with Implications for the Education of Women.* New York: King's Crown Press, 1951.

26. DONOHUE, WILMA, and TIBBITTS, CLARK (eds.). *Growing in the Older Years.* Ann Arbor: University of Michigan Press, 1951.

27. DOTSON, FLOYD. "Patterns of Voluntary Association among Urban Working-Class Families," *American Sociological Review,* XVI, No. 5 (October, 1951), 687–93.

28. DRUCKER, A. J., and REMMERS, H. H. "Citizenship Attitudes of Graduated Seniors at Purdue University, U.S. College Graduates, and High-School Pupils," *Journal of Educational Psychology,* XLII, No. 4 (April, 1951), 231–35.

29. DUBLIN, LOUIS I., in collaboration with MORTIMER SPIEGELMAN. *The Facts of Life from Birth to Death.* New York: Macmillan Co., 1951.

30. EISSLER, RUTH S., FREUD, ANNA, HARTMAN, H., and KRIS, E. (eds.).

The Psychoanalytic Study of the Child, Vol. VI. New York: International Universities Press, 1951.

31. ELLIS, ALBERT. *The Folklore of Sex.* New York: Charles Boni, 1951.
32. ELLIS, ALBERT, and BEECHLEY, ROBERT M. "A Comparison of Child Guidance Clinic Patients Coming from Large, Medium, and Small Families," *Journal of Genetic Psychology,* LXXIX (September, 1951), 131–44.
33. FABIAN, ABRAHAM A. "Clinical and Experimental Studies of School Children Who Are Retarded in Reading," *Quarterly Journal of Child Behavior,* Vol. III (1951).
34. FORD, CLELLAN S., and BEACH, FRANK A. *Patterns of Sexual Behavior.* New York: Harper & Bros., 1951.
35. FRENKEL-BRUNSWIK, E. "Patterns of Social and Cognitive Outlooks in Children and Parents," *American Journal of Orthopsychiatry,* XXI (1951), 543–58.
36. GELLERMAN, SAUL W. "The Relation between Social Attitudes and a Projected Thema of Frustration by Parents," *Journal of Social Psychology,* XXXIV (November, 1951), 183–90.
37. GOMBERG, M. ROBERT, and LEVINSON, FRANCES T. (eds.). *Diagnosis and Process in Family Counseling: Evolving Concepts through Practice.* New York: Family Service Association of America, 1951.
38. GOODE, WILLIAM J. "Economic Factors and Marital Stability," *American Sociological Review,* XVI, No. 6 (December, 1951), 802–12.
39. GRAHAM, FRANCES K., CHARWAT, WANDA A., HONIG, ALICE S., and WELTZ, PAULA C. "Aggression as a Function of the Attack and the Attacker," *Journal of Abnormal and Social Psychology,* XLVI (1951), 512–20.
40. GRANT, VERNON W. "Preface to a Psychology of Sexual Attachment," *Journal of Social Psychology,* XXXIII (1951), 187–208.
41. GRIFFITHS, W. "Behavior Difficulties of Children as Perceived and Judged by Parents, Teachers, and Children Themselves," *Journal of Home Economics,* XLIII (1951), 794–95.
42. HACKER, HELEN MAYER. "Women as a Minority Group," *Social Forces,* XXX, No. 1 (October, 1951), 60–69.
43. HANDLIN, OSCAR. *The Uprooted: The Epic Story of the Great Migrations That Made the American People.* Boston: Little, Brown & Co., 1951.
44. HARRIS, MARY JORDAN, and STAAB, JOSEPHINE. "The Relationship of Current Net Income to the Socioeconomic Status of Southern Farm Families," *Rural Sociology,* XVI, No. 4 (December, 1951), 353–58.
45. HAVIGHURST, ROBERT J., EATON, WALTER H., BAUGHMAN, JOHN W., and BURGESS, ERNEST W. *The American Veteran Back Home: A Study of Veteran Readjustment.* New York: Longmans, Green & Co., Inc., 1951.
46. HAY, DONALD G. "Social Participation in Four Rural Communities of the Northeast," *Rural Sociology,* XVI, No. 1 (March, 1951), 127–35.

47. HENRY, JULES. "Family Structure and the Transmission of Neurotic Behavior," *American Journal of Orthopsychiatry*, XXI (October, 1951), 800–818.

48. HENRY, JULES, and WARSON, SAMUEL. "Family Structure and Psychic Development," *American Journal of Orthopsychiatry*, XXI (October, 1951), 59–73.

49. HIERONYMUS, A. N. "A Study of Social Class Motivation: Relationships between Anxiety for Education and Certain Socio-economic and Intellectual Variables," *Journal of Educational Psychology*, XLII, No. 4 (April, 1951), 193–205.

50. HILGARD, JOSEPHINE R. "Sibling Rivalry and Social Heredity," *Psychiatry*, Vol. XIV (November, 1951).

51. HILL, GEORGE W., and TARVER, JAMES D. "Indigenous Fertility in the Farm Population of Wisconsin, 1848–1948," *Rural Sociology*, XVI, No. 4 (December, 1951), 359–63.

52. HILL, REUBEN. "Interdisciplinary Workshop on Marriage and Family Research," *Marriage and Family Living*, XII, No. 1 (winter, 1951), 13–28.

53. ———. "Review of Current Research on Marriage and the Family," *American Sociological Review*, XVI, No. 5 (October, 1951), 694–701.

54. HOLLINGSHEAD, AUGUST B. "Age Relationships and Marriage," *American Sociological Review*, XVI, No. 4 (August, 1951), 492–99.

55. HORROCKS, JOHN E., and BUKER, MAE E. "A Study of the Friendship Fluctuations of Preadolescents," *Journal of Genetic Psychology*, LXXVII (June, 1951), 131–44.

56. JACOBSON, A. H. "Conflict in Attitudes toward the Marital Roles of Husband and Wife," *Research Studies of the State College of Washington*, XIX (1951), 103–6.

57. KARPMAN, BENJAMIN, LURIE, LOUIS A., LIPPMAN, HYMAN S., RABINOVITCH, REGINALD S., LOURIE, LAWSON G., and LOWREY, DAVID M. "Psychopathic Behavior in Infants and Children," *American Journal of Orthopsychiatry*, XXI (April, 1951), 223–72.

58. KATES, SOLIS L. "Suggestibility, Submission to Parents and Peers, and Extrapunitiveness, and Impunitiveness in Children," *Journal of Psychology*, XXXI (1951), 233–41.

59. KENT, DONALD P. "Subjective Factors in Mate Selection: An Exploratory Study," *Sociology and Social Research*, XXXV, No. 6 (July-August, 1951), 391–98.

60. KIRKPATRICK, CLIFFORD, and COTTON, JOHN. "Physical Attractiveness, Age, and Marital Adjustment," *American Sociological Review*, XVI, No. 1 (February, 1951), 81–86.

61. KISER, CLYDE V., and WHELPTON, P. K. (eds.). Social and Psychological Factors Affecting Fertility, Vol. II. New York: Milbank Memorial Fund, 1951.

62. KOHLMANN, ELEANORE L. "Teen-Age Interest in Children," *Journal of Home Economics*, XLIII, No. 1 (January, 1951), 23–26.

63. KOLLER, MARVIN R. "Some Changes in Courtship Behavior in Three

Generations of Ohio Women," *American Sociological Review*, XVI, No. 3 (June, 1951), 366–70.

64. LANDIS, PAUL H. *Two Generations of Rural and Urban Women Appraise Marital Happiness* ("Rural Sociology Series on the Family," No. 2; Bull. 524.) Pullman: Washington Agricultural Experiment Stations, Institute of Agricultural Sciences, State College of Washington, 1951.

65. LANGDON, GRACE, and STOUT, IRVING W. *These Well Adjusted Children.* New York: John Day Co., 1951.

66. LITTLE, SUE WARREN, and COHEN, LOUIS D. "Goal Setting Behavior of Asthmatic Children and of Their Mothers for Them," *Journal of Personality*, Vol. XIX (June, 1951).

67. LOCKE, HARVEY J. *Predicting Adjustment in Marriage: A Comparison of a Divorced and a Happily Married Group.* New York: Henry Holt & Co., 1951.

68. LOWRIE, SAMUEL HARMAN. "Dating Theories and Student Responses," *American Sociological Review*, XVI, No. 3 (June, 1951), 334–40.

69. MAAS, HENRY S. "Some Social Class Differences in the Family Systems and Group Relations of Pre- and Early Adolescents," *Child Development*, XXII, No. 2 (June, 1951), 145–53.

70. McGUIRE, CARSON. "Family Backgrounds and Community Patterns," *Marriage and Family Living*, XIII, No. 1 (February, 1951), 160–64.

71. MARCUS, PEGGY. "In-law Relationship Adjustment of Couples Married between Two and Eleven Years," *Journal of Home Economics*, XLIII, No. 1 (January, 1951), 35–37.

72. MARMOR, JUDD. "Psychological Trends in American Family Relationships," *Marriage and Family Living*, XIII, No. 4 (November, 1951), 145–47.

73. MERTON, ROBERT K., WEST, PATRICIA S., JAHODA, MARIE, and SELVIN, HANAN C. (eds.). *Social Policy and Social Research in Housing.* (*Journal of Social Issues*, Vol. VII, Nos. 1–2.) New York: Association Press, 1951.

74. MILNER, ESTHER. "A Study of the Relationship between Reading Readiness in Grade One School Children and Patterns of Parent-Child Interaction," *Child Development*, XXII, No. 2 (June, 1951), 95–113.

75. MONAHAN, THOMAS P. "One Hundred Years of Marriages in Massachusetts," *American Journal of Sociology*, LVI, No. 6 (May, 1951), 534–45.

76. ———. *The Pattern of Age at Marriage in the United States.* 2 vols. Philadelphia: Stephenson Bros., 1951.

77. MOWRER, ERNEST R., and MOWRER, HARRIET. "The Social Psychology of Marriage," *American Sociological Review*, XVI, No. 1 (February, 1951), 27–36.

78. MUDD, EMILY HARTSHORNE. *The Practice of Marriage Counseling.* New York: Association Press, 1951.

79. NIMKOFF, MEYER F. "Technology, Biology, and the Changing Fam-

266   *Identity and Interpersonal Competence*

ily," *American Journal of Sociology*, LVII, No. 1 (July, 1951), 20–26.

80. NOTCUTT, B., and SILVA, A. L. M. "Knowledge of Other People," *Journal of Abnormal and Social Psychology*, XLVI (1951), 30–37.

81. NYE, IVAN. "Adolescent-Parent Adjustment—Socio-economic Level as a Variable," *American Sociological Review*, XVI, No. 3 (June, 1951), 341–49.

82. OGBURN, WILLIAM FIELDING. "How Technology Changes Society," *Sociology and Social Research*, XXXVI, No. 2 (November-December, 1951), 75–83.

83. PHILLIPS, E. L. "Parent-Child Similarities in Personality Disturbances," *Journal of Clinical Psychology*, VII (1951), 188–90.

84. REMMERS, H. H., and DRUCKER, A. J. "Teen-Agers' Attitudes toward Problems of Child Management," *Journal of Educational Psychology*, XLII, No. 2 (February, 1951), 105–13.

85. ROHWER, ROBERT A. "Family Farming as a Value," *Rural Sociology*, XVI, No. 4 (December, 1951), 330–39.

86. ROSE, ARNOLD M. "The Adequacy of Women's Expectations for Adult Roles," *Social Forces*, XXX, No. 1 (October, 1951), 69–77.

87. ROTH, JULIUS, and PECK, ROBERT F. "Social Class and Social Mobility Factors Related to Marital Adjustment," *American Sociological Review*, XVI, No. 4 (August, 1951), 478–87.

88. SCHWARTZ, SHEPARD. "Mate-Selection among New York City's Chinese Males," *American Journal of Sociology*, LVI, No. 6 (May, 1951), 562–68.

89. SEARS, PAULINE S. "Doll Play Aggression in Normal Young Children: Influence of Sex, Age, Sibling Status, Father's Absence," *Psychological Monographs*, LXV, No. 6 (1951), 1–42.

90. SHEFFIELD, ALFRED D., and SHEFFIELD, ADA ELIOT. *The Mind of a "Member": New Bearings for Service to Home and Work Relations.* New York: Exposition Press, 1951.

91. SHUEY, AUDREY M. "Intelligence of College Women as Related to Family Size," *Journal of Educational Psychology*, XLII, No. 4 (April, 1951), 215–22.

92. SKIDMORE, REX A., and McPHEE, WILLIAM M. "The Comparative Use of the California Test of Personality and the Burgess-Cottrell-Wallin Schedule in Predicting Marital Adjustment," *Marriage and Family Living*, XIII, No. 3 (summer, 1951), 121–26.

93. SLIMP, ELEANOR. "Life Experiences of Schizophrenic Children," *Smith College Studies in Social Work*, Vol. XXI (1951).

94. SPERLING, MELITTA. "The Neurotic Child and His Mother: A Psychoanalytic Study," *American Journal of Orthopsychiatry*, XXI, No. 2 (April, 1951), 351–64.

95. STENDLER, CELIA B. "Social Class Differences in Parental Attitudes toward School at Grade I Level," *Child Development*, XXII, No. 1 (March, 1951), 37–47.

96. STERNBERG, HARRIET. "Fathers Who Apply for Child Guidance,"

Smith College Studies in Social Work, Vol. XXII, No. 1 (October, 1951).

97. STOTT, LELAND H. "The Problem of Evaluating Family Success," *Marriage and Family Living,* XIII, No. 4 (November, 1951), 149–53.

98. STOTT, LELAND H., and BERSON, MINNIE P. "Some Changes in Attitudes Resulting from a Preparental Education Program," *Journal of Social Psychology,* XXXIV (November, 1951), 191–202.

99. STOUT, IRVING W., and LANGDON, GRACE. "A Study of the Home Life of Well Adjusted Children in 3 Areas of the U.S." *Journal of Educational Psychology,* XXV (October, 1951), 67–85.

100. STRODTBECK, FRED L. "Husband-Wife Interaction over Revealed Differences," *American Sociological Review,* XVI, No. 4 (August, 1951), 468–73.

101. SUNDAL, A. PHILIP, and MCCORMICK, THOMAS C. "Age at Marriage and Mate Selection: Madison, Wisconsin, 1937–1943," *American Sociological Review,* XVI, No. 1 (February, 1951), 37–48.

102. TARVER, JAMES D. "Age at Marriage and Duration of Marriages of Divorced Couples," *Sociology and Social Research,* XXXVI, No. 2 (November-December, 1951), 102–6.

103. ———. "Trend in Age at Marriage of Wisconsin Men and Women, 1909–1940," *American Sociological Review,* XVI, No. 2 (April, 1951), 246–47.

104. TASCH, RUTH JACOBSON. "The Role of the Father in the Family," *Journal of Experimental Education,* XX (1951), 319–61.

105. TERMAN, L. M. "Correlates of Orgasm Adequacy in a Group of 556 Wives," *Journal of Psychology,* XXXII (1951), 115–72.

106. THOMAS, JOHN L. "The Factor of Relation in the Selection of Marriage Mates," *American Sociological Review,* XVI, No. 4 (August, 1951), 487–91.

107. ———. "Religious Training in the Roman Catholic Family," *American Journal of Sociology,* LVII, No. 2 (September, 1951), 178–83.

108. THORPE, ALICE C. "How Married College Students Manage," *Marriage and Family Living,* XIII (November, 1951), 104–5.

109. THURSTON, JOHN R., and MUSSEN, PAUL H. "Infant Feeding Gratification and Adult Personality," *Journal of Personality,* XIX (June, 1951), 449–58.

110. TURNER, RALPH H. "The Nonwhite Female in the Labor Force," *American Journal of Sociology,* LVI, No. 5 (March, 1951), 438–47.

111. ULLMAN, A. D., DEMONE, H. W., and STEARNS, A. W. "Does Failure Run in Families? A Further Study of One Thousand Unsuccessful Careers," *American Journal of Psychiatry,* CVII (March, 1951), 667–76.

112. VALIEN, PRESTON, and VAUGHN, RUTH E. "Birth Control Attitudes and Practices of Negro Mothers," *Sociology and Social Research,* XXXV, No. 6 (July-August, 1951), 415–21.

113. VINCENT, CLARK E. "Trends in Infant Care," *Child Development,* XXII, No. 3 (September, 1951), 199–210.

114. WHETTEN, NATHAN L. "Suburbanization as a Field for Sociological Research," *Rural Sociology*, XVI, No. 4 (December, 1951), 319–30.

115. WHYTE, WILLIAM H., JR. "The Wives of Management," *Fortune*, XLIV, No. 4 (October, 1951), 86 ff.

116. ——. "The Corporation and the Wife," *ibid.*, No. 5 (November, 1951), pp. 109 ff.

117. WILEY, J. H. "A Scale To Measure Parental Attitudes toward Certain Aspects of Children's Behavior," *Speech Monographs*, XVIII (1951), 132–33.

118. WINCH, ROBERT F. "Further Data and Observations on the Oedipus Hypothesis: The Consequence of an Inadequate Hypothesis," *American Sociological Review*, XVI, No. 6 (December, 1951), 784–95.

119. WINSTEL, BEULAH. "The Use of a Controlled Play Situation in Determining Certain Effects of Maternal Attitudes on Children," *Child Development*, XXII, No. 4 (December, 1951), 299–311.

120. ZETTERBERG, HANS L. "The Religious Conversion as a Change of Social Roles," *Sociology and Social Research*, XXXVII, No. 3 (November-December, 1951), 159–66.

1952

1. ABERLE, DAVID F., and NAEGELE, KASPAR D. "Middle-Class Fathers' Occupational Role and Attitudes toward Children," *American Journal of Orthopsychiatry*, XXII (April, 1952), 366–78.

2. BACH, GEORGE R. "Some Diadic Functions of Childhood Memories," *Journal of Psychology*, XXXIII (1952), 87–98.

3. BARNES, C. A. "A Statistical Study of the Freudian Theory of Levels of Psychosexual Development," *Genetic Psychology Monographs*, XLV (1952), 105–74.

4. BARUCH, DOROTHY W., medical collaboration with HYMAN MILLER. *One Little Boy.* New York: Julian Messner, Inc., 1952.

5. BEE, LAWRENCE S. "Evaluating Education for Marriage and Family Living," *Marriage and Family Living*, XIV, No. 2 (May, 1952), 97–103.

6. BEND, EMIL. "Marriage Offers in a Yiddish Newspaper—1935 and 1950," *American Journal of Sociology*, LVIII, No. 1 (July, 1952), 60–66.

7. BENEDEK, THERESE F. *Psychosexual Functions in Women.* New York: Ronald Press Co., Inc., 1952.

8. BENSON, PURNELL. "The Interests of Happily Married Couples," *Marriage and Family Living*, XIV, No. 4 (November, 1952), 276–80.

9. BERDIE, RALPH F. "The Parent as a Rival Sibling," *Journal of Clinical Psychology*, VIII (1952), 95–96.

10. BIRD, CHARLES, MONACHESI, ELIO D., and BURDICK, HARVEY. "The Effect of Parental Discouragement of Play Activities upon the Attitudes of White Children toward Negroes," *Child Development*, XXIII, No. 4 (December, 1952), 295–306.

11. ——. "Infiltration and the Attitudes of White and Negro Parents

and Children," *Journal of Abnormal and Social Psychology*, XLVII, No. 3 (July, 1952), 687–99.
12. BOSSARD, JAMES H. S., and SANGER, WINOGENE PRATT. "The Large Family System—a Research Report," *American Sociological Review*, XVII, No. 1 (February, 1952), 3–9.
13. BRESSLER, MARVIN. "Selected Family Patterns in W. I. Thomas' Unfinished Study of the Bintl Brief," *American Sociological Review*, XVII, No. 5 (October, 1952), 563–71.
14. BRETSCH, HOWARD S. "Social Skills and Activities of Socially Accepted and Unaccepted Adolescents," *Journal of Educational Psychology*, XLIII, No. 8 (December, 1952), 449–58.
15. BROWN, JAMES STEPHEN. "The Conjugal Family and the Extended Family Group," *American Sociological Review*, XVII, No. 3 (June, 1952), 297–306.
16. ———. *The Farm Family in a Kentucky Mountain Neighborhood.* (Kentucky Agricultural Experiment Station Bull. 587.) Lexington: Kentucky Agricultural Experiment Station, University of Kentucky, August, 1952.
17. ———. *The Family Group in a Kentucky Mountain Farming Community.* (Kentucky Agricultural Experiment Station Bull. 588.) Lexington: Kentucky Agricultural Experiment Station, University of Kentucky, June, 1952.
18. BROWN, LILLIAN PENN, GATES, HELEN D., NOLDER, EVANGELINE L., and VAN FLEET, BARBARA. "Personality Characteristics of Exceptional Children and of Their Mothers," *Elementary School Journal*, LII (1952), 286–90.
19. BUELL, BRADLEY, and ASSOCIATES. *Community Planning for Human Services.* New York: Columbia University Press, 1952.
20. BURGESS, ERNEST W. "Family Living in the Later Decades," *Annals of the American Academy of Political and Social Science*, CCLXXIX (1952), 106–14.
21. BURLINGHAM, DOROTHY. *Twins: A Study of Three Pairs of Identical Twins.* New York: International Universities Press, 1952.
22. BURMA, JOHN H. "Research Note on the Measurement of Interracial Marriage," *American Journal of Sociology*, LVII, No. 6 (May, 1952), 587–89.
23. CARR, LOWELL J., and STERMER, JAMES EDSON. *Willow Run: A Study of Industrialization and Cultural Inadequacy.* New York: Harper & Bros., 1952.
24. CASS, LORETTA KEKEISEN. "An Investigation of Parent-Child Relationships in Terms of Awareness, Identification, Projection, and Control," *American Journal of Orthopsychiatry*, XXII (April, 1952), 305–13.
25. ———. "Parent-Child Relationships and Delinquency," *Journal of Abnormal and Social Psychology*, XLVII, No. 1 (January, 1952), 101–4.
26. CAVA, ESTHER LADEN, and RAUSH, HAROLD L. "Identification and the

Adolescent Boy's Perception of His Father," *Journal of Abnormal and Social Psychology,* XLVII, No. 4 (October, 1952), 855–56.

27. CHRISTENSEN, HAROLD T. "Dating Behavior as Evaluated by High-School Students," *American Journal of Sociology,* LVII, No. 6 (May, 1952), 580–86.

28. CHRISTENSEN, HAROLD T., and PHILBRICK, ROBERT E. "Family Size as a Factor in the Marital Adjustments of College Couples," *American Sociological Review,* XVII, No. 3 (June, 1952), 306–12.

29. CLARKE, ALFRED C. "An Examination of the Operation of Residential Propinquity as a Factor in Mate Selection," *American Sociological Review,* XVII, No. 1 (February, 1952), 17–22.

30. CONNOR, RUTH, and HALL, EDITH FLINN. "The Dating Behavior of College Freshmen and Sophomores," *Journal of Home Economics,* XLIV, No. 4 (April, 1952), 278–81.

31. CUTTS, NORMA E., and MOSELEY, NICHOLAS. *Better Home Discipline.* New York: Appleton-Century-Crofts, 1952.

32. DILLER, JULIET C., and FULLER, EARL W. "Adjusted and Maladjusted Student Nurses," *Journal of Social Psychology,* XXXVI (1952), 45–52.

33. DINKEL, ROBERT M. "Occupation and Fertility in the United States," *American Sociological Review,* XVII, No. 2 (April, 1952), 178–83.

34. DRUCKER, A. J., CHRISTENSEN, HAROLD T., and REMMERS, H. H. "Some Background Factors in Socio-sexual Modernism," *Marriage and Family Living,* XIV, No. 4 (November, 1952), 334–37.

35. DYMOND, ROSALIND F., HUGHES, ANNE S., and RAABE, VIRGINIA L. "Measurable Changes in Empathy with Age," *Journal of Consulting Psychology,* XVI (1952), 202–6.

36. EHRMANN, WINSTON W. "Student Cooperation in a Study of Dating Behavior," *Marriage and Family Living,* XIV, No. 4 (November, 1952), 322–26.

37. EISSLER, RUTH S., FREUD, ANNA, HARTMAN, H., and KRIS, E. (eds.). *The Psychoanalytic Study of the Child,* Vol. VII. New York: International Universities Press, 1952.

38. ELIAS, GABRIEL. "A Measure of 'Homelessness,'" *Journal of Abnormal and Social Psychology,* XLVII, No. 1 (January, 1952), 62–66.

39. ELLIS, ALBERT, and DOORBAR, RUTH R. "Recent Trends in Sex, Marriage, and Family Research," *Marriage and Family Living,* XIV, No. 4 (November, 1952), 338–40.

40. FAIRCHILD, JOHNSON E. (ed.). *Women, Society, and Sex.* New York: Sheridan House, 1952.

41. FISCHER, A. E. "Sibling Relationships, with Special Reference to the Problem of the Second Child," *Journal of Pediatrics,* XL (1952), 254–59.

42. FREEMAN, HOWARD E., and SHOWEL, MORRIS. "Familism and Attitude toward Divorce," *Sociology and Social Research,* XXXVI, No. 5 (May-June, 1952), 312–18.

43. FRENCH, DAVID G. *An Approach to Measuring Results in Social Work: A Report on the Michigan Reconnaissance Study of Evalua-*

tive Research in Social Work Sponsored by the Michigan Welfare League. New York: Columbia University Press, 1952.

44. FRIEDMAN, STANLEY M. "An Empirical Study of the Castration and Oedipus Complexes," *Genetic Psychology Monographs*, XLVI (1952), 61–130.

45. FRUMKIN, ROBERT M. "The Indirect Assessment of Marital Adjustment," *Marriage and Family Living*, XIV, No. 3 (August, 1952), 215–18.

46. GINSBURG, SOL WIENER. "The Psychological Aspects of Eating," *Journal of Home Economics*, XLIV, No. 5 (May, 1952), 325–28.

47. GIST, NOEL P. "Ecological Decentralization and Rural-urban Relationships," *Rural Sociology*, XVII, No. 4 (December, 1952), 328–35.

48. GRACE, HARRY A., and LOHMANN, JOAN JENKINS. "Children's Reactions to Stories Depicting Parent-Child Conflict Situations," *Child Development*, XXIII, No. 1 (March, 1952), 61–74.

49. GRIFFITHS, WILLIAM. *Behavior Difficulties of Children as Perceived and Judged by Parents, Teachers, and Children Themselves.* Minneapolis: University of Minnesota Press, 1952.

50. HARTLEY, RUTH E. *Growing through Play: Experiences of Teddy and Bud.* New York: Columbia University Press, 1952.

51. HARTLEY, RUTH E., FRANK, LAWRENCE K., and GOLDENSON, ROBERT M. *New Play Experiences for Children.* New York: Columbia University Press, 1952.

52. ———. *Understanding Children's Play.* New York: Columbia University Press, 1952.

53. HASTORF, A. H., and BENDER, J. E. "A Caution Restricting the Measurement of Empathic Ability," *Journal of Abnormal and Social Psychology*, XLVII, No. 2 (April, 1952), 574–76.

54. HAVIGHURST, ROBERT J. "Social Class and Basic Personality Structure," *Sociology and Social Research*, XXXVI, No. 6 (July-August, 1952), 355–63.

55. HAWKINS, HAROLD, and WALTERS, JAMES. "Family Recreation Activities," *Journal of Home Economics*, XLIV, No. 8 (October, 1952), 623–26.

56. HELFANT, KENNETH. "Parents' Attitudes vs. Adolescent Hostility in the Determination of Adolescent Sociopolitical Attitudes," *Psychological Monographs*, LXVI, No. 13 (1952), 1–23.

57. HENRY, JULES, and BOGGS, JOAN WHITEHORN. "Child Rearing, Culture, and the Natural World," *Psychiatry*, XV, No. 3 (August, 1953), 261–71.

58. HENTIG, HANS VON. "The Sex Ratio—a Brief Discussion Based on United States Census Figures," *Social Forces*, XXX, No. 4 (May, 1952), 443–49.

59. HERBERT, ELIZABETH SWEENEY. "When the Homemaker Goes To Work," *Journal of Home Economics*, XLIV, No. 4 (April, 1952), 257–59.

60. HILL, G. W., and TARVER, J. D. "Marriage and Divorce Trends in

Wisconsin, 1915–45," *Milbank Memorial Fund Quarterly*, XXX (January, 1952), 5–17.

61. HIMES, JOSEPH S., JR. "Value Consensus in Mate Selection among Negroes," *Marriage and Family Living*, XIV, No. 4 (November, 1952), 317–21.

62. HOLLINGSHEAD, AUGUST B. "Marital Status and Wedding Behavior," *Marriage and Family Living*, XIV, No. 4 (November, 1952), 308–11.

63. HOPSON, ARTHUR. "The Relationship of Migratory Marriages to Divorce in Tennessee," *Social Forces*, XXX, No. 4 (May, 1952), 449–55.

64. HULSE, WILFRED C. "Childhood Conflict Expressed through Family Drawings," *Journal of Projective Techniques*, XVI (1952), 66–79.

65. ISCH, MARIA JEFFRE. "Fantasied Mother-Child Interaction in Doll Play," *Journal of Genetic Psychology*, LXXXI (December, 1952), 233–58.

66. ITKIN, WILLIAM. "Some Relationships between Intra-family Attitudes and Pre-parental Attitudes toward Children," *Journal of Genetic Psychology*, LXXX (June, 1952), 221–52.

67. JACOBSON, ALVER HILDING. "Conflict of Attitudes toward the Roles of the Husband and Wife in Marriage," *American Sociological Review*, XVII, No. 2 (April, 1952), 146–50.

68. JANSEN, LUTHER T. "Measuring Family Solidarity," *American Sociological Review*, XVII, No. 6 (December, 1952), 727–33.

69. JENSEN, OLIVER. *The Revolt of American Women: A Pictorial History of the Century of Change from Bloomers to Bikinis—from Feminism to Freud.* New York: Harcourt, Brace & Co., 1952.

70. JOHNSON, ELMER H. "Family Privacy in a Multi-unit Dwelling," *Marriage and Family Living*, XIV, No. 3 (August, 1952), 219–25.

71. JOHNSON, THOMAS F. "Conceptions of Parents Held by Adolescents," *Journal of Abnormal and Social Psychology*, XLVII, No. 4 (October, 1952), 783–89.

72. KALLMAN, FRANZ J., and BONDY, EVA. "Applicability of the Twin Study Method in the Analysis of Variations in Mate Selection and Marital Adjustment," *American Journal of Human Genetics*, IV (1952), 209–22.

73. KENNEDY, RUBY JO REEVES. "Single or Triple Melting-Pot? Intermarriage in New Haven, 1870–1950," *American Journal of Sociology*, LVIII, No. 1 (July, 1952), 56–59.

74. KEPHART, WILLIAM M., and MONAHAN, THOMAS P. "Desertion and Divorce in Philadelphia," *American Sociological Review*, XVII, No. 6 (December, 1952), 719–27.

75. KEPHART, WILLIAM M., and STROHM, ROLF B. "The Stability of Gretna Green Marriages," *Sociology and Social Research*, XXXVI, No. 5 (May-June, 1952), 291–96.

76. KING, CHARLES E. "The Burgess-Cottrell Method of Measuring Marital Adjustment Applied to a Non-white Southern Urban Population," *Marriage and Family Living*, XIV, No. 4 (November, 1952), 280–85.

77. KLATSKIN, ETHELYN HENRY. "Shifts in Child Care Practices in Three Social Classes under an Infant Care Program of Flexible Methodology," *American Journal of Orthopsychiatry*, XXII (1952), 52–61.

78. KLUCKHOHN, FLORENCE R. "American Family, Past and Present, and America's Women." In MOWRER, O. H. (ed.), *Patterns for Modern Living*, Part I: *Psychological Patterns*, pp. 25–140. Chicago: Delphian Society, 1952.

79. KORNITZER, MARGARET. *Child Adoption in the Modern World.* New York: Philosophical Library, 1952.

80. LANGDON, GRACE, and STOUT, IRVING W. *The Discipline of Well-adjusted Children.* New York: John Day Co., 1952.

81. LASKO, JOAN KALHORN. "Parent-Child Relationships: Report from the Fels Research Institute," *American Journal of Orthopsychiatry*, XXII (April, 1952), 300–304.

82. LEE, EVERETT S., and LEE, ANNE S. "The Differential Fertility of the American Negro," *American Sociological Review*, XVII, No. 4 (August, 1952), 437–47.

83. LEE, MARGIE ROBINSON. "Background Factors Related to Sex Information and Attitudes," *Journal of Educational Psychology*, XLIII, No. 8 (December, 1952), 467–85.

84. LEE, ROSE HUM. "Delinquent, Neglected, and Dependent Chinese Boys and Girls of the San Francisco Bay Region," *Journal of Social Psychology*, XXXVI (1952), 15–34.

85. LEVY, DAVID M., and HESS, AUDREY. "Problems in Determining Maternal Attitudes toward Newborn Infants," *Psychiatry*, XV, No. 3 (August, 1952), 273–86.

86. LILLYWHITE, JOHN D. "Rural-urban Differentials in Divorce," *Rural Sociology*, XVII, No. 4 (December, 1952), 348–55.

87. LLOYD, R. GRANN. "Parent-Youth Conflicts of College Students," *Sociology and Social Research*, XXXVI, No. 4 (March-April, 1952), 227–30.

88. LOCKE, HARVEY J., and KARLSSON, GEORG. "Marital Adjustment and Prediction in Sweden and the United States," *American Sociological Review*, XVII, No. 1 (February, 1952), 10–17.

89. LOWRIE, SAMUEL HARMON. "Sex Differences and Age of Initial Dating," *Social Forces*, XXX, No. 4 (May, 1952), 456–61.

90. LU, YI-CHUANG. "Marital Roles and Marriage Adjustment," *Sociology and Social Research*, XXXVI, No. 6 (July-August, 1952), 364–68.

91. ——. "Parent-Child Relationship and Marital Roles," *American Sociological Review*, XVII, No. 3 (June, 1952), 357–61.

92. ——. "Parental Role and Parent-Child Relationship," *Marriage and Family Living*, XIV, No. 4 (November, 1952), 294–97.

93. ——. "Predicting Roles in Marriage," *American Journal of Sociology*, LVIII, No. 1 (July, 1952), 51–55.

94. MCGUIRE, J. CARSON. "Family Life in Lower and Middle Class Homes," *Marriage and Family Living*, XIV, No. 1 (February, 1952), 1–6.

95. McGuire, J. Carson. "Conforming, Mobile, and Divergent Families," *ibid.*, No. 2 (May, 1952), pp. 109–15.
96. Marchand, Jean, and Langford, Louise. "Adjustments of Married Students," *Journal of Home Economics*, XLIV, No. 2 (February, 1952), pp. 113–14.
97. Marcson, Simon. "Intermarriage and Generational Status," *Phylon*, XII (1951), 357–63.
98. Maslow, A. H., and Sakoda, J. M. "Volunteer-Error in the Kinsey Study," *Journal of Abnormal and Social Psychology*, XLVII (1952), 259–62.
99. Monahan, Thomas P. "How Stable Are Remarriages?" *American Journal of Sociology*, LVIII, No. 3 (November, 1952), 280–88.
100. Motz, Annabelle Bender. "The Role Conception Inventory: A Tool for Research in Social Psychology," *American Sociological Review*, XVII, No. 4 (August, 1952), 465–71.
101. Nelson, Lowry. "Education and the Changing Size of Mormon Families," *Rural Sociology*, XVII, No. 4 (December, 1952), 335–42.
102. Nowlis, Vincent. "The Search for Significant Concepts in a Study of Parent-Child Relationships," *American Journal of Orthopsychiatry*, XXII (April, 1952), 286–99.
103. Nye, Ivan. "Adolescent-Parent Adjustment: Age, Sex, Sibling Number, Broken Homes, and Employed Mothers as Variables," *Marriage and Family Living*, XIV, No. 4 (November, 1952), 327–32.
104. Ort, Robert S. "A Study of Role-Conflicts as Related to Class Level," *Journal of Abnormal and Social Psychology*, XLVII, No. 2 (April, 1952), 425–32.
105. Pan, Ju-Shu. "A Comparison of Factors in the Personal Adjustment of Old People in the Protestant Church Homes for the Aged and Old People Living Outside of Institutions," *Journal of Social Psychology*, XXXV (1952), 195–203.
106. Pfeiffer, Marie Stoll, and Scott, Dorothy D. "Factors in Family Happiness and Unity," *Journal of Home Economics*, XLIV, No. 6 (June, 1952), 413–14.
107. Poffenberger, Shirley, Poffenberger, Thomas, and Landis, Judson T. "Intent toward Conception and the Pregnancy Experience," *American Sociological Review*, XVII, No. 5 (October, 1952), 616–20.
108. Powell, Reed M. "Sociometric Analysis of Informal Groups—Their Structure and Function in Two Contrasting Communities," *Sociometry*, XV, Nos. 3–4 (August-November, 1952), 367–99.
109. Preston, Malcolm G., Peltz, William L., Mudd, Emily Hartshorne, and Froscher, Hazel B. "Impressions of Personality as a Function of Marital Conflict," *Journal of Abnormal and Social Psychology*, XLVII, No. 2 (April, 1952), 326–36.
110. Radke-Yarrow, Marian, Trager, Helen, and Miller, Jean. "The Role of Parents in the Development of Children's Ethnic Attitudes," *Child Development*, XXIII, No. 1 (March, 1952), 13–53.
111. Rockwood, Lemo D. "A Proposal for the Direction of Family Life

Research in the Next Decade," *Journal of Home Economics,* XLIV (January, 1952), 23–27.

112. SCHNEPP, GERALD J., and JOHNSON, MARY MARGARET. "Do Religious Background Factors Have Predictive Value?" *Marriage and Family Living,* XIV, No. 4 (November, 1952), 301–4.

113. SCHNEPP, GERALD J., and ROBERTS, LOUIS A. "Residential Propinquity and Mate Selection on a Parish Basis," *American Journal of Sociology,* LVIII, No. 1 (July, 1952), 45–50.

114. SCHOEPPE, AILEEN, HAGGARD, ERNEST A., and HAVIGHURST, ROBERT J. "Some Factors Affecting Sixteen-Year-Olds' Success in Five Developmental Tasks," *Journal of Abnormal and Social Psychology,* XLVII, No. 4 (October, 1952), 42–52.

115. SCHOEPPE, AILEEN, and HAVIGHURST, ROBERT J. "A Validation of Development and Adjustment Hypotheses of Adolescence," *Journal of Educational Psychology,* XLIII, No. 6 (October, 1952), 339–53.

116. SEWELL, WILLIAM H. "Infant Training and the Personality of the Child," *American Journal of Sociology,* LVIII, No. 2 (September, 1952), 150–59.

117. SEWELL, WILLIAM H., and MUSSEN, PAUL H. "The Effects of Feeding, Weaning, and Scheduling Procedures on Childhood Adjustment and the Formation of Oral Symptoms," *Child Development,* XXIII, No. 3 (September, 1952), 185–91.

118. SHELDON, WILLIAM D., and CARRILLO, LAWRENCE. "Relation of Parents, Home, and Certain Developmental Characteristics to Children's Reading Ability," *Elementary School Journal,* LII (1952), 262–70.

119. SMITH, WILLIAM M., JR. "Rating and Dating: A Re-study," *Marriage and Family Living,* XIV, No. 4 (November, 1952), 312–17.

120. SOPCHAK, ANDREW L. "Parental 'Identification' and 'Tendency toward Disorders' as Measured by the Minnesota Multiphasic Personality Inventory," *Journal of Abnormal and Social Psychology,* XLVII, No. 2 (April, 1952), 159–65.

121. SPAULDING, CHARLES B. "A Patterned Response to Segregation of the Sexes," *Sociology and Social Research,* XXXVII, No. 2 (November-December, 1952), 92–97.

122. SPERRY, IRWIN V. "Cooperative Research in Family Life," *Journal of Home Economics,* XLIV, No. 3 (March, 1952), 177–80.

123. STAPLES, RUTH. "Appreciations and Dislikes Regarding Grandmothers as Expressed by Granddaughters," *Journal of Home Economics,* XLIV, No. 5 (May, 1952), 340–43.

124. STAUDT, VIRGINIA M. "Attitudes of College Students toward Marriage and Related Problems. II. Age, Educational, Familial, and Economic Factors in Marriage," *Journal of Psychology,* XXXIV, No. 2 (1952), 95–106.

125. STENDLER, CELIA BURNS. "Critical Periods in Socialization and Overdependency," *Child Development,* XXIII, No. 1 (March, 1952), 3–12.

126. STRODTBECK, FRED L. "The Interaction of a 'Henpecked' Husband

and His Wife," *Marriage and Family Living*, XIV, No. 4 (November, 1952), 305–8.

127. TARVER, JAMES D. "Intra-family Farm Succession Practices," *Rural Sociology*, XVII, No. 3 (September, 1952), 267–71.

128. TAVES, MARVIN J. "Farm versus Village Living: A Decade of Change," *Rural Sociology*, XVII, No. 1 (March, 1952), 47–55.

129. TAYLOR, PAULINE S. "The Employment of Rural Women," *Journal of Home Economics*, XLIV, No. 1 (January, 1952), 16–18.

130. TURBEVILLE, GUS. "The Negro Population in Duluth, Minnesota, 1950," *Sociology and Social Research*, XXXVI, No. 4 (March-April, 1952), 231–38.

131. TURNER, RALPH H. "Children and Women's Work," *Sociology and Social Research*, XXXVI, No. 6 (July-August, 1952), 377–81.
Children," *Journal of Abnormal and Social Psychology*, XLVII, No.

132. UĞUREL-SEMIN, REFIA. "Moral Behavior and Moral Judgment of 2 (April, 1952), 463–74.

133. WALLIN, PAUL. "Two Conceptions of the Relation between Love and Idealization," *Research Studies of the State College of Washington*, XX (1952), 21–35.

134. WALTERS, JAMES, and OJEMANN, RALPH H. "A Study of the Components of Adolescent Attitudes concerning the Role of Women," *Journal of Social Psychology*, XXXV (1952), 101–10.

135. WHELPTON, P. K., and KISER, CLYDE (eds.). *Social and Psychological Factors Affecting Fertility*, Vol. III. New York: Milbank Memorial Fund, 1952.

136. WHITE, ROBERT W. *Lives in Progress: A Study in the Natural Growth of Personality*. New York: Dryden Press, 1952.

137. WILLIAMS, MELVIN J. "Counseling with Parents and Teachers on the Preschool Level," *Marriage and Family Living*, XIV, No. 1 (February, 1952), 19–22.

138. WILLIAMSON, ROBERT C. "Economic Factors in Marital Adjustment," *Marriage and Family Living*, XIV, No. 4 (November, 1952), 298–301.

139. WITMER, HELEN LELAND, and KOTINSKY, RUTH (eds.). *Personality in the Making: The Fact-finding Report of the Midcentury White House Conference on Children and Youth*. New York: Harper & Bros., 1952.

1953

1. ADLER, LETA McKINNEY. "The Relationship of Marital Status to Incidence of and Recovery from Mental Illness," *Social Forces*, XXXII, No. 2 (December, 1953), 185–94.

2. ALBRECHT, RUTH. "Relationships of Older People with Their Own Parents," *Marriage and Family Living*, XV, No. 4 (November, 1953), 296–98.

3. ANDERSON, W. A. "Some Factors Associated with Family Informal Participation." (Mimeograph Bull. 36.) Ithaca: Cornell University Agricultural Experimental Station, Department of Rural Sociology, 1953.

4. BEIER, ERNEST G., and RATZEBURG, FRED. "The Parental Identifications of Male and Female College Students," *Journal of Abnormal and Social Psychology*, XLVIII, No. 4 (October, 1953), 569–72.

5. BENDER, I. E., and HASTORF, A. H. "On Measuring Generalized Empathic Ability (Social Sensitivity)," *Journal of Abnormal and Social Psychology*, XLVIII, No. 4 (October, 1953), 503–6.

6. BENNETT, THELMA, and WALTERS, JAMES. "Personal and Social Adjustment of College Home Economics Freshmen," *Journal of Home Economics*, XLV, No. 1 (January, 1953), 29–31.

7. BLOOD, ROBERT O., JR. "Consequences of Permissiveness for Parents of Young Children," *Marriage and Family Living*, XV, No. 3 (August, 1953), 209–12.

8. ———. "A Situational Approach to the Study of Permissiveness in Child-rearing," *American Sociological Review*, XVIII, No. 1 (February, 1953), 84–87.

9. BOODISH, HYMAN. "An Experiment in Group Counseling on Marriage and the Family," *Marriage and Family Living*, XV, No. 2 (May, 1953), 121–25.

10. BOSSARD, JAMES H. S. *Parent and Child: Studies in Family Behavior.* Philadelphia: University of Pennsylvania Press, 1953.

11. BOWERMAN, CHARLES E. "Assortative Mating by Previous Marital Status: Seattle, 1939–1946," *American Sociological Review*, XVIII, No. 2 (April, 1953), 170–77.

12. BROWN, MURIEL W. *With Focus on Family Living: The Story of Four Experiments in Community Organization for Family Life Education.* Washington: Government Printing Office, 1953.

13. BURGESS, ERNEST W., and WALLIN, PAUL. *Engagement and Marriage.* Philadelphia: J. B. Lippincott Co., 1953.

14. CHRISTENSEN, HAROLD T. "Rural-urban Differences in the Spacing of the First Birth from Marriage: A Repeat Study," *Rural Sociology*, XVIII (1953), 60.

15. ———. "Studies in Child Spacing. I. Premarital Pregnancy as Measured by the Spacing of the First Birth from Marriage," *American Sociological Review*, XVIII, No. 1 (February, 1953), 53–59.

16. CHRISTENSEN, HAROLD T., ANDREWS, ROBERT, and FREISSER, SOPHIE. "Falsification of Age at Marriage," *Marriage and Family Living*, XV, No. 4 (November, 1953), 301–4.

17. CHRISTENSEN, HAROLD T., and BOWDEN, OLIVE P. "Studies in Child Spacing. II. The Time-Interval between Marriage of Parents and Birth of Their First Child, Tippecanoe County, Indiana," *Social Forces*, XXXI, No. 4 (May, 1953), 346–51.

18. CHRISTENSEN, HAROLD T., and MEISSNER, HANNA H. "Studies in Child Spacing. III. Premarital Pregnancy as a Factor in Divorce," *American Sociological Review*, XVIII, No. 6 (December, 1953), 641–44.

19. CLEMENS, A. H. *The Cana Movement in the United States: Summary of a Survey Made under the Auspices of the Marriage Coun-*

seling Center of the Catholic University of America. Washington: Catholic University of America Press, 1953.

20. Cowles, May L. "Changes in Family Personnel, Occupational Status, and Housing Occurring over the Farm Family's Life Cycle," *Rural Sociology*, XVIII, No. 1 (March, 1953), 35–44.

21. Crist, John R. "High School Dating as a Behavior System," *Marriage and Family Living*, XV, No. 1 (February, 1953), 23–28.

22. Despert, J. Louise. *Children of Divorce*. New York: Doubleday & Co., 1953.

23. Ditzion, Sidney. *Marriage, Morals, and Sex in America: A History of Ideas*. New York: Bookman Associates, 1953.

24. Dymond, Rosalind. "The Relation of Accuracy of Perception of the Spouse and Marital Happiness," *American Psychologist*, VIII (1953), 344.

25. Eissler, Ruth S., Freud, Anna, Hartman, H., and Kris, E. (eds.). *The Psychoanalytic Study of the Child*, Vol. VIII. New York: International Universities Press, 1953.

26. Elias, G. *Family Adjustment Test*. Chicago: Psychometric Affiliates, 1953.

27. Ellingson, R. J. "Response to Physiological Stress in Normal and Behavior Problem Children," *Journal of Genetic Psychology*, LXXXIII (September, 1953), 19–29.

28. Farber, Maurice L. "English and Americans: Values in the Socialization Process," *Journal of Psychology*, XXXVI (1953), 243–50.

29. Feinberg, Mortimer R. "Relation of Background Experience to Social Acceptance," *Journal of Abnormal and Social Psychology*, XLVIII, No. 2 (April, 1953), 206–14.

30. Fischer, Paul H. "An Analysis of the Primary Group," *Sociometry*, XVI, No. 3 (August, 1953), 272–76.

31. Folger, John, and Rowan, John. "Migration and Marital Status in Ten Southeastern Cities," *Social Forces*, XXXII, No. 2 (December, 1953), 178–85.

32. Foote, Nelson N. "Love," *Psychiatry*, XVI, No. 3 (August, 1953), 245–51.

33. Freeman, Howard E., and Showel, Morris. "The Role of the Family in the Socialization Process," *Journal of Social Psychology*, XXXVII (1953), 97–101.

34. Frumkin, Robert M. "The Kirkpatrick Scale of Family Interests as an Instrument for the Indirect Assessment of Marital Adjustment," *Marriage and Family Living*, XV, No. 1 (February, 1953), 35–37.

35. ———. "A Use of Imaginative Reconstruction in the Indirect Assessment of Marital Adjustment," *Sociology and Social Research*, XXXVIII, No. 2 (November-December, 1953), 84–88.

36. Golden, Joseph. "Characteristics of the Negro-White Intermarried in Philadelphia," *American Sociological Review*, XVIII, No. 2 (April, 1953), 177–83.

37. Havighurst, Robert J., and Albrecht, Ruth. *Older People*. New York: Longmans, Green & Co., Inc., 1953.

38. HOFFMAN, MARTIN L. "Some Psychodynamic Factors in Compulsive Conformity," *Journal of Abnormal and Social Psychology*, XLVIII, No. 3 (April, 1953), 383–93.

39. HONIGMANN, JOHN J. "A Comparative Analysis of Divorce," *Marriage and Family Living*, XV, No. 1 (February, 1953), 37–43.

40. IOWA STATE DEPARTMENT OF HEALTH, DIVISION OF VITAL STATISTICS. *Marriage and Divorce in Iowa*. (Excerpted from the 1952 *Annual Report*.) Des Moines: Division of Vital Statistics, Iowa State Department of Health, 1953.

41. JACO, E. GARTLY, and BALKNAP, IVAN. "Is a New Family Form Emerging in the Urban Fringe?" *American Sociological Review*, XVIII, No. 5 (October, 1953), 551–57.

42. KERCKHOFF, RICHARD K. "The Profession of Marriage Counseling as Viewed by Members of Four Allied Professions: A Study in the Sociology of Occupations," *Marriage and Family Living*, XV, No. 4 (November, 1953), 340–44.

43. KEYFITZ, NATHAN. "A Factorial Arrangement of Comparisons of Family Size," *American Journal of Sociology*, LVIII, No. 5 (March, 1953), 470–80.

44. KING, CHARLES E. "Marital Adjustment in a Southern Urban Minority Population," *Sociology and Social Research*, XXXVII, No. 6 (July-August, 1953), 399–402.

45. KINSEY, ALFRED C., POMEROY, WARDELL B., MARTIN, CLYDE E., and GEBHARD, PAUL H. *Sexual Behavior in the Human Female*. Philadelphia: W. B. Saunders Co., 1953.

46. KITAGAWA, EVELYN M. "Differential Fertility in Chicago, 1920–1940," *American Journal of Sociology*, LVIII, No. 5 (March, 1953), 481–92.

47. KNOBLOCK, HILDA, and PASAMANICK, BENJAMIN. "Further Observations on the Behavioral Development of Negro Children," *Journal of Genetic Psychology*, LXXXIII (September, 1953), 137–57.

48. KOMAROVSKY, MIRRA. *Women in the Modern World: Their Education and Their Dilemmas*. Boston: Little, Brown & Co., 1953.

49. KYRK, HAZEL. *The Family in the American Economy*. Chicago: University of Chicago Press, 1953.

50. LANDIS, PAUL H. *The Broken Home in Teenage Adjustments*. (Washington Agricultural Experiment Stations Bull. 542.) Pullman: Washington Agricultural Experiment Stations, 1953.

51. LEHMAN, RUTH T. "The Married Home Economics Graduate, 1900–1950," *Marriage and Family Living*, XV, No. 4 (November, 1953), 322–24.

52. LONGWORTH, DONALD S. "Critique of Attempts To Evaluate Marriage Teaching," *Marriage and Family Living*, XV, No. 4 (November, 1953), 308–12.

53. LU, YI-CHUANG. "Home Discipline and Reaction to Authority in Relation to Marital Roles," *Marriage and Family Living*, XV, No. 3 (August, 1953), 223–25.

54. McCARTHY, DOROTHEA. "Some Possible Explanations of Sex Differ-

ences in Language Development and Disorders," *Journal of Psychology*, XXXV (1953), 155–60.

55. McGuire, Carson. "Family and Age Mates in Personality Formation," *Marriage and Family Living*, XV, No. 1 (February, 1953), 17–23.

56. Mangus, A. R. "Sexual Deviation and the Family," *Marriage and Family Living*, XV, No. 4 (November, 1953), 325–31.

57. Marches, Joseph R., and Turbeville, Gus. "The Effect of Residential Propinquity on Marriage Selection," *American Journal of Sociology*, LVIII, No. 6 (May, 1953), 592–95.

58. Marcson, Simon. "Predicting Intermarriage," *Sociology and Social Research*, XXXVII, No. 3 (January-February, 1953), 151–56.

59. Marshall, James. "Children in the Present World Situation," *American Journal of Orthopsychiatry*, XXIII (July, 1953), 454–64.

60. Martin, H. T., and Siegel, L. "Background Factors Related to Effective Group Participation," *Journal of Abnormal and Social Psychology*, XLVIII, No. 4 (October, 1953), 599–600.

61. Martin, Walter T. *The Rural-urban Fringe: A Study of Adjustment to Residence Location.* Eugene: University of Oregon, University Press, 1953.

62. Mitchell, Howard E., Preston, Malcolm G., and Mudd, Emily H. "Anticipated Development of Case from Content of First Interview Record," *Marriage and Family Living*, XV, No. 3 (August, 1953), 226–31.

63. Monahan, Thomas P. "Does Age at Marriage Matter in Divorce?" *Social Forces*, XXXII, No. 1 (October, 1953), 81–87.

64. Montagu, M. F. Ashley (ed.). *The Meaning of Love.* New York: Julian Press, Inc., 1953.

65. Moore, Denise Francq. "Sharing in Family Financial Management by High-School Students," *Marriage and Family Living*, XV, No. 4 (November, 1953), 319–21.

66. Morgan, Winona L. "New Approaches to Child Development," *Journal of Home Economics*, XLV, No. 1 (January, 1953), 13–16.

67. Porter, Blaine M. "Measurement of Parental Acceptance of Children," *Journal of Home Economics*, XLVI, No. 3 (March, 1953), 176–82.

68. Prugh, Dane G., Staub, Elizabeth M., Sands, Harriet H., Kirschbaum, Ruth M., and Lenihan, Ellenora A. "A Study of the Emotional Reactions of Children and Families to Hospitalization and Illness," *American Journal of Orthopsychiatry*, XXIII (January, 1953), 70–106.

69. Ruesch, Jurgen, Block, Jack, and Bennett, Lillian. "The Assessment of Communication. I. A Method for the Analysis of Social Interaction," *Journal of Psychology*, XXXV (1953), 59–80.

70. Rheinstein, Max. "Trends in Marriage and Divorce Law of Western Countries," *Law and Contemporary Problems*, XVIII (1953), 3–19.

71. Roff, Merrill, and Brody, David S. "Appearance and Choice

Status during Adolescence," *Journal of Psychology*, XXXVI (1953), 347–56.
72. SCHOEPPE, AILEEN. "Sex Differences in Adolescent Socialization," *Journal of Social Psychology*, XXXVIII (1953), 175–85.
73. SEARS, R. R., WHITING, J. W. M., NOWLIS, V., and SEARS, P. S. *Some Child-rearing Antecedents of Aggression and Dependency in Young Children.* ("Genetic Psychology Monographs," Vol. XLVII, No. 2 [1953].)
74. SHERRIFFS, A. C., and JARRETT, R. F. "Sex Differences in Attitudes about Sex Differences," *Journal of Psychology*, XXXV (1953), 161–68.
75. SIRJAMAKI, JOHN. *The American Family in the Twentieth Century.* Cambridge: Harvard University Press, 1953.
76. SMITH, ELEANOR, and MONANE, J. H. GREENBERG. "Courtship Values in a Youth Sample," *American Sociological Review*, XVIII, No. 6 (December, 1953), 635–40.
77. SMITH, WILLIAM CARLSON. *The Stepchild.* Chicago: University of Chicago Press, 1953.
78. STAVER, NANCY. "The Child's Learning Difficulty as Related to the Emotional Problem of the Mother," *American Journal of Orthopsychiatry*, XXIII (January, 1953), 131–40.
79. STIEBLING, HAZEL K. "Are Farm Families Catching Up?" *Journal of Home Economics*, XLV, No. 1 (January, 1953), 9–12.
80. STONE, ABRAHAM, and LEVINE, LENA. "The Dynamics of the Marital Relationship," *Mental Hygiene*, XXXVII (1953), 606–14.
81. STONE, CAROL LARSON, and LANDIS, PAUL H. "An Approach to Authority Patterns in Parent–Teen-Age Relationships," *Rural Sociology*, XVIII, No. 3 (September, 1953), 233–42.
82. STROUP, ATLEE L. "Predicting Marital Success or Failure in an Urban Population," *American Sociological Review*, XVIII, No. 5 (October, 1953), 558–62.
83. SULLIVAN, HARRY STACK. *The Interpersonal Theory of Psychiatry.* New York: W. W. Norton & Co., 1953.
84. SUSSMAN, MARVIN B. "The Help Pattern in the Middle Class Family," *American Sociological Review*, XVIII, No. 1 (February, 1953), 22–28.
85. ———. "Parental Participation in Mate Selection and Its Effects upon Family Continuity," *Social Forces*, XXXII, No. 1 (October, 1953), 76–81.
86. TARWATER, JESSE W. "Self-understanding and the Ability To Predict Another's Response," *Marriage and Family Living*, XV, No. 2 (May, 1953), 126–28.
87. TIETZE, CHRISTOPHER, and LEWIT, SARAH. "Patterns of Family Limitation in a Rural Negro Community," *American Sociological Review*, XVIII, No. 5 (October, 1953), 563–64.
88. TUCKMAN, JACOB, LORGE, IRVING, and SPOONER, GEORGE A. "The Effect of Family Environment on Attitudes toward Old People and the Older Worker," *Journal of Social Psychology*, XXXVIII (1953), 207–18.

89. UNITED NATIONS. *Study of Adoption of Children.* New York: Columbia University Press, 1953.

90. VINCENT, CLARK E. "Role Clarification for the Contemporary College-educated Woman," *Journal of Home Economics,* XLV, No. 8 (October, 1953), 567–70.

91. ———. "The Sociology of Knowledge in Critiques of Family Sociology," *Research Studies of the State College of Washington,* XXI (1953), 252–57.

92. WALLIN, PAUL, and VOLLMER, HOWARD M. "Marital Happiness of Parents and Their Children's Attitudes to Them," *American Sociological Review,* XVIII, No. 4 (August, 1953), 424–31.

93. WALTERS, JAMES. "The Measurement of Attitude Components in Family Life Education Research," *Journal of Home Economics,* XLV, No. 10 (December, 1953), 729–32.

94. WATTENBERG, WILLIAM M. "Eleven-Year-old Boys in Trouble," *Journal of Educational Psychology,* XLIV, No. 7 (November, 1953), 409–17.

95. WEBSTER, A. S. *The Development of Phobias in Married Women.* ("Psychological Monographs," Vol. XLVII, No. 17 [1953].)

96. WHITING, JOHN W. M., and CHILD, IRVIN L. *Child Training and Personality: A Cross-cultural Study.* New Haven: Yale University Press, 1953.

97. WHYTE, WILLIAM H., JR. "The Transients. I–IV," *Fortune,* Vol. XLVII, Nos. 5–6, Vol. XLVIII, Nos. 1–2 (May-August, 1953).

98. WILLIAMS, JUDITH R., and SCOTT, ROLAND B. "Motor Development and Its Relationship to Child Rearing Practices in Two Groups of Negro Infants," *Child Development,* XXIV, No. 2 (June, 1953), 103–21.

99. WILLIAMSON, R. C. "Selected Urban Factors in Marital Adjustment," *Research Studies of the State College of Washington,* XXI (1953), 237–41.

100. WILSON, MARGARET S. "Do College Girls Conform to the Standards of Their Parents?" *Marriage and Family Living,* XV, No. 3 (August, 1953), 207–8.

101. WOLFENSTEIN, MARTHA. "Trends in Infant Care," *American Journal of Orthopsychiatry,* XXIII (January, 1953), 120–30.

1954

1. ACKERMAN, NATHAN W. "Interpersonal Disturbances in the Family: Some Unsolved Problems in Psychotherapy," *Psychiatry,* XVII, No. 4 (November, 1954), 359–68.

2. ALBRECHT, RUTH. "Intergeneration Parent Patterns," *Journal of Home Economics,* XLVI, No. 1 (January, 1954), 29–32.

3. ———. "Relationships of Older Parents with Their Children," *Marriage and Family Living,* XVI, No. 1 (February, 1954), 32–35.

4. ———. "The Parental Responsibilities of Grandparents," *ibid.,* No. 3 (August, 1954), pp. 201–4.

5. ALLEN, ROBERT M. "Continued Longitudinal Rorschach Study of a

Child for Years Three to Five," *Journal of Genetic Psychology*, LXXXV (September, 1954), 135-49.

6. ANASTASI, ANNE. "Tested Intelligence and Family Size, Methodological and Interpretive Problems," *Eugenics Quarterly*, I, No. 3 (September, 1954), 155-60.

7. ANDERSON, WILLIAM F., JR. "Attitudes of Parents of Differing Socio-economic Status toward the Teaching Profession," *Journal of Educational Psychology*, XLV, No. 6 (October, 1954), 345-52.

8. AUSUBEL, DAVID P., BALTHAZAR, EARL E., ROSENTHAL, IRENE, BLACKMAN, LEONARD S., SCHPOONT, SEMOUR H., and WELKOWITZ, JOAN. "Perceived Parent Attitudes as Determinants of Children's Ego Structure," *Child Development*, XXV, No. 3 (September, 1954), 173-83.

9. BAYLEY, NANCY. "Some Increasing Parent-Child Similarities during the Growth of Children," *Journal of Educational Psychology*, XLV, No. 1 (January, 1954), 1-21.

10. BEHRENS, MARJORIE L. "Child Rearing and the Character Structure of the Mother," *Child Development*, XXV, No. 3 (September, 1954), 225-38.

11. BEIGEL, HUGO G. "Body Height in Mate Selection," *Journal of Social Psychology*, XXXIX (1954), 257-68.

12. BENNETT, EDWARD M., and JOHANNESEN, DOROTHEA E. "Some Psychodynamic Aspects of Felt Parental Alliance in Young Children," *Journal of Abnormal and Social Psychology*, XLIX, No. 3 (July, 1954), 463-66.

13. BLOM, GASTON E., and NICHOLLS, GRACE. "Emotional Factors in Children with Rheumatoid Arthritis," *American Journal of Orthopsychiatry*, XXIV (1954), 588-601.

14. BOSSARD, JAMES H. S., and BOLL, ELEANOR STOKER. "Security in the Large Family," *Mental Hygiene*, XXXVIII (October, 1954), 529-44.

15. BRESSLER, MARVIN, and KEPHART, WILLIAM M. "Marriage and Family Patterns of an Academic Group," *Marriage and Family Living*, XVI, No. 2 (May, 1954), 121-27.

16. BRIGGS, DENNIE L. "Social Adaptation among Japanese American Youth: A Comparative Study," *Sociology and Social Research*, XXXVIII, No. 5 (May-June, 1954), 293-300.

17. BRIM, ORVILLE G., JR. "The Acceptance of New Behavior in Child Rearing," *Human Relations*, VII (1954), 473-91.

18. BURGESS, ERNEST W. "Economic, Cultural, and Social Factors in Family Breakdown," *American Journal of Orthopsychiatry*, XXIV (1954), 462-70.

19. CAPLOW, THEODORE. *The Sociology of Work*, esp. chaps. x and xi, "Occupations of Women" and "Occupation and Family." Minneapolis: University of Minnesota Press, 1954.

20. CARTER, DON C. "The Influence of Family Relations and Family Experiences on Personality," *Marriage and Family Living*, XVI, No. 3 (August, 1954), 212-15.

21. CENTERS, RICHARD, and BLUMBERG, GODFREY H. "Social and Psycho-

logical Factors in Human Procreation: A Survey Approach," *Journal of Social Psychology*, XL (1954), 245–57.

22. Connor, Ruth, Johannis, Theodore B., Jr., and Walters, James. "Parent-Adolescent Relationships. I. Parent-Adolescent Conflicts: Current and in Retrospect. II. Intra-familial Conceptions of the Good Father, Good Mother, and Good Child," *Journal of Home Economics*, XLVI, No. 3 (March, 1954), 183–91.

23. Dinitz, Simon, Dynes, Russell R., and Clarke, Alfred C. "Preferences for Male or Female Children: Traditional or Affectional?" *Marriage and Family Living*, XVI, No. 2 (May, 1954), 128–30.

24. Dornbusch, Sanford M. "The Prediction of Total Family Unemployment," *American Sociological Review*, XIX, No. 4 (August, 1954), 472–75.

25. Duvall, Evelyn M. *In-laws: Pro and Con: An Original Study of Interpersonal Relations.* New York: Association Press, 1954.

26. Eaton, Joseph W., and Mayer, Albert J. *Man's Capacity To Reproduce: The Demography of a Unique Population.* Glencoe, Ill.: Free Press, 1954.

27. Eissler, Ruth, Freud, Anna, Hartman, H., and Kris, E. (eds.). *The Psychoanalytic Study of the Child*, Vol. IX. New York: International Universities Press, 1954.

28. Ellis, Albert. *The American Sexual Tragedy.* New York: Twayne Publishers, 1954.

29. Ellis, Albert, and Beechley, Robert M. "Emotional Disturbance in Children with Peculiar Given Names," *Journal of Genetic Psychology*, LXXXV (December, 1954), 337–39.

30. Feinberg, Henry. "Achievement of Children in Orphan Homes as Revealed by the Stanford Achievement Test," *Journal of Genetic Psychology*, LXXXV (December, 1954), 217–29.

31. Folsom, Joseph K. "The Burgess-Wallin Report: A Contribution to Eugenics through the Improvement of Marriage," *Eugenics Quarterly*, I, No. 2 (June, 1954), 52–55.

32. Foote, Nelson N. "Changes in American Marriage Patterns and the Role of Women," *Eugenics Quarterly*, I, No. 4 (December, 1954), 254–60.

33. ———. "Research: A New Strength for Family Life," *Marriage and Family Living*, XVI, No. 1 (February, 1954), 13–20.

34. Frumkin, Robert M. "Attitudes of Negro College Students toward Intrafamily Leadership and Control," *Marriage and Family Living*, XVI, No. 3 (August, 1954), 252–53.

35. ———. *The Measurement of Marriage Adjustment.* Washington: Annals of American Research, Public Affairs Press, 1954.

36. Gellhorn, Walter D., assisted by Jacob D. Hyman and Sidney H. Asch (special committee of the Bar of the City of New York). *Children and Families in the Courts of New York City.* New York: Dodd, Mead & Co., 1954.

37. Gillies, Duncan V., and Lastrucci, Carlo L. "Validation of the Effectiveness of a College Marriage Course," *Marriage and Family Living*, XVI, No. 1 (February, 1954), 55–58.

38. GOLDEN, JOSEPH. "Patterns of Negro-White Intermarriage," *American Sociological Review*, XIX, No. 2 (April, 1954), 144–47.

39. GREEN, JAMES WYCHE. "Factors Inducing Decisions To Build Farmhouses," *Rural Sociology*, XIX, No. 3 (September, 1954), 263–70.

40. GRIFFITHS, WILLIAM. "Changing Family Health Patterns: A View of Recent Research," *Journal of Home Economics*, XLVI, No. 1 (January, 1954), 13–16.

41. HAJNAL, JOHN. "Differential Changes in Marriage Patterns," *American Sociological Review*, XIX, No. 2 (April, 1954), 148–54.

42. ———. "Analysis of Changes in the Marriage Pattern by Economic Groups," *ibid.*, No. 3 (June, 1954), pp. 295–302.

43. HANDFORD, NORAH PRUDENCE. "Mothers of Adolescent Girls," *Smith College Studies in Social Work*, XXIV, No. 3 (June, 1954), 9–34.

44. HAWKES, GLENN R., and EGBERT, ROBERT L. "Personal Values and the Empathic Response: Their Interrelationships," *Journal of Educational Psychology*, XLV, No. 8 (December, 1954), 469–76.

45. HILL, REUBEN. "Marriage and Family Research," *Eugenics Quarterly*, I, No. 1 (March, 1954), 58–65.

46. HILL, REUBEN, MOSS, J. JOEL, and WIRTHS, CLAUDINE G. "Eddyville's Families: A Study of Personal and Family Adjustments Subsequent to the Rapid Urbanization of a Southern Town." Chapel Hill: Institute for Research in Social Science, University of North Carolina, 1954. Mimeographed.

47. HILLMAN, CHRISTINE H. "An Advice Column's Challenge for Family-Life Education," *Marriage and Family Living*, XVI, No. 1 (February, 1954), 51–54.

48. HIMELHOCH, JEROME (ed.). "Sexual Behavior in American Society" (a special issue), *Social Problems*, I, No. 4 (April, 1954), 119–86.

49. HIMES, JOSEPH S. "A Value Profile in Mate Selection among Negroes," *Marriage and Family Living*, XVI, No. 3 (August, 1954), 244–47.

50. HOEFLIN, RUTH. "Child Rearing Practices and Child Care Resources Used by Ohio Farm Families with Children," *Journal of Genetic Psychology*, LXXXIV (June, 1954), 271–97.

51. HUGHES, JULIUS H., and THOMPSON, GEORGE G. "A Comparison of the Value Systems of Southern Negro and Northern White Youth," *Journal of Educational Psychology*, XLV, No. 5 (May, 1954), 300–309.

52. JACKSON, JOAN K. "The Adjustment of the Family to the Crisis of Alcoholism," *Quarterly Journal of Studies in Alcohol*, XV (December, 1954), 562–86.

53. KARDINER, ABRAM. *Sex and Morality.* Indianapolis: Bobbs-Merrill Co., Inc., 1954.

54. KAUFMAN, IRVING, PECK, ALICE L., and TAGIURI, CONSUELO K. "The Family Constellation and Overt Incestuous Relations between Father and Daughter," *American Journal of Orthopsychiatry*, XXIV (April, 1954), 266–79.

55. KEPHART, WILLIAM M. "Drinking and Marital Disruption," *Quarterly Journal of Studies in Alcohol*, XV (March, 1954), 63–73.

56. ———. "The Duration of Marriage," *American Sociological Review*, XIX, No. 3 (June, 1954), 287–95.

57. ———. "Some Variables in Cases of Reported Sexual Maladjustment," *Marirage and Family Living*, XVI, No. 3 (August, 1954), 241–43.

58. KERCKHOFF, RICHARD K. "Interest Group Reactions to the Profession of Marriage Counseling," *Sociology and Social Research*, XXXIX, No. 3 (December-January, 1954), 179–83.

59. KING, CHARLES E. "The Sex Factor in Marital Adjustment," *Marriage and Family Living*, XVI, No. 3 (August, 1954), 237–40.

60. KIRKPATRICK, CLIFFORD, and HOBART, CHARLES. "Disagreement, Disagreement Estimate, and Non-empathetic Imputations for Intimacy Groups Varying from Favorite Date to Married," *American Sociological Review*, XIX, No. 1 (February, 1954), 10–19.

61. KLEMER, RICHARD H. "Factors of Personality and Experience Which Differentiate Single from Married Women," *Marriage and Family Living*, XVI, No. 1 (February, 1954), 41–44.

62. KOLLER, MARVIN R. "Studies of Three-Generation Households," *Marriage and Family Living*, XVI, No. 3 (August, 1954), 205–6.

63. KOSTICK, MAX MARTIN. "A Study of Transfer: Sex Differences in the Reasoning Process," *Journal of Educational Psychology*, XLV, No. 8 (December, 1954), 449–58.

64. LANDIS, PAUL H. *Teenage Adjustment in Large and Small Families: Comparison within a High School and College Sample in Washington.* (Washington Agricultural Experiment Station Bull. 549.) Pullman: Washington Agricultural Experiment Station, 1954.

65. LANGFORD, LOUISE M., and ALM, O. W. "A Comparison of Parent Judgments and Child Feelings concerning the Self Adjustment of Twelve-Year-old Children," *Journal of Genetic Psychology*, LXXXV (September, 1954), 39–46.

66. LASKO, J. K. *Parent Behavior toward First and Second Children.* ("Genetic Psychology Monographs," Vol. XLIX, No. 1 [1954].)

67. LAW, SHIRLEY. "The Mother of the Happy Child," *Smith College Studies in Social Work*, XXV, No. 1 (October, 1954), 1–27.

68. LEMASTERS, ERSEL E. "Social Class Mobility and Family Integration," *Marriage and Family Living*, XVI, No. 3 (August, 1954), 226–32.

69. LERNER, ARTHUR. "Attitudes of Male Alcoholic Inmates toward Marriage, Family, and Related Problems," *Mental Hygiene*, XXVIII (July, 1954), 468–82.

70. LOWE, WARNER L. "Group Beliefs and Socio-cultural Factors in Religious Delusions," *Journal of Social Psychology*, XL (1954), 267–74.

71. MACRAE, DUNCAN, JR. "A Test of Piaget's Theories of Moral Development," *Journal of Abnormal and Social Psychology*, XLIX, No. 1 (January, 1954), 14–18.

72. MARTIN, WILLIAM E. "Learning Theory and Identification. III. The

Development of Values in Children," *Journal of Genetic Psychology*, LXXXIV (June, 1954), 211–17.

73. MEAD, MARGARET. "Some Theoretical Considerations on the Problem of Mother-Child Separation," *American Journal of Orthopsychiatry*, XXIV (July, 1954), 471–83.

74. MILLER, HASKELL M. "Marriage and the Family in a Tennessee Valley Area," *Marriage and Family Living*, XVI, No. 3 (August, 1954), 233–36.

75. MONAHAN, THOMAS P., and KEPHART, WILLIAM M. "Divorce and Desertion by Religious and Mixed-religious Groups," *American Journal of Sociology*, LIX, No. 5 (March, 1954), 454–65.

76. MORRIS, DON P., SOROKER, ELEANOR, and BURRUSS, GENETTE. "Follow-up Studies of Shy, Withdrawn Children. I. Evaluation of Later Adjustment," *American Journal of Orthopsychiatry*, XXIV (1954), 743–54.

77. MOTT, SINA M. "Concept of Mother—a Study of Four- and Five-Year-old Children," *Child Development*, XXV, No. 2 (June, 1954), 99–106.

78. MOWRER, ERNEST R. "Some Factors in the Affectional Adjustment of Twins," *American Sociological Review*, XIX, No. 4 (August, 1954), 468–71.

79. MOWRER, O. H. "Learning Theory and Identification. I. Introduction," *Journal of Genetic Psychology*, LXXXIV (June, 1954), 197–99.

80. MUELLER, KATE HEVNER. *Educating Women for a Changing World.* Minneapolis: University of Minnesota Press, 1954.

81. MUMMERY, DOROTHY V. "Family Backgrounds of Assertive and Non-assertive Children," *Child Development*, XXV, No. 1 (March, 1954), 63–80.

82. NEUBECK, GERHARD. "Factors Affecting Group Psychotherapy with Married Couples," *Marriage and Family Living*, XVI, No. 3 (August, 1954), 216–20.

83. NIEMAN, LIONEL J. "The Influence of Peer Groups upon Attitudes toward the Feminine Role," *Social Problems*, II (1954), 104–11.

84. NIMKOFF, MEYER F. "The Family in the United States," *Marriage and Family Living*, XVI, No. 4 (November, 1954), 390–96.

85. NORTHWAY, MARY I. "A Plan for Sociometric Studies in a Longitudinal Programme of Research in Child Development," *Sociometry*, XVII (August, 1954), 272–82.

86. PAN, JU-SHU. "Institutional and Personal Adjustment in Old Age," *Journal of Genetic Psychology*, LXXXV (September, 1954), 155–58.

87. PATON, JEAN M. *The Adopted Break Silence: The Experiences and Views of Forty Adults Who Once Were Adopted Children.* Philadelphia: Life History Study Center, 1954.

88. PENNECK, JEAN L., BREW, MARGARET L., and TILLINGHAST, ROSE C. *Farm Family Spending and Saving in Illinois, with a Comparison of Survey and Home-Accounts Data.* (Agriculture Information Bull. 101.) Washington: Government Printing Office, 1954.

89. PERLIS, MILDRED E. "The Social Functions of Marriage Wit," *Marriage and Family Living*, XVI, No. 1 (February, 1954), 49–50.

90. REAGAN, BARBARA B. *Condensed vs. Detailed Schedule for Collection of Family Expenditure Data.* Washington: Home Economics Research Branch, Agricultural Research Service, U.S. Department of Agriculture, 1954.

91. REUSS, CARL F. "Research Findings on the Effects of Modern-Day Religion on Family Living," *Marriage and Family Living*, XVI, No. 3 (August, 1954), 221–25.

92. RISDON, RANDALL. "A Study of Interracial Marriages Based on Data for Los Angeles County," *Sociology and Social Research*, XXXIX, No. 2 (November-December, 1954), 92–95.

93. ROGERS, CARL R., and DYMOND, ROSALIND (eds.). *Psychotherapy and Personality Change: Co-ordinated Research Studies in the Client-centered Approach.* Chicago: University of Chicago Press, 1954.

94. ROHRER, W. C., and SCHMIDT, J. F. *Family Type and Social Participation.* ("Maryland Agricultural Experiment Station Miscellaneous Publications," No. 196.) College Park: Maryland Agricultural Experiment Station, June, 1954.

95. SCHNEIDERMAN, LEO. "Social Perception as a Function of Identification," *Journal of Psychology*, XXXVII (1954), 155–62.

96. SCHNEYER, SOLOMON. "The Marital Status of Alcoholics: A Note on an Analysis of the Marital Status of 2,008 Patients of Nine Clinics," *Quarterly Journal of Studies in Alcohol*, XV (June, 1954), 325–30.

97. SCHNORE, LEO F. "The Separation of Home and Work: A Problem for Human Ecology," *Social Forces*, XXXII, No. 4 (March, 1954), 336–43.

98. ———. "The Separation of Home and Work in Flint, Michigan." Ann Arbor: University of Michigan, Institute for Human Adjustment, 1954. Mimeographed.

99. SCUDDER, RICHARD, and ANDERSON, C. ARNOLD. "Range of Acquaintance and of Repute as Factors in Prestige Rating Methods of Studying Social Status," *Social Forces*, XXXII, No. 3 (March, 1954), 248–53.

100. SEWARD, JOHN P. "Learning Theory and Identification. II. The Role of Punishment," *Journal of Genetic Psychology*, LXXXIV (June, 1954), 201–10.

101. SHELDON, PAUL M. "The Families of Highly Gifted Children," *Marriage and Family Living*, XVI, No. 1 (February, 1954), 59–60, 67.

102. SINGER, JEROME L. "Projected Familial Attitudes as a Function of Socioeconomic Status and Psychopathology," *Journal of Consulting Psychology*, XVIII (April, 1954), 99–104.

103. SMITH, MADORAH E. "Mental Test Ability in a Family of Four Generations," *Journal of Genetic Psychology*, LXXXV (December, 1954), 321–35.

104. SMITH, WILLIAM M., JR. "Family Plans for Later Years," *Marriage and Family Living*, XVI, No. 1 (February, 1954), 36–40.

105. SPERRY, IRWIN V. "Use of Projective Techniques in the Study of Children and Families," *Journal of Home Economics,* XLVI, No. 4 (April, 1954), 241–44.
106. SPIEGEL, JOHN P. "New Perspectives in the Study of the Family," *Marriage and Family Living,* XVI, No. 1 (February, 1954), 4–12.
107. STAPLES, RUTH, and SMITH, JUNE WARDEN. "Attitudes of Grandmothers and Mothers toward Child Rearing Practices," *Child Development,* XXV, No. 2 (June, 1954), 91–97.
108. STENDLER, CELIA BURNS. "The Learning of Certain Secondary Drives by Parisian and American Middle Class Children," *Marriage and Family Living,* XVI, No. 3 (August, 1954), 195–200.
109. STEPHENSON, CHESTER M. "Married Female School Teachers," *Marriage and Family Living,* XVI, No. 3 (August, 1954), 251.
110. STOLZ, LOIS MEEK, et al. *Father Relations of War-born Children.* Stanford, Calif.: Stanford University Press, 1954.
111. STOTT, LELAND H. "The Longitudinal Approach to the Study of Family Life," *Journal of Home Economics,* XLVI, No. 2 (February, 1954), 79–82.
112. STRAUSS, ANSELM. "Strain and Harmony in Japanese-American War-Bride Marriages," *Marriage and Family Living,* XVI, No. 2 (May, 1954), 99–106.
113. STRODTBECK, FRED L. "The Family as a Three-Person Group," *American Sociological Review,* XIX, No. 1 (February, 1954), 23–29.
114. SUSSMAN, MARVIN B. "Family Continuity: Selective Factors Which Affect Relationships between Families at Generational Levels," *Marriage and Family Living,* XVI, No. 2 (May, 1954), 112–20.
115. TABACK, MATTHEW. "Family Studies in the Eastern District. I. Family Structure and Its Changing Pattern," *Milbank Memorial Fund Quarterly,* XXXII (October, 1954), 343–82.
116. TAYLOR, CARL C. "The Family Farm in the New Society," *Rural Sociology,* XIX, No. 3 (September, 1954), 271–80.
117. THOMAS, JOHN L., S.J. "Out-Group Marriage Patterns of Some Selected Ethnic Groups," *American Catholic Sociological Review,* XV, No. 1 (March, 1954), 9–18.
118. TURNER, F. BERNADETTE. "Common Characteristics among Persons Seeking Professional Marriage Counseling," *Marriage and Family Living,* XVI, No. 2 (May, 1954), 143–44.
119. VAN AMERONGEN, SUZANNE TAETS. "Initial Psychiatric Family Studies," *American Journal of Orthopsychiatry,* XXIV (January, 1954), 73–83.
120. VANCE, RUPERT B. "The Ecology of Our Aging Population," *Social Forces,* XXXII, No. 4 (March, 1954), 330–35.
121. VINCENT, CLARK E. "The Unwed Mother and Sampling Bias," *American Sociological Review,* XIX, No. 5 (October, 1954), 562–67.
122. WALLIN, PAUL. "Marital Happiness of Parents and Their Children's Attitude to Marriage," *American Sociological Review,* XIX, No. 1 (February, 1954), 20–23.
123. ———. "Sex Differences in Attitudes to 'In-laws'—a Test of a

Theory," *American Journal of Sociology*, LIX, No. 5 (March, 1954), 466–69.

124. WESTOFF, CHARLES F. "Differential Fertility in the United States, 1900 to 1952," *American Sociological Review*, XIX, No. 5 (October, 1954), 549–61.

125. WHELPTON, P. K., and KISER, CLYDE (eds.). *Social and Psychological Factors Affecting Fertility*, Vol. IV. New York: Milbank Memorial Fund, 1954.

126. WHELPTON, PASCAL K. *Cohort Fertility: Native White Women in the United States*. Princeton: Princeton University Press, 1954.

127. ———. "Future Fertility of American Women," *Eugenics Quarterly*, I (March, 1954), 4–15.

128. WHITESIDE-TAYLOR, KATHERINE. *Parent Cooperative Nursery Schools*. New York: Bureau of Publications, Teachers College, 1954.

129. WILKENING, EUGENE A. "Change in Farm Technology as Related to Familism, Family Decision Making, and Family Integration," *American Sociological Review*, XIX, No. 1 (February, 1954), 29–37.

130. ———. "Techniques of Assessing Farm Family Values," *Rural Sociology*, XIX, No. 1 (March, 1954), 39–49.

131. WILLIAMSON, ROBERT C. "Socio-economic Factors and Marital Adjustment in an Urban Setting," *American Sociological Review*, XIX, No. 2 (April, 1954), 213–16.

132. WINCH, ROBERT, KTSANES, THOMAS, and KTSANES, VIRGINIA. "The Theory of Complementary Needs in Mate-Selection: An Analytic and Descriptive Study," *American Sociological Review*, XIX, No. 3 (June, 1954), 241–49.

133. YOUNG, KIMBALL. *Isn't One Wife Enough? The Story of Mormon Polygamy*. New York: Henry Holt & Co., Inc., 1954.

134. YOUNG, LEONTINE. *Out of Wedlock: A Study of the Problems of the Unmarried Mother and Her Child*. New York: McGraw-Hill Book Co., Inc., 1954.

135. ZIMMERMAN, CARLE C., and BRODERICK, CARLFRED B. "Nature and Role of Informal Family Groups," *Marriage and Family Living*, XVI, No. 2 (May, 1954), 107–11.

136. ZNANIECKI, FLORIAN. "The Dynamics of Social Relations," *Sociometry*, XVII, No. 4 (November, 1954), 299–303.

The family research output in the United States from 1945 through 1954 was meager or immense, depending upon the standard of comparison. Related to the volume of research in even the minor specialities of natural science, it was minute. The upward trend within the decade is encouraging only in relation to previous output; in relation to the hopes that are coming to rest upon social science for the development of human resources, the advance in quantity is discouragingly slow. From the standpoint of anyone who attempts to keep up with the literature in the field, on the other hand, it is clear that a regular abstracting service is in order, and it is gratifying that the National Council on Family Relations is endeavoring to satisfy this need through the medium of its quarterly journal, *Marriage and Family Living.* Thus far, regrettably, the means for thorough and careful coverage are insufficient, as apparently likewise in the neighboring field of child development (e.g., *Child Development Abstracts*). It is to be hoped that ways can be found whereby the foregoing Bibliography will be the last that has to be published without adequate annotations, as the disciplines and professions which produce and utilize family research improve their channels of communication. In 1955, it is already evident, we shall harvest a bumper crop of family research.

The problems of quantity, however, are ultimately of less account than the quality of findings reported. Like the famous mousetrap, a piece of work of vital importance will find its way into scientific thought, though published in Urdu. It is far easier to find the means of translation and dissemination than to conceive the project whose findings will be worthy of universal attention.

By virtue of reading through the listing for each year of family research, one observes recurrences not only of names but also of themes. It might thus appear that a brief, descriptive way to summarize the 1,031 entries would be in terms of a thematic analysis. This was attempted, along the lines of the usual divisions of subject matter found in family textbooks: demography, dating and courtship, mate selection, marital relations, parent-child relations, institutional structure and change, and divorce and instability. Despite some fluctuations in certain categories (e.g., decline in studies of effects of war separation) and notable stability in others (e.g., mate selection according to propinquity), the result seemed rather sterile of meaning as a basis for evaluation, which would have been our only purpose in classification.

More promising for a time seemed thematic analysis according to theoretical approach or reference to problems of the current period. Professor Reuben Hill, of the University of North

Carolina, has already presented some analysis of research trends in terms of theoretical and conceptual approaches and intends to do more. Whether evaluation in these terms will lead to the sharpening of factional lines or to their blurring and whether the sharpening or the blurring of such differences is ultimately the more productive cannot be foreseen. While strong theoretical preferences are exhibited in the items, these do not yet seem a basis for evaluation of past work, at least the kind of basis we were seeking.

On the other hand, it soon became apparent that its mere reference to, or stimulation by, contemporary problems did not automatically make a piece of research relevant and useful to its subjects. Many pieces of work on aging or on ambiguities in the roles of women, for example, have recently appeared, of a flat, descriptive nature that indicates nothing of what is emergent or potential under varying conditions. This is not a matter, by the way, of whether their content is statistical; as a matter of fact, the demographic work on the speed of trends in marriage, fertility, and divorce is of the most significance of almost anything published within the decade. Relevance, in other words, is a matter of bearing on potential courses of conduct, and here the field is so wide open as almost to defy generalization.

To make a long story short, we tried various schemes of classification. There is a legend that in each field of research there are unfilled gaps and neglected areas. These turn out, upon close inspection, to be artifacts of the scheme of classification applied. Such schemes are limited in number only by the imagination, and choice among them is almost a matter of arbitrary preference. We ended up, therefore, with simply a presentation of the data available as to the content of family research for the last ten years and the proposal that others should join in an effort to apply criteria for evaluation on a regular and systematic basis.

It has often been thought that critical scrutiny of previous research would somehow lead to the improvement of future products. But in reflecting upon the output of the past decade, it has become clear that the effects of such a review depend heavily upon the criteria employed.

At an earlier stage in the preparation of this volume, it appeared that the technical competence of family researchers was the strategic point of attack at which the most rapid progress could be made. If a larger number of able young scholars could be attracted into this field, it is no doubt true that the standards of family research would tend to rise. On the other hand, after laboriously devising the following list of technical criteria whereby each item of published work might be classified and evaluated, some doubts arose as to the effect of limiting scrutiny of family research to these questions alone:

1. Professional? Was it conducted by a well-trained, full-time scholar, by an experienced research organization, or by a casual amateur?

2. Cumulative? Was it built upon the methods, theory, and findings of previous research in a way to advance the process of generalization? Does it open up the way, in turn, for further investigation?

3. Theoretically oriented? Was there explicit testing of hypotheses stated before the investigation, or was it merely exploratory and descriptive?

4. Quantitative? How successful was the effort to specify operationally and to measure the principal variables utilized in the study?

5. Predictive? If relationships among the variables were stated in general form, was the test of prediction applied to their verification?

6. Longitudinal? Do the results show merely cross-sectional distributions at a moment, or do they show changing relationships in time?

7. Controlled? Are comparisons made between outcomes known to be subject to equivalent conditions through methods of design and analysis?

8. Experimental? Are the principal generalizations which accrue finally subjected to strictly experimental validation, utilizing appropriate control groups?

9. Representative? To how broad a describable universe can the findings be generalized by sampling theory?

10. Interdisciplinary? To what extent do the generalizations adduced interrelate several levels of abstraction?

A published study may merit all ten of the honorific adjectives by which we caption the generally accepted technical criteria of good research, and yet the contribution may be only an exercise in virtuosity, trivial and irrelevant to the concerns of its subjects.

It is evident that the postwar generation of family researchers is receiving better technical training than ever before. The standard of their output in this respect can therefore be confidently expected to rise, as is partly borne out by inspection of the items published from year to year in the past decade. It is far less clear that the items published over the ten-year period show a trend, as yet, toward higher relevance or importance. The problem of how to evaluate family research in these terms is difficult and controversial.

Perhaps it is significant that family research in the last ten years has been subjected to repeated critiques. In May, 1945, the *American Journal of Sociology* celebrated its first half-century of existence by publishing critical reviews of the various fields of sociology. Professors Mirra Komarovsky and the late Willard Waller, of Barnard College, analyzed trends in "Studies of the Family" (*American Journal of Sociology*, L, No. 6 [May, 1945], 443–51) by dividing previous work into three periods. They characterized 1896–1915 as the period of large-scale historical and institutional constructions of an evolutionary slant, alongside moralistic attacks on social evils; 1916–25, they felt, was the decade in which empirical and value-neutral field studies of families, utilizing statistics, ousted the previous speculative or library approach. From 1926 through 1944, they believed, the dominant trend was toward a social-psychological approach, despite the obstacles of bias and prejudice to scientific examination of the intimacies of family life. To some extent they deplored a decline in cognizance of the broader societal setting of family behavior and also the tendency to utilize middle-class assumptions.

Bracketing the other end of the decade is "A Critique of Contemporary Marriage and Family Research" by Professor Hill (*Social Forces*, XXXIII, No. 3 [March, 1955], 268–77; also *Eugenics Quarterly*, I [1954], 58–63). Hill also indorses the doubts of other critics of the adjustment approach and favors a greater emphasis upon research related to the dynamics of family development, with a view to eventual practical application.

Between these two articles have appeared ten other assessments of family research, that is, an average of more than one per year:

KELLEY, IDA B., and NESBITT, MARGARET. "The Family, Education, and Child Adjustment," *Review of Educational Research,* XVI (1946), 71–80.

BURGESS, ERNEST W. "The Family and Sociological Research," *Social Forces,* XXVI (1947), 1–6.

COTTRELL, LEONARD S., JR. "The Present Status and Future Orientation of Research on the Family," *American Sociological Review,* XIII (1948), 123–36.

KOLB, WILLIAM L. "Sociologically Established Family Norms and Democratic Values," *Social Forces,* XXVI (1948), 451–56.

NIMKOFF, MEYER F. "Trends in Family Research," *American Journal of Sociology,* LIII (1948), 477–82.

WINCH, ROBERT F. "The Study of Personality in the Family Setting," *Social Forces,* XXVIII (1950), 310–16.

MOWRER, ERNEST R., and MOWRER, HARRIET R. "The Social Psychology of Marriage," *American Sociological Review,* XVI (1951), 27–36.

BARRON, MILTON L. "Research on Intermarriage: A Survey of Accomplishments and Prospects," *American Journal of Sociology,* LVII (1951), 249–55.

ROCKWOOD, LEMO D. "A Proposal for the Direction of Family Life Research for the Next Decade," *Journal of Home Economics,* XLIV (1952), 23–27.

ELLIS, ALBERT, and DOORBAR, RUTH R. "Recent Trends in Sex, Marriage, and Family Research," *Marriage and Family Living,* XIV (1952), 338–40.

Indeed the tendency toward an annual review may have become explicitly regularized at last, with the appearance of the following by the abstracts editor of *Marriage and Family Living:*

EHRMANN, WINSTON. "A Review of Family Research in 1954 (with Selected Bibliography)," *Marriage and Family Living,* XVII (1955), 169–76.

For everyone who has written a critique of family research in the last ten years, there are probably ten others who have thought seriously about the matter. Rather than summarize the various criteria that have been suggested, as if these were definitive or complete, it appears the part of wisdom and good planning to propose simply that the process of criticism continue on a regular and systematic basis, with no attempt by any group or person to dominate the process of evaluation.

Any person should be free to suggest a new and apt criterion, but he should also be bound to present it in a form which can be applied by anyone else. What this means, in other words, is that any criterion would be welcomed if it could be translated into an objective measure of the relative worth of actual items of research. Unfortunately, at the present time much of the resistance to evaluation of research is based on just these two shortcomings of previous critiques: (1) they appear more as the subjective attitudes and preferences of particular individuals than as generally accepted values, which seem virtually unattainable beyond the matter of technical standards, and (2) being stated in terms of praise or blame rather than in terms of operational measures, they do not lead to every observer's making the same ranking by each criterion.

Let us take a simple example. Throughout this work we have steadily complained about the prevalence of the remedial outlook in family research, as against research oriented toward identifying the conditions of optimal family development. Now whether or not others in the field accept this distinction as a valid criterion of what direction ought to be taken in the future is of less importance than whether the distinction can be reliably made among all articles and monographs. If each piece of published work can be successfully classified according to this criterion, then trends and direction from year to year can be characterized publicly. We would be confident that the effect of evaluating family research by whatever criteria anyone felt important enough to advance and apply would rapidly lead to further research of higher relevance. Instead of judging past research, even for just a decade back, we would propose the permanent establishment of a regular procedure for annual evaluation of forthcoming work, with self-conscious attention to the clarification of explicit criteria through discussion among practitioners in the field.

This recommendation is not given because we are without definite attitudes and preferences as to the direction which should be emphasized in future research. These should be evident in the preceding chapters, although our emphasis upon American research may conceal our feeling that much more comparative study of family behavior among both industrial and underdeveloped countries is in order. We are eager to elaborate, as fast as possible, and apply our concept of the reflexivity quotient. And we are convinced that, despite the favorable trend, further study of actual interaction in the family cannot be overemphasized. Indeed, a host of feelings comes to mind about points at which improvement is possible; the domestication of the psychoanalytic writers by scientific method, for example, seems to us the more important because of what they can potentially contribute. But our voice is only one, and shouting louder is not the way to create a chorus.

If a regular and public procedure for application of suggested criteria were to be established, we believe that family researchers would choose their problems in a more rational and considered way than merely through delayed response to current crises. The function of self-examination in research, as in other fields of planning, is neither to perpetuate existing patterns nor to give further weight to transient fads but to bring about appropriate development in a progressive and cumulative way.

Index